John,

Happy Birthday!
    Hope you have
a good average
this next year!

with
Dale

THE
POWER HITTERS

BY DONALD HONIG

CRESCENT BOOKS
NEW YORK · AVENEL, NEW JERSEY

ACKNOWLEDGMENTS

Baseball is a team game and so must be the writing of any book about it. I am deeply indebted to a number of people for their generous support and encouragement during the writing and editing of "The Power Hitters." I would especially like to thank Steve Zesch for his editing work along with Ron Smith, Joe Hoppel and Craig Carter of The Sporting News. Also, for their good advice and wise counsel, I am grateful to these keen students of baseball history: Stanley Honig, David Markson, Lawrence Ritter, Andrew Aronstein, Douglas Mulcahy, Louis Kiefer, Mary Gallagher and Thomas, Michael and James Brookman.

For assistance in photo research, a heartfelt thanks to the spirited Pat Kelly and her staff at the National Baseball Hall of Fame and Museum at Cooperstown, and to the always-helpful Mike Aronstein of Photo File.

A special word of thanks to Bill Deane, senior research assistant at the National Baseball Hall of Fame and Museum.

—Donald Honig

This 1993 edition published by Crescent Books, distributed by Outlet Book Company, Inc., a Random House Company, 40 Engelhard Avenue, Avenel, New Jersey 07001.

Random House
New York • Toronto • London • Sydney • Auckland

Library of Congress Cataloging-in-Publication Data
Honig, Donald.
    The power hitters / Donald Honig.
        p.   cm.
    Originally published: St. Louis, Mo. : Sporting News, c1989.
    Includes index.
    ISBN 0-517-09303-0
    1. Baseball players—United States—Biography. 2. Home runs (Baseball) I. Title.
GV865.A1H6195   1993
796.357'092'273—dc20
    [B]   93-6638
                                               CIP

Contents

For My Daughter Catherine

INTRODUCTION

They are among the royal figures of sports, baseball's equivalent of heavyweight champions. They generate strength and power, and evoke awe and excitement. They are the great home run hitters. With one swing of the bat, they can decide a game —or a season. Many of baseball's unforgettable occasions are the product of the sudden and breathtaking rise and flight of the home run, that enthralling blow that the eyes follow for several wondrous moments while exhilaration sweeps over the body.

For the first two decades of this century, baseball was played with a "dead ball." Runs were coaxed across home plate with the help of sacrifice bunts and stolen bases. This was "scientific" baseball, with John McGraw in the dugout and Ty Cobb on the field as its foremost practitioners. But in 1920, Babe Ruth and the lively ball changed all of that. Where before, home runs had been few and far between, and many of them hit inside the park, the ball was now soaring over the fence with greater frequency. If this deprived the game of some of its science, then it brought to it a greater and more pleasing element of entertainment.

The players herein are the elite among home run hitters, some of whom are associated with singular glorious demonstrations of their specialty: Ruth and his "called shot" in the 1932 World Series, Ted Williams and his game-winning blast in the 1941 All-Star Game, Hank Greenberg and his pennant-winning grand slam on the final day of the 1945 season and Reggie Jackson and his memorable power display in the 1977 World Series.

In baseball history, home run glory has come to players not necessarily associated with the game's premier blow over the long run: Gabby Hartnett and his dramatic "Homer in the Gloamin'," which helped the Chicago Cubs win the National League pennant in 1938; Bobby Thomson's fabled "Shot Heard Round the World," which gave the New York Giants the 1951 N.L. pennant in a playoff with the Brooklyn Dodgers; Bill Mazeroski's ninth-inning home run in the seventh game of the 1960 World Series, crowning the Pittsburgh Pirates world champions; Carlton Fisk's 12th-inning home run caroming off Fenway Park's left-field foul pole in Game 6 of the 1975 World Series; Chris Chambliss swatting a ninth-inning home run in the final game of the 1976 American League Championship Series, propelling the New York Yankees into their first World Series since 1964; George Brett's monumental shot at Yankee Stadium that sealed the pennant for the Kansas City Royals in 1980; Rick Monday's two-out, ninth-inning homer that gave the Los Angeles Dodgers the pennant in 1981, and Kirk Gibson's Hollywood-script pinch-hit homer that won the opening game of the 1988 World Series for the Dodgers. And there have been others.

One of the exalted parts of home run lore is Roger Maris's 61-homer season in 1961, a feat that Maris never again came even close to duplicating. It stands in baseball history as the American League counterpart to Hack Wilson's 56-home run season for the Cubs in 1930—league records set by men who for one superb season performed far beyond themselves, but did it in the one aspect of the game that would leave them imperishably inscribed upon baseball's honor roll.

The men in this book are slugging legends who hit home runs over the length of their careers. They are the men who year after year brought tension to home plate, apprehension to the mound and pure excitement to the fans. They are the power and the might of baseball.

The Sultan Of Swat

Nobody hit the heart out of a baseball like Babe Ruth. And nobody ever hit a baseball with more flair, gusto, drama or majesty. No, Ruth did not invent the home run. What he did was bring glamour and spectacle to the art of hitting one; he made the home run a thing of impact and distance. He was a monarch of his time, and like all mighty monarchs, he remade something over into his own image. "When you are looking at Babe Ruth," one writer said, "you are looking at baseball."

Great theatrical performers all possess a keen sense of timing, and though he did not work before footlights, Ruth *was* theater. No ball player ever demonstrated surer timing, and not just at home plate. This Goliath of players and the lively ball coincided at precisely the right time, captivating a fandom that had been left bitter and disillusioned by the 1919 World Series scandal. Ruth symbolized the new culture hero—the home run hitter. His knockout swing was like a new invention and those soaring home runs were like feats of exploration dispatched into the unknown.

His very name became descriptive of things grandiose and incomparable. To this day, an impressively long home run need only be described as "Ruthian" and the idea is conveyed. Call a man "The Babe Ruth of football" or "The Babe Ruth of basketball," and no more need be said.

Like George Washington, who never said "I cannot tell a lie," but has nevertheless enjoyed enhanced nobility for supposedly saying so, Ruth probably did not call his shot in the 1932 World Series. Still, people *want* it to be true, because the idea of it is the essence of this man who is part legend, part child, part buffoon and all ball player. Everything about Ruth—eater, drinker, womanizer, home run hitter, Yankee symbol—was wonderfully outsized, unprecedented and inimitable. He was a thunderclap in an echo chamber, and to this day the boom resonates.

Joe Dugan, the third baseman on the Ruth-led

"When you are looking at Babe Ruth, you are looking at baseball."

Yankee teams of the 1920s, recalled a brief exchange with the exalted right fielder.

"We were sitting on a train heading out west," Dugan said. "It was pretty late. Babe was looking out the window. I don't know what prompted it, but all of a sudden I asked him, 'Babe, what kind of kid were you?' He turned and looked at me and said, 'I was a good kid.' Then he looked back out the window again, at his own reflection in the glass, and said, 'Maybe a little lonely.' "

The truth was, Dugan, like the rest of his teammates, was as fascinated by Ruth as the rest of the populace was.

"There was nothing like him," said pitcher Waite

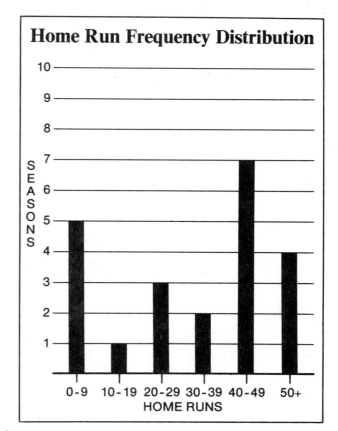

Home Run Frequency Distribution

At St. Mary's Industrial School, George Herman Ruth sometimes toiled as a lefthanded catcher.

Jack Dunn, owner of the Baltimore Orioles of the International League. Ruth was his "Baby."

Ruth (top center) with Providence in 1914. Sitting third from the left is Manager Wild Bill Donovan, who would take over as Yankee pilot the following season.

The top four starters for the Boston Red Sox in 1916 were (left to right) Carl Mays, Ernie Shore, Babe Ruth and Dutch Leonard. They combined to post 76 victories that season.

Hoyt, probably the most cosmopolitan of Ruth's teammates. "It wasn't just the home runs, but the whole man, the whole personality. He was wild and he was innocent. He could be self-centered, but most of the time he was incredibly generous. He could be impractical and irresponsible when it came to things like money and taking care of himself. But then you'd see him outside of the park after a game standing for hours signing autographs for the kids, joking with them, enjoying the hell out of himself. *For hours!* And remember, this was no ordinary ball player, this was one of the most famous people in the world. Did I ever try to figure him out? No. He was enough just to take as he was without trying to figure out."

Fittingly for a man who was nearly unstoppable at home plate, a man who roared through life like a force of nature, recognizing no discipline or authority except those limits imposed by his gargantuan appetites, the beginning of his tale shows an unruly Baltimore street kid whose spirited ways were the despair of his parents, who finally realized they could not control him. In 1902, when George was seven years old, his father, a saloonkeeper, and mother turned him over to St. Mary's Industrial School for Boys.

Being installed at St. Mary's was a turning point in Ruth's life. The home, in Baltimore, was run by the Xaverian Brothers, a strict, stern, yet fair Catholic order. The school's "prefect of discipline" was Brother Matthias, who, at 6-foot-6 and 250 muscular pounds, proved an excellent choice for the job. There was more than brawn to this man, however. For Ruth, he would become "the greatest man I ever knew."

Ruth adjusted well and comfortably to life at St. Mary's. It was never Brother Matthias' intention to break any boy's spirit—this was not a reform school—but to save him from the wild side, to channel his energies, develop whatever abilities the

boy had and to build character. With George Herman Ruth, a unique blend of vigor and talent, what finally came to the fore most compellingly was his gift for baseball, both as hitter and pitcher. Ruth could hit a baseball with great power, but even more impressive, as Ruth matured, was the lefthander's smoking fastball.

Word of Ruth's exploits eventually reached the ears of Jack Dunn, owner of the International League's Baltimore Orioles. One cold February day in 1914, Dunn walked through the gates of St. Mary's and signed the 19-year-old Ruth to a contract. A good and responsible man, Dunn assured the Brothers he would take care of their prodigy, to the extent that his coddling of Ruth led to the famous nickname—George was, in the eyes of the Oriole players, "Dunn's baby," and this soon became "Babe."

Baltimore's rookie lefthander was an immediate success. By early July, he had posted a 14-6 record, throwing an imposing fastball that was attracting plenty of attention. Normally, Dunn held on to his young stars for several years, watching their value appreciate. In 1914, however, he was feeling a financial pinch—the newly formed Federal League, a self-proclaimed major league, had installed an outpost in Baltimore that was siphoning off Oriole fans.

As a result, Dunn decided to sell some of his stars, including Ruth, whom he offered first to Connie Mack. But the Philadelphia Athletics patriarch was not interested. John McGraw was, but before the lord of the New York Giants could make an offer, Boston Red Sox Owner Joseph Lannin snatched up Ruth, pitcher Ernie Shore and catcher Ben Egan for about $25,000. (Ten years later, Ruth, in Yankee pinstripes, was the toast of New York and baseball's No. 1 gate attraction, a situation that hardly helped McGraw's already choleric disposition.)

Ruth got into a few games with the Red Sox, then

**A trim young Ruth, magic wand in hand (right), emerged as a baseball legend
when he joined the Yankees and began hitting balls out of sight.**

The hard-throwing Babe Ruth was a 24-game winner in 1917.

"He was magical," said Boston teammate Harry Hooper.

was farmed out to Providence, where he helped the Grays to the International League pennant with 8-3 pitching, good for an overall league record of 22-9. He returned to Boston at the end of the season and wound up with a 2-1 big-league record. The Red Sox were very high on the lean young southpaw with the big fastball. "I kind of like the way he swings the bat, too," noted Manager Bill Carrigan.

Ruth arrived for spring training in 1915 eager to start work. In an era when rookies had as much stature in camp as a torn uniform, the 20-year-old Babe was an anomaly.

"They had never seen a rookie like him," Shore said. "I don't mean just his ability; it was his attitude. You see, away from the ball park, in a restaurant or in a hotel, he was awkward and unsure of himself. But on the field, well, he just bustled over with self-confidence. He wanted to take batting practice with the regulars. Well, a rookie doesn't do that, much less a rookie pitcher. But he pushed himself in whenever he could.... It was like the ball field was his natural domain ... and, hell, I guess it was.

"Carrigan got a big kick out of him. Bill was a tough man himself and he admired spunk in somebody else, especially a rookie. Babe wasn't arrogant or anything like that. He was comfortable, that's all. And when he was comfortable, everything came out of him, that whole personality, the mischief, the laughter, the whole business."

Since the founding of the Boston Red Sox with the American League in 1901, Boston fans had enjoyed the prowess of Jimmy Collins (the top third

baseman of his time), Cy Young, Tris Speaker and Smoky Joe Wood, a 34-game winner in 1912. But neither they nor anyone else was prepared for the young Babe Ruth in 1915. Ruth unfurled an 18-8 record, batted .315 and slugged a dead ball for a team-leading four homers, his first career shot coming May 6 off the Yankees' Jack Warhop at the Polo Grounds. He captivated the city with his ingenuous, gale-force personality, as well. Here was a package that could be matched neither by the beloved Speaker, with his machine-like consistency, nor Ty Cobb, with his deadly precision. In the words of one writer, Ruth "was a man who transcended his immediate environment and demonstrated new, unprecedented levels of achievement."

"He was magical," recalled Harry Hooper, the Red Sox's right fielder. "A real showman. And it just poured out of him naturally. You either have that in you or you don't. And the fans knew it right away. The minute we'd all come out on the field to warm up, you'd hear them yelling, 'Babe, Babe.' And he'd laugh and wave and lift up his cap. They loved him and he loved them. It was real, right from the beginning."

In 1916, Ruth was 23-12 with a league-best 1.75 earned-run average, capping the year with a 14-inning, complete-game victory over the Brooklyn Robins as the Red Sox claimed their second straight World Series title. He won a career-high 24 games the following year, then went 13-7 in 1918 as he began a transition to the outfield. Despite playing in just 95 games, Ruth shared the league lead with 11 home runs—the first of his dozen homer titles—

Ruth was usually the center of attention.

Yankee righthander Waite Hoyt.

Ruth and the catcher follow the flight of one of the Bambino's career 714 home runs.

and then helped pitch Boston to another World Series title with two victories over the Chicago Cubs. As a topper, he increased his Series scoreless streak to 29⅔ innings, a record not broken until 1961 by Whitey Ford.

But it was in 1919 that the miracle of Babe Ruth began in earnest. No longer willing to allow such a natural resource to spend so much time on the bench, the club did the inevitable, converting Ruth to a full-time player (though Babe did do some mound work that year, running up a 9-5 record).

If Manager Ed Barrow had harbored any doubts about the move ("I'd be the laughingstock of baseball if I changed the best lefthander in the game into an outfielder," he had argued the year before), they were settled in an exhibition game that spring against the New York Giants in Tampa. Ruth caught hold of a pitch and sent it on a memorable ride, so momentous that Hooper, more than half a century later, could still feel the exhilaration of the moment:

"You watch the outfielder—he tells you how far it's going," Hooper said. "Well, I looked up once at that ball and then I watched the right fielder. It was Ross Youngs. He was running and running into right-center, getting smaller and smaller. There was no wall or grandstand out there, just a low rail fence, way, way out. Youngs finally stopped at the fence and put his hands on his hips and stood there and watched that ball come down. Then he turned around and looked back toward the infield."

The dimensions of the blow initially stunned Ruth's teammates. "I don't think anybody even went over to shake Babe's hand when he came back to the bench," Hooper said. "But then after a few minutes we started going over to him, one by one. Babe? He didn't think he had done anything wonderful. To him it was just another wallop."

Another wallop? It was later paced off to an estimated 579 feet. In the universe of baseball, it was like the sun-blast of a new age. People simply did not hit a baseball that far in 1919.

For the second straight season, Ruth was the A.L. home run leader, this time breaking Gavvy Cravath's modern major league record with an astounding 29 blows (Cravath had hit 24 for the Phillies in 1915; the A.L. record had been 16, set by the Athletics' Socks Seybold in 1902). The 24-year-old slugger now stood taller in Boston than the Bunker Hill Monument. Red Sox fans were prepared to sit back and enjoy what was promising to be a monumental career for this most entertaining performer. And so they would have—except there was a fox in the hen coop.

The fox's name was Harry Frazee, who had bought the club after the 1916 season and had a knack for producing Broadway musicals that hit the stages of the Great White Way like so many soaked cabbages. To escape a debt that had been helped along by his glittering turkeys, Frazee began selling his star players. On January 3, 1920, he reshaped Red Sox history—for the worse—by selling

Ruth to the Yankees for $125,000.

It was probably an inevitable union, Babe Ruth and New York. The big man with the oversized, rollicking personality and thunderous home run bat was a perfect match for the Big City as it rolled into the rip-roaring 1920s: The Jazz Age, Prohibition, speakeasies, the Charleston, giddy prosperity, Jack Dempsey, Red Grange, Charles Lindbergh—and Babe Ruth.

Ruth's arrival in New York led the New York Times to speculate, "It would not be surprising if Ruth surpassed his record of 29 circuit clouts next summer." On July 19, Ruth eclipsed his record, hitting numbers 30 and 31 against the Chicago White Sox. The next day's New York Tribune carried this report:

"It is now just past midseason and Ruth, with 31 home runs already to his credit, might, within the probabilities of mathematics, reach the utterly amazing total of 50 home runs for the season, a mark never even dreamed of before the advent of Ruth."

The Yankees' new outfielder reached the magical pinnacle, finishing with 54 homers, not to mention an .847 slugging average that remains an all-time record. (The Yankees, despite a third-place finish, also cashed in by becoming the first team in history to draw 1 million fans.) What followed in 1921 was unfathomable: 59 home runs, 171 runs batted in and 177 runs scored, all modern major league records at the time, all distinctly Ruthian achievements. And for the first time in club history, the Yanks were American League champions.

"He is the most destructive force ever known in baseball," summed up Manager Miller Huggins.

Ruth was, of course, swatting a livelier ball, just as everyone else was. No one else, however, was quite like the Babe, who out-homered every team in the league in 1920 and led the runner-up in the individual race, the St. Louis Browns' George Sisler, 54-19. In 1921, he outpaced teammate Bob Meusel and the Browns' Ken Williams, 59-24, while the Giants' George Kelly topped the National League with 23 home runs.

Ruth simply was unrivaled when it came to the home run, and not just because of the incredible yearly totals or inconceivable distances his shots traveled. A Ruthian clout was surrounded by drama, excitement and flair, all of which made him the decade's most dominant and revered figure, athlete or otherwise.

"The effect he had on people was amazing," Hoyt said. "If they heard he was on a train, you'd see them standing out in the fields and on the platforms of small depots just to catch a glimpse of him as the train shot by. He was always getting mobbed in hotels and restaurants. But one time, it was the strangest thing. It wasn't long after I'd joined the club in 1921. We were walking through a crowded lobby, and you know how those places are—hubbubs of activity and noise. Suddenly you didn't hear a sound, and suddenly nobody was moving.

The Babe enjoyed the spotlight and was a photographer's delight.

Ruth and Rogers Hornsby at the 1926 Series.

The crowds loved Ruth, and vice versa.

Ruth prepares to uncoil with his powerful home run swing.

The Babe in his heyday.

They were all just staring at Babe, like he was something from another part of the solar system. They weren't coming over to shake his hand or ask for his signature, they were just staring at him. In fact, I recall saying something about it to him when we got into the elevator, something like, 'Babe, they were looking at you like you were from another planet.' He just laughed."

And so the power of the home run. It is initially a conquest of man over man, of batter over pitcher, but when it becomes airborne it is more, a soaring spectacle of strength and distance, sports' most enthralling moment.

Ruth would have led the American League in home runs every season from 1918 through 1931 had it not been for an act of defiance and an intestinal abscess. The former occurred after the 1921 season, when Babe and a few teammates disobeyed baseball's rule that prohibited World Series participants from barnstorming after the Series. Ruth figuratively thumbed his nose at the first-year commissioner of baseball, Judge Kenesaw Mountain Landis, who sternly warned him not to go. When the Babe and his accomplices returned, they were fined and suspended for the first six weeks of the 1922 season. Ruth got into 110 games and hit 35 home runs, four fewer than the Browns' Williams, the A.L. leader.

In 1925, the Babe's intestinal abscess—popularly known as "the bellyache heard round the world"—kept him out of the lineup until June 1. He played in just 98 games, batted 359 times and hit 25 home runs; the home run leader, Meusel, hit 33 home

For a little boy, an unforgettable moment.

Babe Ruth is there and that means a smile on every face.

Yankee Manager Joe McCarthy (left), Ruth and fellow slugger Lou Gehrig. It was the spring of 1931, McCarthy's first year as skipper.

runs in 624 at-bats.

In the five seasons after his 59 home runs, Ruth peaked at 47 homers in 1926. But in 1927, as the kingpin of the acknowledged "Greatest Team of All Time," he exploded to his magical 60, a number that would become the most fabled in baseball. It was Ruth at his peak, and the figure gradually developed the allure of the unapproachable, the unbreakable. It was the ultimate baseball record, and it had been set by the right man. When Roger Maris hit 61 home runs in 1961, the feat was attended by resentment as well as applause: Maris needed the longer schedule (by eight games) to break the record, his detractors argued, and was worthy of a place next to Ruth only if an asterisk qualified his performance. If the record had belonged to anyone but Ruth, the carping would not have been as heated. The furor was unfair to Maris (he *still* would have totaled 59 home runs if the 154-game schedule had been in effect), but it served to underscore once again the stature of Babe Ruth.

Ruth provided the occasion of No. 60 with what dramatics were available—the Yankees had long since clinched the flag—in the team's penultimate game of the 1927 season. Facing Washington left-hander Tom Zachary with the score tied 2-2 and a man on base in the bottom of the eighth inning, the Babe lashed a towering shot into Yankee Stadium's right-field bleachers. Zachary bounded off the mound, pleading to the umpire, "Foul! Foul!" But No. 60 was clearly fair, appending the reluctant

pitcher forever to the Ruth legend.

"Nobody ever got a livelier reception per capita than Ruth did as he paced around," wrote Bill Hanna of the New York Herald Tribune. "(Coach Art) Fletcher's cap went up in the air first, then (coach Charlie) O'Leary's—and O'Leary hates to expose his bald head—and the other players rushed to congratulate the Babe. All of the fans—grandstand, bleachers and boxes—stood and cheered and waved their handkerchiefs. The crowd was small, the ovation deafening."

If anyone ever minimized the moment, it was Yankee equipment manager Pete Sheehy, who, nevertheless, captured the essence of the Ruthian feat.

"There wasn't the excitement you'd imagine," Sheehy would say. "He had already hit 59 another year and the feeling was that next year he would probably hit 62."

Ruth continued his massive hitting into the 1930s, now paired in the lineup with Lou Gehrig, a slugger nearly his equal. The legend of Ruth's might and power continued growing to such stupendous proportions that one feels compelled to consult the record book for reaffirmation. And it's there, all right, all the documentation for the career that spanned 22 seasons: the 12 home run titles, those batting averages—10 times over .340, with a career high of .393 in 1923. The 11 seasons of more than 40 homers, including four over 50 and an average of 46 home runs per year from 1920 through 1933. Thirteen times he drove in more than 100 runs, includ-

Lou Gehrig greets Ruth as he crosses home plate after his "called shot" against the Cubs in the 1932 World Series. The catcher is Gabby Hartnett and the umpire is Roy Van Graflan.

Ruth with Yankee Manager Miller Huggins in the late 1920s.

By 1938, Ruth was aging quickly and a coach for the Brooklyn Dodgers.

ing an average of 151 RBIs from 1926 through 1932.

Yes, the lively ball was in full spirit, but take Ruth out of that "Golden Age of Hitting" and it becomes significantly less precious: In the 1920s, Ruth hit more than 40 home runs eight times; only five other players did it once (Cy Williams, Rogers Hornsby, Gehrig, Chuck Klein and Mel Ott). The Yankees, meanwhile, were beginning their rise to baseball supremacy, winning pennants from 1921-23 and 1926-28, and World Series titles in 1923, 1927 and 1928.

In his heyday, Ruth was asked to explain his extraordinary slugging (aside, of course, from his unique physical gifts). "My theory," Babe said, "is that the bigger the bat, the faster the ball will travel. It's the weight of the bat that drives the ball. Some of my bats weigh as much as 52 ounces."

(Hornsby disagreed, maintaining it was bat speed that drove the ball and that necessitated a lighter stick. Today's power hitters agree with Hornsby.)

That the Babe could whip a 52-ounce bat with such ease gives some idea of his strength. In his youth, before high living gave him that pillow belly, he was an impressive physical specimen, about 195 pounds well proportioned on his 6-foot-2 frame. Contemporaries said his hands were as strong as iron, the palms heavily calloused from gripping the bat handle as tightly as possible. That also explained part of the Ruth hitting credo: a fiercely gripped bat would reduce any "give" when he made contact.

How did teams pitch to this wrecking machine?

"Most pitchers that I have talked to dislike giving Ruth a ball on the inside," Walter Johnson said. "I'd figure just the other way." Said Ty Cobb: "Babe can hit anything, but the best ball to give him is a slow curve, high, on the outside." Said Hoyt, "Pitch him high and it was dangerous, but pitch him low and he'd absolutely kill it. A lot of guys worked him inside even though he was a dead pull hitter. They were afraid to go outside with him, you see, because they feared decapitation. I've seen him hit line drives that the first baseman would go up for and the ball would end up in the seats. Can you imagine one of those things hit straight back at the pitchers?"

Next to walking the big Bam, many pitchers relied on slow curves, a strategy shunned by noted fireballer Lefty Grove. "I saw them try it," Grove said. "Burn it in and then slow up. But he was too quick, he could adjust in the middle of his swing. You could fool Gehrig once in a while with a slow curve, but never Babe."

The final word belonged to White Sox catcher Ray Schalk: "I've come to the rather hopeless conclusion that there isn't any way to fool Babe."

In 1932, at the age of 37, Ruth enjoyed the last of his signature seasons, rapping 41 homers (second now, to Philadelphia's Jimmie Foxx) with 137 RBIs and a .341 batting mark. Ruth, however, still had left in his nearly depleted bag of magic his best piece of theater—a single moment that would strain cre-

dulity yet achieve credibility only because baseball's Jovian figure was involved. And showman that he was, Ruth saved it for the grandest stage of all, the World Series.

The Babe had long since proved himself a superior performer in Series play, what with his scoreless innings streak as a pitcher and his two three-homer games against the St. Louis Cardinals, one each in the 1926 and 1928 Series. But if the legend of Ruth needed some ultimate, glittering capstone, the great man was about to set one in place.

The scene has become familiar to all who know baseball and the story of Babe Ruth. Chicago's Wrigley Field was in a state of emotional extremity for the third game of the 1932 World Series, a championship showdown that had evolved into a vicious war after the New Yorkers denounced the Cubs as "cheapskates" for voting Mark Koenig—a key late-season acquisition and former Yankee shortstop—only half a share of Series money. The verbal abuse flying from dugout to dugout was vitriolic even by baseball standards.

Ruth, batting in the fifth inning with the score tied, 4-4, aroused a crowd even under normal circumstances, but now the fans were screaming from close range, still smarting over his three-run homer in the first, while the Chicago bench unleashed salvo after salvo of verbal gunfire. As the Babe answered in kind, Chicago righthander Charlie Root maneuvered the count to 2-2.

At this point, Ruth gestured toward the field with his right hand, holding up one finger. What he was saying or implying has been debated ever since. His teammates insisted he was pointing to the centerfield bleachers, indicating a home run was forthcoming; the Cubs claimed Ruth was pointing to Root, the raised finger indicating he still had one strike left. The gesture has had almost as many interpretations as it had witnesses.

What happened next is beyond dispute. Ruth sent Root's next delivery winging on an explosive journey to center field for one of the longest home runs ever hit in Wrigley Field. With that, the mists close in and embrace the event, shielding it forever.

"What do you think of that big monkey calling his shot and getting away with it?" said Gehrig, the on-deck hitter, after the game.

"If he had," Root would fume, "I would have knocked him on his ass with the next pitch."

Ruth himself was evasive about the "called" shot for the rest of his life, sometimes saying he did, at other times laughing at the absurdity of it. "I didn't exactly point to any spot," Ruth would tell Chicago sportswriter John Carmichael at one point. "All I wanted to do was give that thing a ride out of the park, anywhere. I used to pop off a lot about hitting homers, but mostly among the Yankees. (Earle) Combs and (Tony) Lazzeri and Fletcher used to yell, 'Come on, Babe, hit one.' So, I'd come back, 'OK, you bums, I'll hit one.' Sometimes I did, sometimes I didn't. Hell, it was fun."

The moment was perhaps best summed up by

In 1938, the Babe changed uniforms again and coached first base for the
Brooklyn Dodgers.

Ruth's Milestone Home Runs

	Date	Place	Pitcher	Club
1	May 6, 1915	New York	Jack Warhop	New York
100	Sept. 24, 1920	New York	Jim Shaw	Washington
200	May 12, 1923	Detroit	Herman Pillette	Detroit
300	Sept. 8, 1925	Boston	Buster Ross	Boston
400	Sept. 2, 1927	Philadelphia	Rube Walberg	Philadelphia
500	Aug. 11, 1929	Cleveland	Willis Hudlin	Cleveland
600	Aug. 21, 1931	St. Louis	George Blaeholder	St. Louis
700	July 13, 1934	Detroit	Tommy Bridges	Detroit
Last	May 25, 1935	Pittsburgh	Guy Bush	Pittsburgh

Billy Herman, the Cubs' second baseman. "I don't think he called it," Herman said. "But it doesn't matter what I say or anybody else says. A lot of people will always believe it—because the man involved was Babe Ruth."

The following season, the thunder was reduced to 34 home runs, and in 1934, to 22. Ruth was now approaching his 40th birthday and had been agitating the club to become manager. He'd had a chilly relationship with skipper Joe McCarthy, whom the Yankees had no intention of replacing. "If he can't manage himself," General Manager Ed Barrow said, "how can he expect to manage a team?"

Ruth was released that winter so that he could sign with the Boston Braves, a wretched club that hoped to feed a starving attendance with the magic of Ruth's name. Signed as a player and vice president, Ruth also was offered vague promises about a potential managing job but for now was accorded "assistant manager" status.

By now, however, it was all over. Ruth was overweight and almost immobile in the field, far removed from the days when he was regarded as one of baseball's best outfielders, principally because of his strong arm. The mighty swing seldom made contact (he fanned 24 times in 72 N.L. at-bats) and on May 30, the Babe appeared in his last game. There was one last glow from the sun that was now below the horizon. On May 25, at Pittsburgh's spacious Forbes Field, the Babe launched three home runs of breathtaking distance, numbers 712, 713 and 714. A week later, he retired.

Ruth's relationship with baseball all but ended with his retirement. In 1938, he was a coach and batting practice attraction with the Brooklyn Dodgers, but after that, never again put on a uniform for pay.

Ruth's 714 career home runs were for decades considered an insurmountable total. Never mind that Hank Aaron would come along and wallop 755 (aided by an additional 3,965 at-bats)—Ruth remains baseball's symbol of home run power. The Yankee slugger is, for many people, the symbol of baseball itself, an image frozen in time.

"When he entered a clubhouse or a room, when he appeared on the field, it was as if he was a whole parade," Hoyt remembered. "There seemed to be flags waving, bands playing constantly.

"To me, there was one—and always will be, but one—Babe Ruth."

RUTH'S CAREER RECORD

Born Feb. 6, 1895, Baltimore, Md.   Died Aug. 16, 1948, New York, N.Y.
Batted and threw lefthanded.   Elected to Hall of Fame, 1936.

Year	Club	League	G.	AB.	R.	H.	HR.	RBI.	B.A.
1914—Balt.-Prov.		Int.	46	121	22	28	1	....	.231
1914—Boston		Amer.	5	10	1	2	0	0	.200
1915—Boston		Amer.	42	92	16	29	4	21	.315
1916—Boston		Amer.	67	136	18	37	3	16	.272
1917—Boston		Amer.	52	123	14	40	2	10	.325
1918—Boston		Amer.	95	317	50	95	●11	64	.300
1919—Boston		Amer.	130	432	★103	139	★29	★112	.322
1920—New York		Amer.	142	458	★158	172	★54	★137	.376
1921—New York		Amer.	152	540	★177	204	★59	★171	.378
1922—New York		Amer.	110	406	94	128	35	99	.315
1923—New York		Amer.	152	522	★151	205	★41	★131	.394
1924—New York		Amer.	153	529	★143	200	★46	121	★.378
1925—New York		Amer.	98	359	61	104	25	66	.290
1926—New York		Amer.	152	495	★139	184	★47	★145	.372
1927—New York		Amer.	151	540	★158	192	★60	164	.356
1928—New York		Amer.	154	536	★163	173	★54	●142	.323
1929—New York		Amer.	135	499	121	172	★46	154	.345
1930—New York		Amer.	145	518	150	186	★49	153	.359
1931—New York		Amer.	145	534	149	199	●46	163	.373
1932—New York		Amer.	133	457	120	156	41	137	.341
1933—New York		Amer.	137	459	97	138	34	103	.301
1934—New York		Amer.	125	365	78	105	22	84	.288
1935—Boston		Nat.	28	72	13	13	6	12	.181
American League Totals			2475	8327	2161	2860	708	2192	.343
National League Totals			28	72	13	13	6	12	.181
Major League Totals			2503	8399	2174	2873	714	2204	.342

WORLD SERIES RECORD

Year	Club	League	G.	AB.	R.	H.	HR.	RBI.	B.A.
1915—Boston		Amer.	1	1	0	0	0	0	.000
1916—Boston		Amer.	1	5	0	0	0	1	.000
1918—Boston		Amer.	3	5	0	1	0	2	.200
1921—New York		Amer.	6	16	3	5	1	4	.313
1922—New York		Amer.	5	17	1	2	0	1	.118
1923—New York		Amer.	6	19	8	7	3	3	.368
1926—New York		Amer.	7	20	6	6	4	5	.300
1927—New York		Amer.	4	15	4	6	2	7	.400
1928—New York		Amer.	4	16	9	10	3	4	.625
1932—New York		Amer.	4	15	6	5	2	6	.333
World Series Totals			41	129	37	42	15	33	.326

PITCHING RECORD

Year	Club	League	G.	IP.	W.	L.	Pct.	ERA.
1914—Balt.-Prov.		Int.	35	245	22	9	.710	......
1914—Boston		Amer.	4	23	2	1	.667	3.91
1915—Boston		Amer.	32	218	18	8	.692	2.44
1916—Boston		Amer.	44	324	23	12	.657	★1.75
1917—Boston		Amer.	41	326	24	13	.649	2.02
1918—Boston		Amer.	20	166	13	7	.650	2.22
1919—Boston		Amer.	17	133	9	5	.643	2.97
1920—New York		Amer.	1	4	1	0	1.000	4.50
1921—New York		Amer.	2	9	2	0	1.000	9.00
1930—New York		Amer.	1	9	1	0	1.000	3.00
1933—New York		Amer.	1	9	1	0	1.000	5.00
Major League Totals			163	1221	94	46	.671	2.28

WORLD SERIES PITCHING RECORD

Year	Club	League	G.	IP.	W.	L.	Pct.	ERA.
1916—Boston		Amer.	1	14	1	0	1.000	0.64
1918—Boston		Amer.	2	17	2	0	1.000	1.06
World Series Totals			3	31	3	0	1.000	0.87

★ Denotes led league.   ● Denotes tied for lead.

The Pride Of the Yankees

The story is neatly shaped by stirring success and stark tragedy. A dramatist might argue that a critical element is missing, that we have a son who was loving and dutiful, a husband who was adored and adoring, an athlete who was heroic and enduring, and then a victim who, nevertheless, was almost martyr-like in his stoicism.

Where tragedy balances the heroism, there is no contrast for the modesty, the shyness, the humility. As far as any recording angel knows, there was no ego, no temperament, no outbursts. "He showed up every day, he played, he gave no trouble, he never complained," said his longtime manager, Joe McCarthy.

There seems not to have been a secret Lou Gehrig, or if there was anything raging or unpleasant about him, he kept it behind drawn shades and locked doors. This enormously strong, endearingly handsome Yankee slugger was, by most accounts, a Momma's boy. It was not spoken disdainfully, but simply as fact.

Only once did Gehrig rebel against maternal authority, and it was no small act of self-assertion. When he was 30 years old, he tore loose and married Eleanor Twitchell, a bright, spirited young lady who was independent, sophisticated and, most crucially, not to be cowed by the formidable Mrs. Gehrig. Lou's mother disapproved of Eleanor—she disapproved of all of "Louie's" girls, but probably this one more than the others because Eleanor was her equal and more. But for once, Gehrig stood his ground and married the woman he loved.

Before Eleanor came on the scene, Mrs. Gehrig had been confronted by one other force that her powerful will could not conquer. This was something as foreign to her as an igloo, but for her son seemed to be as natural as breathing. It was called baseball.

The ball field was the one place where young Lou could let all restraints fly and assert the essence of Lou Gehrig. Free of his mother, he was his own man—powerful and dominant. If there were frus-

Lou Gehrig, pride of the Yankees.

trations, he dealt with them here, attacking the baseball and hitting shuddering line drives and long home runs in all directions. Given his physical strength, the outlet was a fortunate one.

Ever dutiful to his parents, both German immigrants, young Louis also hit the books with dedication—when he wasn't stealing time to indulge his lust for baseball and football. He starred on the baseball team at New York City's Commerce High, laying one of the first cornerstones to the Gehrig legend when, on a trip to Chicago, he blasted a homer over Wrigley Field's right-field wall during an annual intercity championship tournament.

Gehrig moved on to Columbia University to

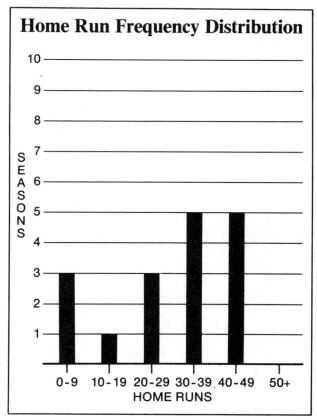

Columbia Lou.

Gehrig (right) with Hartford Manager Pat
O'Connor in 1924.

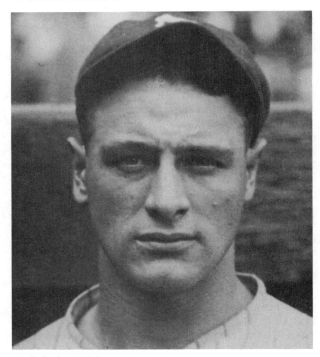

Gehrig in 1926.

All eyes are riveted on Gehrig's powerful swing.

study architecture, a career that would satisfy Momma Gehrig, but what he ultimately built on campus was a reputation as a strong-armed pitcher gifted with a rare slugging talent.

In a 1923 game against Rutgers at New Brunswick, N.J., the muscular young collegian widened the eyes of a Yankee scout, Paul Krichell. "I did not go there to look at Gehrig," Krichell recalled. "I did not even know what position he played. But he played in the outfield against Rutgers and socked a couple of balls a mile. I sat up and took notice. I saw a tremendous youth, with powerful arms and terrific legs. I said, 'Krich, get busy. Here is a kid who can't miss.'"

Krichell informed Yankee General Manager Ed Barrow that he had discovered another Babe Ruth, a revelation that must have sounded like a visit to dreamland. Krichell, however, was a respected judge of talent, not a man to report having seen a cannon where but a rifle was in hand. And Barrow, who a quarter-century earlier had signed an awkward-looking youngster named Honus Wagner, knew that dreams belonged to those who dreamed them. He instructed his scout to stay with this young horse named Gehrig.

A few days later, Krichell saw Gehrig play about four miles north of the Yankee offices, at Columbia's old South Field. It was a day Gehrig hit one of those home runs that become reference points in baseball history, not because someone took out a tape and measured the shot, but because it had strength, youth and promise in its flight. The home run soared over 116th Street and bounced up the steps of the library as if, in the words of one writer, "rushing straight for the history books."

Despite Momma Gehrig's moody disapproval, Gehrig soon signed a Yankee contract. Thus was born a part of baseball lore, a story that justifies every scout's faith and hope and optimism, the story of a vast and unexpected sighting. It is an emotional experience scouts yearn to have, that they probably rehearse having. One need only note what Yankee scout Tom Greenwade said more than a quarter-century later when he first laid eyes on a young switch-hitting Oklahoman named Mantle: "I knew how Paul Krichell felt when he saw Gehrig for the first time."

The Yankees sent Gehrig to Hartford in the Eastern League for most of the 1923 and 1924 seasons, and Lou responded as he always would—with raw power. Gehrig bombed 24 home runs in only 59 games in his first year at Hartford, then 37 homers while batting .369 in 1924. Recalled to brand-new Yankee Stadium in the waning days of the 1923 campaign, he hoisted his first of 493 big-league homers on September 27, in Boston, off the Red Sox's Bill Piercy. Gehrig played first base that day only because Wally Pipp, the regular, had sprained his ankle while stepping off a streetcar that morning—a twist of fate that foreshadowed a more popular bit of legend by two years.

Indeed, the feats of the strapping young Gehrig were fast becoming known throughout the insular world of baseball, a realm that quivers from sole to crown whenever an exciting new talent is turned loose, just as it did after the 1923 season. The Yankees were trying to make a deal with Louisville of the American Association for their talented young center fielder, Earle Combs. The manager at Louisville was McCarthy.

"The Yankees were anxious to buy Combs," McCarthy recalled, "and they were offering a good price for him. But we'd heard about this kid Gehrig they had at Hartford and we said that if they'd throw him into the deal, we'd shake hands on it. They really wanted Combs in the worst way, and

The infield of the 1927 Yankees featured (left to right) Gehrig, second baseman
Tony Lazzeri, shortstop Mark Koenig and third baseman Joe Dugan.

Gehrig takes time on a 1927 barnstorming tour in
Los Angeles to show the kids how it's done.

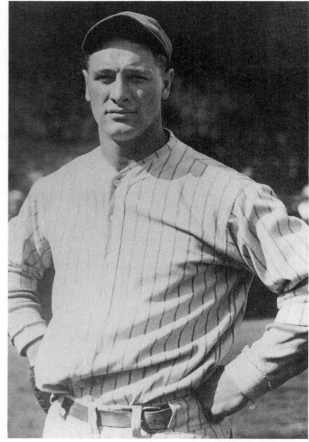

If Babe Ruth was the King, Gehrig was the Crown
Prince.

Lou's devotion to Momma Gehrig never wavered.

we figured they'd give us Gehrig. But they wouldn't do it and that impressed me. I said to myself, 'This Gehrig kid must be pretty good.' We finally dealt Combs to the Yankees and they kept Gehrig. That was a good thing for me, because when I took over the Yankees in 1931 I had both of them—Combs in center field and Gehrig on first base."

The Yankees were grooming Gehrig as their first baseman despite having a perfectly adequate man at the post in Pipp. The 32-year-old Pipp had been a steady performer with the team for 10 years, playing on pennant winners in 1921, 1922 and 1923. Over the previous three seasons (1922-24), he had batted a cumulative .310—obviously not a man to be casually pushed aside. Nor did the Yankees move him. The 1925 season opened with Pipp at first base and Gehrig on the bench.

Through April and May, Gehrig appeared in only 11 games. Twenty-one years old, eager, anxious, possessing a talent nearly as colossal as Ruth's —but he never complained. No one knew what he was thinking, few people ever did.

On June 1, Gehrig was sent up to pinch hit for shortstop Pee Wee Wanninger in what became game No. 1 of his record string of 2,130 consecutive games played. Less than a month earlier, Wanninger had replaced Everett Scott at shortstop, ending Scott's consecutive-game streak at 1,307, the major league record Gehrig would shatter. Thus does the endlessly weaving game of baseball often cross-reference its history.

The next day, legend has it, Pipp reported to the park feeling ill. He had a headache, the story goes, sometimes alluding to a beaning Pipp supposedly suffered during batting practice. Pipp, however, had been struggling (like the Yanks) all season, batting only .244. Manager Miller Huggins, probably waiting for the chance, inserted Gehrig at first base. And that was that, until May 2, 1939.

"Miller Huggins shot the works," wrote John Kieran in the next day's New York Herald Tribune. "Facing a drop into the cellar with a former championship team, he yanked out three of his regulars at the Stadium yesterday, sent his youngsters out to play and the revamped Yankees came crashing through to victory over the world champion Senators. . . . Aaron Ward, Wally Pipp and Wally Schang were benched in favor of Howard Shanks, Lou Gehrig and Benny Bengough. The youngsters romped about the greensward in joyous fashion

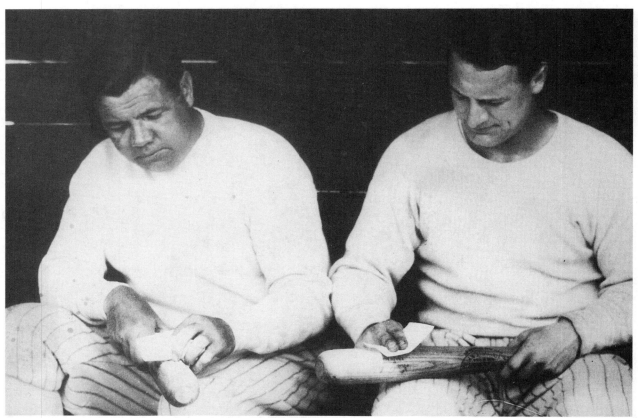

Ruth (left) and Gehrig smoothing their bats with sandpaper.

Gehrig receiving three nattily dressed visitors at Yankee Stadium in the early
1930s: Groucho, Chico and Harpo Marx.

Baseball's three long-ball symbols of the early 1930s were (left to right) Gehrig, Jimmie Foxx and Ruth.

and contributed more than their share of the 16 soaring safeties amassed by the Yankees. . . . Gehrig got a single in the second, a double in the third and a single in the fifth. Now then, boys, all together—Rah, Rah, Rah, Columbia!"

In the following issue of The Sporting News, correspondent Joe Vila noted: "The expected shakeup of the Yankees materialized last week with fair results. Manager Huggins took the bull by the horns, benched Wally Pipp and had Aaron Ward on the sidelines much of the time for unsuccessful efforts to hit the ball at opportune moments. It was the first time Pipp had been laid off, except for injuries, since he became a member of the New York American League team 10 years ago and, of course, he felt humiliated. In his place, Huggins inserted Buster Gehrig, the former Columbia University star, who responded nicely with some solid walloping."

The new man played in 126 games that year and batted .295, the same as he would in his last full season, 1938 (what was promising in 1925, however, would prove ominous in '38). Among his 129 hits were 20 home runs, a modest figure by later standards but, with the home run in its infancy, good enough to rank sixth in the league.

A year later, Gehrig helped swat the Yankees to the pennant and played in his first of seven World Series. For the year, he batted .313, collected a league-high 20 triples and drove in 107 runs, the first of 13 consecutive seasons with 100 or more runs batted in, a major league record he shares with Jimmie Foxx. Gehrig, however, proved to be an RBI

machine unlike anyone who ever played—including the "Beast"—driving in more than 150 runs in a record seven seasons.

Gehrig's mighty coupling with Ruth didn't start until his third full season. This was the thunderous year of the 1927 Yankees, arguably baseball's most talented alignment. And among the game's most legendary array of bats was the deadliest one-two lineup punch ever seen: Ruth in the No. 3 slot and Gehrig batting fourth, a pairing devised by Huggins to ensure Ruth was pitched to.

Together, Ruth and his crown prince slammed 107 home runs (60 for Babe, 47 for Lou), nearly one-fourth of the league's 439 homers that year. Gehrig's 47 blows were, in fact, the most hit in one season by any player other than Ruth. He batted .373, set a major league record with 175 RBIs (eclipsing by four the mark established by Ruth in 1921) and was voted the A.L. Most Valuable Player. Gehrig and Ruth claimed the top two spots in the league in homers, RBIs, runs scored, walks, total bases and slugging average.

It was a devastating performance by this slugging tandem, though Roger Maris (61 homers) and Mickey Mantle (54) would top the two-man mark with 115 homers in 1961. Yet placed within the proper context, the dominance of the Ruth-Gehrig duo is clear-cut: In 1961, 20 other A.L. batters besides Maris and Mantle hit at least 20 home runs; in 1927; no A.L. player other than Ruth or Gehrig hit more than 18 homers. Then there's the matter of RBIs (Gehrig 175, Ruth 164, Maris 142, Mantle 128)

Gehrig and Yankee rookie Joe DiMaggio going through spring drills in 1936.

Discussing his teammates Ruth and Gehrig (above), Yankee pitcher George Pipgras said of Lou, "He was the quiet one."

Gehrig is greeted by the Yankee batboy after slamming a home run in the 1937 World Series. The New York Giants' catcher is Harry Danning.

Gehrig and Yankee Owner Jacob Ruppert have just agreed on Lou's 1935 contract. Gehrig had won the Triple Crown in 1934.

and batting average (Gehrig .373, Ruth .356, Mantle .317, Maris .269).

Ruth and Gehrig remain baseball's most famous slugging duo, and not merely because of their awesomely impressive numbers.

They established their supremacy first, at the dawn of the age of the lively ball and, therefore, set standards and made impressions that were the deepest and most lasting.

Statistically, Ruth and Gehrig might run neck and neck, but there were profound differences between the teammates, both on and off the field. They were different personalities and different hitters. Ruth had been the unsupervised Baltimore street kid who had run wild until lassoed by the prefects of St. Mary's; Gehrig had grown up smothered by the love of an overly protective mother. Ruth was loud, coarse, vulgar; Gehrig was quiet, shy, modest. Ruth was a prodigal spender; Gehrig was frugal. At home plate, Ruth was a pull hitter, driving long, majestically high home runs; Gehrig was a slasher, hitting blistering line drives in all directions. Ruth the hitter was more fearsome than Gehrig; Gehrig the personality was less fathomable

to the opposition and therefore more troubling. "We never threw at Gehrig," Lefty Grove said. "You didn't want to get him mad. Best let him sleep."

George Pipgras, who starred on the mound for the Yankees during the Ruth-Gehrig era, recalled the pair of monumental teammates.

"They were very different, you know," he said. "Babe was outgoing and friendly—he loved people, he loved giving autographs. Lou was the quiet one; sometimes he gave the impression that he didn't much care about people. Maybe it was shyness. I remember one time we were coming into some town in the South to play an exhibition game. When the bus pulled up to the ball park there was a great crowd of people outside waiting for autographs. Lou sort of froze up. He didn't like a lot of people around him. I could see he didn't want to get off the bus. Finally I said to him, 'Lou, just wait until Babe gets off. He'll draw them away and then you can sneak off.' And that's just what happened."

As great as Gehrig was, Ruth was always a little better, always more. The Babe had "saved" baseball. He was the game's grand personality, an ap-

By the mid-1930s, Gehrig was known as baseball's "Iron Man."

A nationwide poll was taken in the summer of 1938 to determine "The Most Popular First Baseman." The winner was Gehrig, shown here with his prize, a new automobile.

proachable idol and down-to-earth god. Gehrig seemed to accept Ruth as unique and was able to live with his subordinate place in the hierarchy without envy or resentment. Or maybe it was simply a matter of suppression. Bob Shawkey, the Yankees' manager in 1930, remembered a scene during spring training. Ruth was in the batting cage, hoisting one terrific shot after another into the blazing Florida sunshine. Gehrig was sitting on the bench, hand to chin, watching, his eyes rising with each disappearing Ruthian clout.

"His face never changed expression," Shawkey said. "I was taken by his fascination with Ruth and couldn't help watching him, a little smile on my face. When he noticed me, he looked at me for a moment and then turned quickly away, as if he had been caught thinking something he didn't want anybody to know about."

Gehrig once told a writer: "I'm not a headline guy and we may as well just face it. I'm just the guy who's in there every day, the fellow who follows Babe in the batting order. When Babe's turn at bat is over, whether he strikes out or belts a home run, the fans are still talking about him when I come up to bat. If I stood on my head at the plate, nobody'd pay any attention."

Gehrig, however, was soon a terror all his own. He led the league in RBIs in 1927, 1928, 1930, 1931

—when he set the current A.L. standard with 184 RBIs—and 1934. In home runs, he tied Ruth for the lead in 1931 with 46 and reached his peak with a league-high 49 homers in both 1934 (when he won the Triple Crown) and 1936 (when he received his second MVP award).

By all accounts, Gehrig was not a home run hitter in the mold of Ruth or Foxx, or like Ted Williams and Ralph Kiner, who came later. They were men who drove the ball not only hard but high and far—aesthetic home runs that were a treat for the eye. Gehrig's four-baggers often were line drives— terrific, savagely struck line drives that had a furious and primitive quality to them.

"He hit smashers," said Tommy Henrich, Gehrig's teammate from 1937-39. "In all directions. He hit them as hard and far to left field as to right. And I mean he really *smashed* them. I've never seen anyone hit line drives like that." It was not uncommon for a Gehrig home run to rocket off a girder and shoot all the way back to the infield. A Ruth home run, on the other hand, took off and soared away to some never-never land, not to be seen again.

By 1935, Ruth was gone and Gehrig should have been the toast of New York. But, as had been frequently pointed out, Gehrig was born to be upstaged, a product not only of his retiring personali-

35

To Yankee Manager Joe McCarthy (left), Gehrig was much more than a great baseball player.

After leaving the Yankee lineup in 1939, Gehrig (left) remained with the team and helped any way he could. Through his ordeal, wife Eleanor (right) remained a great comfort for the venerable slugger.

ty, but due to incredible circumstances as well. The classic example occurred June 3, 1932, his single greatest day in baseball. Gehrig ripped four consecutive home runs against the Philadelphia Athletics to tie a major league record, only to find the biggest headlines going to the sudden retirement of New York Giants Manager John McGraw. And in the World Series that year, despite batting .529 against the Chicago Cubs, not to mention eight RBIs, nine runs scored or the two home runs in Game 3, Gehrig was shoved into the wings by the great showman's most celebrated moment—Ruth's alleged "called shot" in the same third game. Still, Gehrig's performance wasn't lost on Chicago Manager Charlie Grimm, who noted, "I didn't think I would ever see a ball player that good." In the World Series, few could rival Gehrig, who helped lead the Yanks to titles in 1927, 1928, 1932 and 1936-38 and set Series records in 1928 for most home runs (four) and RBIs (nine) in a four-game Series. In seven Series overall, he batted .361 with 10 homers and 35 RBIs.

And then, in 1936, there was the arrival of Joe DiMaggio, a man as shy and bland of personality as Gehrig, but one who played with a white-hot pride and intensity that overshadowed everyone else on the field, including Gehrig. And ultimately, the two shining achievements of these Yankee teammates is symbolic of the public's perception of each. DiMaggio's 56-game hitting streak was filled with drama, tension and excitement, while Gehrig's string of 2,130 consecutive games played was one of passive

endurance; truly heroic, yes, but the product of consistent excellence and a stoic commitment to the job at hand.

Gehrig was the man who never missed a beat, a slugger the equal of Ruth and Williams but one who never brought to the plate the same kind of electricity that crackled through anxious crowds when they batted. The torch was passed at Yankee Stadium on opening day 1939, when Williams doubled to right field for his first major league hit. As the strong, slender, 20-year-old Red Sox rookie whirled around first base, the man he passed was just days from the end of his remarkable career. In fact, he was dying.

The first indication of Gehrig's illness appeared in his final statistics for 1938: 29 home runs (his lowest total since 1928), 114 RBIs (lowest since 1926) and a .295 batting average (his first sub-.300 season since his rookie compaign). These could have been the ragged edges of what had been a long and relentlessly played career; some people thought so. But they began thinking about it more deeply the following spring when they saw Gehrig swinging and running to virtually no purpose.

"His best shots," one teammate said, "went to left field. He just couldn't seem to pull a ball. And when he ran he simply got nowhere, like a guy on a treadmill."

Nevertheless, Gehrig tried to work himself into shape, as if conditioning would restore his reflexes. He accomplished little, but considering that he was suffering from amyotrophic lateral sclerosis, a dis-

Gehrig arriving in Minnesota in June 1939 en route to the Mayo Clinic.

"Lou Gehrig Appreciation Day" at Yankee Stadium on July 4, 1939.

Gehrig's Milestone Home Runs

	Date	Place	Pitcher	Club
1	Sept. 27, 1923	Boston	Bill Piercy	Boston
100	June 17, 1928	St. Louis	Alvin Crowder	St. Louis
200	June 20, 1931	St. Louis	George Blaeholder	St. Louis
300	April 30, 1934	Washington	Earl Whitehill	Washington
400	July 10, 1936	New York	Lloyd Brown	Cleveland
Last	Sept. 27, 1938	New York	Dutch Leonard	Washington

ease that slowly strangles the muscles, it is remarkable that he accomplished anything at all.

"You'd see him in the clubhouse trying to get his uniform on," teammate Wes Ferrell recalled. "He'd fumble with the buttons, then seem to take forever to lace his spikes. Somebody said that one morning Lou was bent over for so long trying to tie his laces that he finally just pitched forward and tumbled over. Nobody knew what was wrong. You couldn't imagine *anything* being wrong with Lou. What the hell, he was 'The Iron Man.'"

Something terrible was amiss; McCarthy knew that much, and for the Yankee skipper, for whom Gehrig was like a son, it was a vexing problem because of the streak. You can bench a man for a game or two, but when he is riding an unbroken string of service that had reached 2,122 games entering the season, you move prudently.

"I had a feeling that once I took him out, it would all be over," McCarthy said. "I didn't know what was wrong, but that it was something very serious (and) becoming more and more obvious."

Eight games into the 1939 season, Gehrig was batting just .143. He was playing with a sluggishness afield that was beginning to tighten the lips of some of his teammates, who were in search of a fourth straight pennant. On April 30 at Yankee Stadium, Gehrig played what would be his final game.

"In the ninth, (Washington's) Buddy Myer slapped one down to me, and in other years I would have stuck the ball into my back pocket," Gehrig said. "But it was a hard play for me and I tossed to (Johnny) Murphy, who had covered the bag. When I returned to the bench, the boys said, 'Great play, Lou.' I thought to myself, 'Heavens, has it reached that stage?'"

On May 2 in Detroit, Gehrig asked to see McCarthy in the manager's hotel room. He had already decided to withdraw from the lineup, and McCarthy sensed his favorite player was troubled.

"He asked me how much longer I thought he should stay in, when I thought he should get out," McCarthy said. "'Right now,' I told him. He didn't say anything right away, just sat there. Then he said, 'Well, that's what I wanted to know. That's the way I feel, too. I'm not doing the ball club any good.'

"His reflexes were shot. I was afraid of his getting hit with a pitched ball. He wouldn't have been able

to get out of the way, that's how bad it was. That was my chief concern, to get him out of there before he got hurt."

The following day, Gehrig told a reporter he was puzzled by his rapid collapse. "I just can't understand it," he said. "I am not sick . . . maybe a rest will do me good."

On June 19, on his 36th birthday, Gehrig learned of his illness after days of tests conducted at the Mayo Clinic in Rochester, Minn. He was told he had approximately two years to live.

Finally, there came the day that was his alone in the sunshine: July 4, 1939, "Lou Gehrig Appreciation Day" at Yankee Stadium. He thanked everyone in a moving speech, and in this moment of supreme poignance, said that while he may have been given "a bad break," he still considered himself "the luckiest man on the face of the earth."

On June 2, 1941, Henry Louis Gehrig died, 16 years to the day he had replaced Wally Pipp at first base for the New York Yankees.

GEHRIG'S CAREER RECORD

Born June 19, 1903, New York, N.Y. Died June 2, 1941, Riverdale, N.Y.
Batted and threw lefthanded. Elected to Hall of Fame, 1939.

Year	Club	League	G.	AB.	R.	H.	HR.	RBI.	B.A.
1921—Hartford		East.	12	46	5	12	0	....	.261
1922—					(Not in Organized Ball)				
1923—New York		Amer.	13	26	6	11	1	9	.423
1923—Hartford		East.	59	227	54	69	24	....	.304
1924—New York		Amer.	10	12	2	6	0	5	.500
1924—Hartford		East.	134	504	111	186	37	....	.369
1925—New York		Amer.	126	437	73	129	20	68	.295
1926—New York		Amer.	155	572	135	179	16	107	.313
1927—New York		Amer.	★155	584	149	218	47	★175	.373
1928—New York		Amer.	154	562	139	210	27	●142	.374
1929—New York		Amer.	154	553	127	166	35	126	.300
1930—New York		Amer.	●154	581	143	220	41	★174	.379
1931—New York		Amer.	155	619	★163	★211	●46	★184	.341
1932—New York		Amer.	★156	596	138	208	34	151	.349
1933—New York		Amer.	152	593	★138	198	32	139	.334
1934—New York		Amer.	●154	579	128	210	★49	★165	★.363
1935—New York		Amer.	149	535	★125	176	30	119	.329
1936—New York		Amer.	●155	579	★167	205	●49	152	.354
1937—New York		Amer.	★157	569	138	200	37	159	.351
1938—New York		Amer.	●157	576	115	170	29	114	.295
1939—New York		Amer.	8	28	2	4	0	1	.143
Major League Totals			2164	8001	1888	2721	493	1990	.340

WORLD SERIES RECORD

Year	Club	League	G.	AB.	R.	H.	HR.	RBI.	B.A.
1926—New York		Amer.	7	23	1	8	0	3	.348
1927—New York		Amer.	4	13	2	4	0	5	.308
1928—New York		Amer.	4	11	5	6	4	9	.545
1932—New York		Amer.	4	17	9	9	3	8	.529
1936—New York		Amer.	6	24	5	7	2	7	.292
1937—New York		Amer.	5	17	4	5	1	3	.294
1938—New York		Amer.	4	14	4	4	0	0	.286
World Series Totals			34	119	30	43	10	35	.361

The Beast

"In the early 1930s," former White Sox ace right-hander Ted Lyons was saying, "we had a kid third baseman, whose name eludes me at the moment. I was pitching against the Philadelphia Athletics and in the middle of the game this kid trots over to the mound from third base. 'Ted,' he says, 'I have a date tonight with a really gorgeous blonde. We're going to dinner and then later on, well, who knows?'

" 'So what?' I asked.

" 'So do me a favor—pitch him outside. I want to be in shape for tonight.'

"Well," Lyons continued, "you know who he was talking about, don't you, who he wanted pitched outside? Jimmie Foxx. And I don't think that fellow was far wrong, either, because if there was any righthanded batter capable of hitting one that could ruin your night, it was Jimmie."

Strength, power, dread, respect—invariably such qualities are woven into the tales of the mighty home run hitters. And among the most classic of the tales are the ones told of Jimmie Foxx.

Foxx was the paragon of the home run hitter in its purest form: he had brute strength, a compelling presence at the plate and he hit home runs that were like exploratory shots, streaking to where no baseball had gone before, and making the journey with a suddenness that, in Lyons' words, "could shock a crowd into silence for a moment and then rouse them into shouts and applause."

Even Wes Ferrell, notoriously hot-tempered on the mound, admitted he was left spellbound by a booming Foxx home run. "He could hit that thing so hard and so far and so high that I just had to stand out there and admire it," Ferrell said. "A man hit a ball like that? You couldn't get mad."

Only Ruth was capable of hitting home runs that evoked similar enchantment. "You'd throw a home run to one of those guys," Ferrell said, "and then spin around on the mound and watch it go . . . all of a sudden you weren't the pitcher who'd fed it up but a spectator, just watching the beauty of that

Jimmie Foxx. They called him "the righthanded Babe Ruth."

thing like everybody else. The guys who lifted one over the fence into the first row of the bleachers, those were the guys you cussed out. But not Ruth or Foxx; they hit home runs the way home runs were meant to be hit."

Some players maintain that it doesn't matter how far the ball travels, just so it clears the fence. But it matters for the spectator, because baseball is a pageant of spectacles and exhibitions, and the long, soaring home run is the ultimate spectacular. And it also matters to that man on the pitching mound.

"Don't let anybody tell you there's no difference between the 350-foot home run and the 500-footer," said Bob Shawkey, winner of 196 games with the

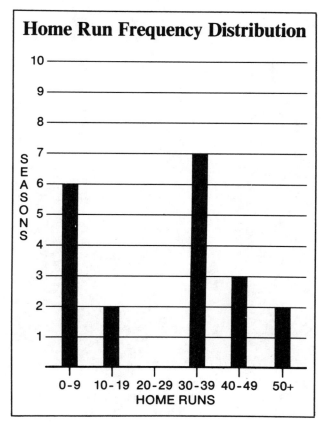

Former Philadelphia Athletics star Frank (Home Run) Baker (right) was the man who first noticed the power potential of Foxx (left). He signed Jimmie for Easton of the Eastern Shore League in 1924.

This picture, taken in the early 1920s, is reputed to be the first of Jimmie Foxx (seated, second from right at age 13) in a baseball uniform.

Athletics and New York Yankees. "The guy who can hit it 500 feet—like Ruth or Foxx—scares the hell out of you. You're much more careful with him because he's still strong enough to pop it out of the park even if you've fooled him and he hasn't hit it square. You try extra hard not to make a mistake with him, and that's generally when you make your mistakes."

Lyons concurred. "I used to feel very self-conscious when a guy like Babe or Jimmie was up at the plate," he said. "They take the game right out of your control and make you feel fatalistic about every pitch you throw them. . . . You could be pitching the game of your life and you look up and there's Ruth or Foxx or Gehrig standing there and you find yourself wishing you were in China."

When it came to a show of strength, no challenge was too big—or small—for Foxx. Before one game, he was putting on an exhibition in batting practice, dispatching one shot after another to faraway places. "Ah, for Pete's sake," somebody remarked,

"you're so doggone big and strong, what would you do if you had to hit-and-run like we do?"

Foxx was indignant. "I can hit-and-run," he insisted. "I can hit behind the runner anytime I want to."

Sure enough, Foxx came up with a man on first and received the hit-and-run sign.

"The pitch comes in," recalled Yankee outfielder Tommy Henrich, "the runner takes off, Jimmie chokes up and punches the ball—on a line into the right-field seats. He hit behind the runner, all right; he hit behind the outfielders, too."

Foxx began building the muscles that would one day disturb the equilibrium of American League pitchers when he was a youngster working on his father's dairy farm in Sudlersville, Md. Jimmie developed steel-like wrists and fingers from milking cows and a thick, powerful upper torso from wrestling heavy milk cans onto trucks and off again at railroad sidings.

"When he was 16," said fellow Athletic Jimmie

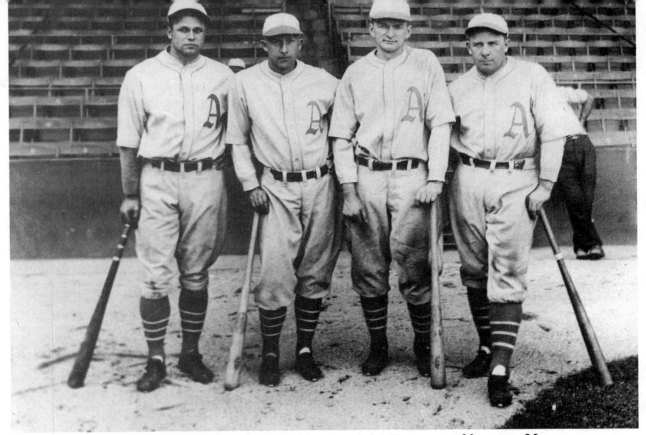

Connie Mack's 1929 championship infield featured (left to right) Foxx, second baseman Max Bishop, shortstop Joe Boley and third baseman Jimmie Dykes.

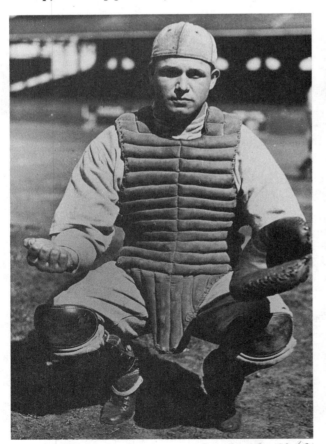

Foxx hit the big leagues as a catcher, but the A's already had Mickey Cochrane. Consequently, he learned to play first base, his position through most of his career.

Ruth and Foxx.

Foxx and Connie Mack.

Dykes, "he already had the physique of a heavy-weight fighter. The first time he took his shirt off in the clubhouse, everybody looked at him and had the same thought: 'Lord, what's he going to be like in a half-dozen years?' Well, in a half-dozen years, he was hitting 58 home runs. But right from the beginning he looked like bullets would bounce off him."

At 14, Foxx already was playing semipro ball on the diamonds that had been carved out of Maryland's dairy belt, hitting baseballs for eye-catching distances. He pitched, played the infield and was a natural catcher, which is usually where 14-year-old kids end up when they look as if they've been put together by a welder. (Catcher and third base were the two positions Foxx always believed were his best.) Jimmie also could run, recalling with pride his days at Sudlersville High, "where I starred in the dash events and the high jump and was considered one of the fastest trackmen in Maryland."

While playing for a semipro team in Ridgely, Md., Foxx made a habit of depositing home runs into the backyard of Buck Herzog, the former National League infielder who owned a house in back of left field. Those calling cards failed to attract Herzog's attention, but another former major leaguer did take notice.

One morning in 1924, Jimmie opened the Foxx mailbox and found a penny post card addressed to him.

"He told me about it once," Dykes said. "It must have made quite an impression on him. He said, 'I never got any mail, but here was this card with my name on it, inviting me to come over to Easton and try out for the ball club.' "

The card was signed "Frank Baker." And like any baseball-happy kid, Jimmie knew Frank Baker was "Home Run" Baker, the slugging third baseman on Connie Mack's all-conquering Athletic teams of the pre-war years and a member of the "$100,000 in-field." Almost as excited over the post card as Jimmie was his father, Dell, a former semipro catcher who said to his husky son, "Let's go. If nothing else, it'll be an experience."

Father and son headed down the pike to Easton, where Baker was managing the Maryland town's entry in the Eastern Shore League. Duly impressed with the 16-year-old strongboy's abilities, Baker signed him to a contract as his catcher.

It was at this point that old loyalties came to bear upon the life and destiny of James Emory Foxx.

Many a man who had played for Mack never forgot the old tactician's fatherly consideration and gentle ways. Some remained devoted to him for the rest of their lives, including Baker, who alerted Mack when he discovered the extent of his new recruit's mammoth potential.

At the same time, according to Foxx, New York Yankees scout Paul Krichell (who the year before had signed Lou Gehrig) had been on his way to give the big kid a serious look when he received a call to clean up an urgent problem on a Yankee farm club.

Jimmie (right, left photo) with a different breed of Fox, Detroit outfielder Pete.
Jimmie "looked like he had been put together by a welder."

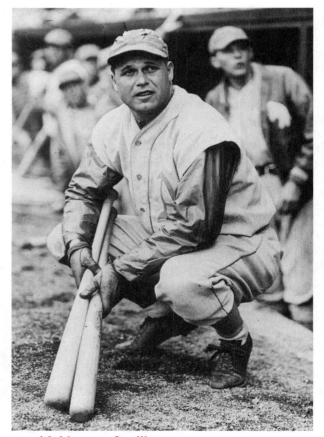

Foxx evidently was as competent with a shotgun as he was with his more familiar
weapon—a baseball bat.

Foxx as a member of the Boston Red Sox in 1936.

When Baker learned of the Yankees' interest, he told Foxx, "I have a chance to make a deal for you with either New York or Philadelphia. Mr. Mack is a wonderful man. I'd advise you to take the A's." The youngster assented.

(Dwell on this for a moment: If Foxx had been sold to New York, the Yankees lineup in a few years would have featured the back-to-back bulge of Ruth, Gehrig and Foxx, who in all likelihood would have caught or played third base).

When the A's called up Foxx that August, Mack remarked, "Now I'll be accused of robbing the cradle."

"I didn't play in any games," Foxx said, "but I did make a western swing with the club. Mr. Mack just wanted to break me in slowly."

For most of the next two seasons, he sat beside Mack and learned, serving only a brief apprenticeship at Providence of the International League in 1925. It wasn't just Foxx's youthfulness that was limiting his playing time—the Athletics already had a budding sensation named Mickey Cochrane behind the plate. But by 1927, Mack began to explore Foxx's versatility, playing him in 61 games, mostly at first base. Foxx batted .323 and belted his first three career homers. He played in 118 games the following year—most of them at third base—and batted .328 with 13 home runs, not a staggering figure, but apparently some of those shots had a special, majestic quality.

"All of his blows soar high and far. They are mighty ones, clouts that come from arms that swing milk cans during the winter," Baseball Magazine reported at the end of the season.

"The wise men of the sport are predicting that this 6-foot, 180-pound youngster is swinging a bat that threatens to cast a shadow over the wonderful achievements of the mighty Babe Ruth."

In the universe of baseball, this was (and still is) the absolute pinnacle of flattery. Ruth was the touchstone of slugging devastation and Foxx was but 20 years old.

Further in this 1928 article, it is painful to note what is said about an upright young man who in the twilight of his life would become known for his financial problems, heavy drinking and, ultimately, his indigence:

"The beckoning of the primrose roadways and the glitter and glare of the white lights made no impression upon him. In the five years that he has been in baseball, Foxx has saved enough money to be the owner of a 200-acre dairy farm near Sudlersville, Maryland, his birthplace. When the last hand is out at the end of the diamond season, Foxx hurries to his farm, where he works from sun-up until it fades in the west each day of the winter."

The writer quotes a practical and diligent Foxx as saying: "I looked around when I came into this game and found that the good players knew as much about finance as they did baseball. I saw that the easygoing fellows in the sport . . . were not getting along as well as the fellows who were saving."

Posing for this picture at the 1937 All-Star Game in Washington was a veritable Who's Who of American League sluggers: (left to right) Lou Gehrig, Joe Cronin, Bill Dickey, Joe DiMaggio, Charlie Gehringer, Foxx and Hank Greenberg.

Foxx receives his 1938 Most Valuable Player award as Boston's coming attraction, young Ted Williams, joins in the festivities.

In 1929, Foxx took over as the Athletics' regular first baseman, joining with left fielder Al Simmons, pitcher Lefty Grove and Cochrane to form the nucleus of one of baseball's most potent teams ever. In his first full season, Foxx whaled 33 home runs, collected 117 runs batted in and batted .354. It was his first of 13 consecutive seasons with 100 or more RBIs, a major league record he shares with Gehrig, and the first of 12 consecutive years with 30 or more home runs, a major league record that is his alone.

Bolstered by Foxx's robust slugging, the Athletics ran off with three straight pennants from 1929-31. In his only three World Series, Foxx batted .350, .333 and .348 and totaled four home runs. In Game 5 of the 1930 Series, Foxx broke up a scoreless duel with a ninth-inning, two-run homer off the Cardinals' Burleigh Grimes that, according to Grimes, "knocked the concrete loose in the center-field bleachers. He hit it so hard I couldn't feel sorry for myself." Describing the clout Foxx hit in the fourth game of the 1931 Series, Cardinal bullpen occupant Jim Lindsey made the classic comment, "We were watching it for two innings."

"That was a crowning thrill when I hit that homer off old Burleigh Grimes in the 1931 Series," Foxx admitted a few years later. "I really felt sorry for Grimes afterward. Honest, I did."

As the 1930s unfolded, Ruth was king and Gehrig crown prince—according to Yankee fans. But to the baseball world at large it was Foxx, not Gehrig, who was monarch-in-waiting. By 1932, Ruth's scepter, though still potent, was swinging in a deepening twilight. Despite his 41 home runs that season, the acknowledged "owner and sole proprietor" of the home run would fail to claim at least a share of the league crown for the first time since 1925. And not only was Ruth second, it was by a large margin.

Foxx tagged a lordly 58 home runs, the most ever by a righthanded batter and, at the time, third only to Ruth's 60 homers in 1927 and 59 in 1921. Also the league leader with 169 RBIs, Foxx was thwarted in his bid for the Triple Crown by the Boston Red Sox's Dale Alexander, who, with almost 200 fewer at-bats, batted .367 to Jimmie's .364. Foxx's heavyweight hitting was reflected in his .749 slugging average (a mark topped in big-league history only by Ruth, four times, Gehrig and Rogers Hornsby) and his first of three A.L. Most Valuable Player awards.

It was clearly Jimmie's breakthrough season, remarkable because he was just 24 and because he eclipsed some already-solid career bests—37 homers and 156 RBIs in 1930. Foxx had solidified his credentials as Ruth's heir apparent, and it wasn't just the numbers. "In almost every park in the American League, Babe now shares with his youthful rival the honors of driving out the longest hit ever," one writer noted that season. "In some parks, the palm may even go to Foxx."

Foxx smashed what many regard as the longest homer ever hit out of Chicago's Comiskey Park, a booming drive over the left-center-field pavilion,

Foxx at spring training in Sarasota, Fla., in March 1940.

and is credited with being the first player to reach the park's center-field bleachers. His monumental homer into the extreme corner of the left-field upper deck at Yankee Stadium supposedly splintered a seat.

In 1933, Foxx was again voted the league's MVP, this time claiming the Triple Crown that had narrowly eluded him in his stunning '32 season. Foxx slammed 48 home runs with 163 RBIs and a .356 batting average, then followed up in 1934 with totals nearly as impressive: 44 homers, 130 RBIs and a .334 batting mark. In 1935, he claimed his third home run title in four seasons, tying for the lead with 36 one-way shots.

In his heyday, Foxx was swinging against some of the most formidable opponents in baseball history in Ruth, Gehrig, Hank Greenberg and Joe DiMaggio. Winning home run and RBI titles in this company was no small task, considering that, from 1929 through 1938, the lowest total for an A.L. RBI lead-

Foxx with the Philadelphia Phillies in 1945, his last year in the big leagues.

Foxx (right) with Chicago Cubs Manager Jimmie Wilson in 1942.

er was 157. Then again, no one had the massive arms of Double-X and, in turn, quite the same power advantage. "Batting strength is in the fingers, wrists and forearms," said Foxx, who drove the ball with a quick cut and light bat because "it's the snap and velocity which drive the ball."

By this time, however, with the Depression and the consequent decline in attendance steadily de-

pleting his resources, Mack had begun breaking up his championship team. One by one the players went, including Simmons, Cochrane, Grove and Foxx, who was sent to the Red Sox in December 1935 for, essentially, $150,000.

With Foxx swinging at Fenway Park's inviting left-field wall, some predicted that Ruth's single-season home run record would fall.

Foxx rekindles some of his baseball memories with his son, Jim, in 1951.

Foxx's Milestone Home Runs

	Date	Place	Pitcher	Club
1	May 31, 1927	Philadelphia	Urban Shocker	New York
100	June 29, 1931	Detroit	Earl Whitehill	Detroit
200	July 15, 1933	Philadelphia	Schoolboy Rowe	Detroit
300	Sept. 15, 1935	Philadelphia	Les Tietje	Chicago
400	June 27, 1938	Cleveland	Bob Feller	Cleveland
500	Sept. 24, 1940	Philadelphia	George Caster	Philadelphia
Last	Sept. 9, 1945	Pittsburgh	Johnny Lanning	Pittsburgh

"I never believed that'" said Grove, who had preceded Foxx to Boston in 1934. "The wall being so close really made no difference, because when Jimmie caught hold of one it went out, no matter where he was playing. If he broke Babe's record, the wall wasn't going to have anything to do with it."

In 1938, Foxx hit 50 home runs and led the league with 175 RBIs and a .349 batting average, failing to win his second Triple Crown only because Greenberg unloaded 58 homers for Detroit. Nevertheless, Foxx received his third MVP designation, becoming the only A.L. player to win the award for two teams and the only major leaguer to hit 50 homers in a season for two clubs.

In 1939, Foxx led the league for the fourth and final time with 35 home runs while batting .360. Two seasons later, he had slipped to 19 homers. Foxx had not yet turned 34, but the deterioration of his abilities had become painfully evident.

"He had been so good," Lyons said, "such a superb player, with so many different facets to his game, that his decline was shocking, mainly because it seemed to happen all at once."

Next to DiMaggio, Ted Williams said, Foxx had been the best player he ever saw, but one who also once boasted that "he could drink 15 of those little bottles of Scotch, those miniatures, and not be affected. Of course, nobody can do that and stay healthy, and it got to Jimmie later on."

The years of dwindling returns were upon Foxx, who continued to drink heavily, invest unwisely and pick up every tab in sight.

"He was good-natured to a fault," Ferrell said. "To a large fault. No matter how much he was hurting in the pocket, Jimmie always grabbed the check."

Foxx suffered a crippling financial blow when a golf course venture in Florida failed.

"He took that golf course thing pretty hard," Ferrell said. "He knew his baseball career was about coming to an end and he'd been counting on the golf course to set him up. Instead, it wiped him out."

In June 1942, Foxx was waived out of the league to the Chicago Cubs. Illness and injuries limited him to just 100 games and eight homers for the year. He sat out the 1943 season, came back for a handful of games with the Cubs in 1944, then finished up with the Phillies in the wartime 1945 campaign. His seven home runs boosted his final career total to 534, second on the all-time long-ball roster (trailing only Ruth) until 1966, when Willie Mays moved ahead.

In retirement, Foxx still had the memories. The former Maryland strongboy, "an inspiration to rural young America," a magazine once had said, struggled through life after baseball. But whatever torments and disappointment ate at Foxx, his disposition never soured. To the end he was smiling, congenial, philosophical, summing up his plight by saying, "I guess I was born to be broke."

FOXX'S CAREER RECORD

Born Oct. 22, 1907, at Sudlersville, Md.　Died July 21, 1967, Miami, Fla.
Batted and threw righthanded.　Elected to Hall of Fame, 1951.

Year Club	League	G.	AB.	R.	H.	HR.	RBI.	B.A.
1924—Easton	E. Sho.	76	260	33	77	10	....	.296
1925—Philadelphia	Amer.	10	9	2	6	0	0	.667
1925—Providence	Int.	41	101	12	33	1	15	.327
1926—Philadelphia	Amer.	26	32	8	10	0	5	.313
1927—Philadelphia	Amer.	61	130	23	42	3	20	.323
1928—Philadelphia	Amer.	118	400	85	131	13	79	.328
1929—Philadelphia	Amer.	149	517	123	183	33	117	.354
1930—Philadelphia	Amer.	153	562	127	188	37	156	.335
1931—Philadelphia	Amer.	139	515	93	150	30	120	.291
1932—Philadelphia	Amer.	154	585	*151	213	*58	*169	.364
1933—Philadelphia	Amer.	149	573	125	204	*48	*163	*.356
1934—Philadelphia	Amer.	150	539	120	180	44	130	.334
1935—Philadelphia	Amer.	147	535	118	185	●36	115	.346
1936—Boston	Amer.	●155	585	130	198	41	143	.338
1937—Boston	Amer.	150	569	111	162	36	127	.285
1938—Boston	Amer.	149	565	139	197	50	*175	*.349
1939—Boston	Amer.	124	467	130	168	*35	105	.360
1940—Boston	Amer.	144	515	106	153	36	119	.297
1941—Boston	Amer.	135	487	87	146	19	105	.300
1942—Boston	Amer.	30	100	18	27	5	14	.270
1942—Chicago	Nat.	70	205	25	42	3	19	.205
1943—Chicago	Nat.				(Did not play)			
1944—Chicago	Nat.	15	20	0	1	0	2	.050
1944—Portsmouth	Pied.	5	2	0	0	0	0	.000
1945—Philadelphia	Nat.	89	224	30	60	7	38	.268
1946—				(Out of Organized Ball)				
1947—St. Petersburg	Fla. Int.	6	6	0	1	....	....	.167
American League Totals		2143	7685	1696	2543	524	1862	.331
National League Totals		174	449	55	103	10	59	.229
Major League Totals		2317	8134	1751	2646	534	1921	.325

WORLD SERIES RECORD

Year Club	League	G.	AB.	R.	H.	HR.	RBI.	B.A.
1929—Philadelphia	Amer.	5	20	5	7	2	5	.350
1930—Philadelphia	Amer.	6	21	3	7	1	3	.333
1931—Philadelphia	Amer.	7	23	3	8	1	3	.348
World Series Totals		18	64	11	22	4	11	.344

PITCHING RECORD

Year Club	League	G.	IP.	W.	L.	Pct.	ERA.
1939—Boston	Amer.	1	1	0	0	.000	0.00
1945—Philadelphia	Nat.	9	23	1	0	1.000	1.57
Major League Totals		10	24	1	0	1.000	1.50

A Giant Among Giants

After 35 years of baseball, John McGraw had good reason to expect no more surprises. So when the curly-haired 16-year-old walked into his Polo Grounds office late in the 1925 season and announced who he was and why he was there, the tough-minded lord of the New York Giants sized him up with a skepticism big-league managers reserve for unknowns who request tryouts.

Melvin Ott was not a total unknown, however. He had been sent to McGraw on the recommendation of a Louisiana lumberman named Harry Williams, a friend of John J. who fielded a semipro team on which the youngster had been catching. On this afternoon, McGraw may have quietly doubted his friend's acumen, for there was nothing prepossessing about this thick-legged, mild-looking kid. But McGraw, with the prospector's faith that all baseball lifers have, nevertheless invited him to work out with the club's rookies, thus setting in motion one of baseball's wonderfully magical stories.

The boy, McGraw discovered, not only was "the most natural hitter I've ever had on any club of mine," but he batted with what was probably the most unorthodox style in all of baseball. The Giant manager watched with amused interest as Ott, a lefthanded hitter, hitched his right foot high off the ground as the pitcher delivered, held it aloft for a moment, then planted it as he whipped the bat through as perfect a swing as McGraw had seen.

McGraw waited to see which pitch would disrupt the boy's timing—fastball, curve or change—but none did. Ott hit each pitch hard, pumping the ball sharply down the right-field line which, in this park, measured a scant 257 feet to the wall.

This, McGraw told himself, was a one-of-a-kind machine that worked flawlessly, a natural (albeit peculiar) hitter who should never be tampered with. He kept Ott on the bench with him for the rest of the season, then vowed the next spring that he'd keep the boy out of the minors, fearful that

Hard-hitting Mel Ott, a giant on the all-time home run charts.

some manager would fuss with the singular batting style.

"I was managing at Toledo that year," Casey Stengel said, "and I'd heard about Ott and asked McGraw if I could have him. The old man cussed me out and said that *nobody* was going to get this kid. He was going to mold Master Melvin *his* way."

Ott became a special project for McGraw, who went about the job carefully and paternally. Until he retired as Giant manager in 1932, by which time Ott was a ripe 23 years old and a star, McGraw's fatherly affection for him never wavered.

"Mel was always an easy kid to like," teammate Freddie Lindstrom said. "He was quiet, polite and

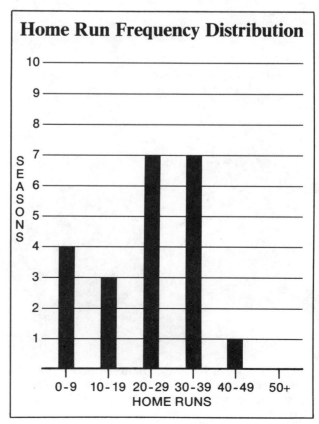

After 35 years of baseball, Giants Manager John McGraw (left) could still be surprised, as he was when he got his first look at Mel Ott, whose unorthodox hitting style and mild manner endeared him to the lord and master of New York baseball.

As the pitch was delivered, Ott raised his right leg high before planting his foot and taking a picture-perfect swing. The youngster reported to the Giants as a catcher but spent most of his big-league career in the outfield.

modest. Always called McGraw 'Mister.' They said that McGraw, who never had any children of his own, was always looking for the perfect son in one of his players. (Christy) Mathewson had filled the role for a long time. Then there was Ross Youngs, who came up around 1918. Youngs was a hustling player—his nickname was 'Pep'—and McGraw was crazy about him. But Youngs contracted Bright's disease (a kidney disorder) and died in 1927, right in the middle of his career. Then Mel came along and McGraw was devoted to him. We all could see it, but nobody minded because Mel was such a sweet kid. Everybody liked him. Why, even in Ebbets Field, which was as hostile a place for a Giant club as you could imagine, there were two Giant players you never heard booed there—Carl Hubbell and Mel."

Lindstrom recalled an incident that underlined the McGraw-Ott relationship. Still a teen-ager, Ott picked up a young woman one night and brought her to the club's hotel. He asked Lindstrom for use of his room and Freddie consented—unwisely because McGraw later heard that a woman had been in Lindstrom's quarters. McGraw, who frowned upon such merrymaking on the road, began berating Lindstrom, who in self-defense eventually con-

fessed that it was Ott who had committed the indiscretion.

"At that," Lindstrom said, "he really blew up. He began calling me immoral and all sorts of things. He refused to believe that Ott had done such a thing —flat out wouldn't hear of it. The more I tried to tell him the truth, the angrier he got. He absolutely refused to believe it. That's how he felt about Mel. I told Mel later, 'Buddy, next time leave me out of it.' "

Ott was the smallest of the top home run hitters at only 5-foot-9 and 165 pounds. Though delivered to McGraw as a catcher, he was ordered to the outfield when he arrived for his first spring training in 1926.

"You ever play the outfield?" McGraw asked.

"Only when I was a kid," said Ott, just turned 17.

McGraw was able to remain poker-faced. ("Catching every day behind the bat would have tied Ott's legs in knots," McGraw would explain, noting the youngster's heavily muscled legs. "He wouldn't last 10 years.")

That this was one of Ott's memorable quotes underlines his reticent personality. One sportswriter who covered the Giants in the 1930s cited how difficult the job could be: "Bill Terry hates writers, Carl

The cozy right-field stands at the Polo Grounds provided an inviting target for the opportunistic Ott.

Ott, touching the plate after a Game 1 home run (left), was one of the heroes in the 1933 World Series. Ott and first baseman Bill Terry (right) celebrate the Giants' five-game victory over Washington.

Four members of the 1936 pennant-winning Giants: (left to right) left fielder Jo-Jo Moore, shortstop Dick Bartell, Ott and catcher Gus Mancuso.

Hubbell doesn't say anything and Mel Ott says even less."

That Ott could have received even more recognition in a city overrun by newsmen and newspapers concerned even the leery Terry.

"One day Terry told me that he'd finally figured out what was wrong with me—I didn't have enough color," said Ott, adored by Giant fans for his boyish charm almost as much as his devastating hitting. "He said I ought to get a red handkerchief and wear it or do something off the beaten path. He even suggested that I get caught in a raid and get pinched. Anything, he said, to get my name in the papers."

But in 1926, Ott was on the bench next to McGraw, learning his trade by watching big leaguers rather than playing in the minors.

"He used to scare me sometimes," Ott said of McGraw. "If some outfielder, either on our club or the opposition, played a ball badly or threw to the wrong base, he'd suddenly turn to me and yell, 'Don't let me ever catch you doing that!'"

Occasionally, Ott would get into a game, mostly as a pinch-hitter. He acquitted himself well, batting .383 in 35 games. The following season, McGraw

began turning his prodigy loose with more frequency. Ott appeared in 82 games—just over half as a pinch-hitter—and batted .282. Among his hits was his first major league home run, July 18 against the Chicago Cubs.

"It wasn't a skyscraper," he remembered. "In fact, it didn't even go into the seats. I hit a shot into center field at the Polo Grounds, the field was wet and Hack Wilson slipped on the grass and fell right on his can and the ball rolled way out to deep center. I came all the way around. That was my first homer."

The 1927 Giants lost the pennant by two games in a grueling race with the runner-up St. Louis Cardinals and league-champion Pittsburgh Pirates. The New York club had a future Hall of Fame infield in Terry at first base, Rogers Hornsby at second, Travis Jackson at shortstop and Lindstrom at third, two other future inductees in center fielder Edd Roush and pitcher Burleigh Grimes—and yet one more in young backup Mel Ott, who was not ready to assume his role on a permanent basis.

As the 1928 season unfolded, it became evident that Ott and the Polo Grounds—more specifically, the right-field corner at the Polo Grounds—would

Ott and Yankee slugger Lou Gehrig at the 1936 World Series.

Ott (right) and Boston Red Sox slugger Jimmie Foxx inspecting some lumber. Between them, they hit more than 1,000 home runs.

become one of baseball's most lethal pairings. With the right-center field wall 449 feet away in the horseshoe, Ott, a natural pull hitter, began whistling shots into the cozier lower stands in the corner, 257 feet away. Of his 511 lifetime homers, 323 were struck in the Polo Grounds, the most hit by one player in one park during a career.

Ott's first full season in 1928 was a solid one—18 home runs and a .322 batting average. A year later, he became a full-fledged star, reigning as one of baseball's heaviest hitters as the National League staged its biggest offensive campaign to date. Ott blasted a career-high 42 home runs, formerly Hornsby's league record, but lost the crown to the Philadelphia Phillies' Chuck Klein, who set a new standard with 43 homers. (Hack Wilson established the still-standing N.L. mark with 56 the next season.) The Giants' 20-year-old right fielder batted .328 and drove in 151 runs, another personal high but second in the league to Wilson's 159 runs batted

Ott in 1939, more than halfway through his illustrious career.

"Nice guys finish last," was the quip attributed to Brooklyn Manager Leo Durocher (right) in obvious reference to Ott, his Giants counterpart.

Manager Ott with Giants Owner Horace Stoneham in 1946.

in.

In 1930, when hits fell in torrents all summer long (the Giants set a modern major league record with a .319 team batting mark), Ott reached his career batting peak with a .349 average which, in this hit-happy season, placed him 12th among qualifiers for the N.L. crown. He added 25 home runs and drove in 119, his second of eight consecutive seasons with more than 100 RBIs, a league record.

In 1932, Ott won his first of six home run titles, tying Klein for the league lead with 38 blasts. Until Ralph Kiner (seven titles) and Mike Schmidt (eight) came along, Ott shared the N.L. record with Philadelphia's dead-ball era slugger Gavvy Cravath with half a dozen homer crowns.

A host of personal achievements already under his belt, Ott broke into his first World Series in 1933 against the Washington Senators. Only 24 years old but already an eight-year veteran, the littlest Giant had a torrid Series, batting .389 and homering twice. His four hits in Game 1 led the Giants

First baseman Johnny Mize (left), infielder Bill Rigney (center) and Ott in the
Giants' Polo Grounds dugout in 1947.

Ott's Milestone Home Runs

	Date	Place	Pitcher	Club
1	July 18, 1927	New York	Hal Carlson	Chicago
100	July 12, 1931	New York	Frank Watt	Philadelphia
200	July 24, 1934	New York	Tex Carleton	St. Louis
300	Aug. 20, 1937	Philadelphia	Larry Crawford	Philadelphia
400	June 1, 1941	New York	Monte Pearson	Cincinnati
500	Aug. 1, 1945	New York	Johnny Hutchings	Boston
Last	April 16, 1946	New York	Oscar Judd	Philadelphia

to a 4-2 victory and he broke up Game 5 with a 10th-inning solo home run that gave New York a 4-3 win and the world championship.

Ott continued hitting home runs throughout the 1930s at a pace that, while never spectacular, was good enough to put him at the top of the league in 1934, 1936, 1937 and 1938.

He was the National League's preeminent power hitter of the decade and, along with Klein, set the high mark for the period from 1931 through 1939 with his 38 homers in 1932. The big bashing was being done in the American League, where, during the same span, the 40-homer mark was reached 14 times by six different players.

Before the start of the 1942 season, Ott replaced Terry as the Giants' manager, vowing to be "a fighting leader of the Giant team." Now 33, his legs didn't have their former spring, but Ott was committed to a full-time role on the field. "When I get into a slump, I'm going to yank myself out of there, of course," he said. "I'm not going to stay in there if I think I'm hurting the team."

Ott, of course, never did do his team damage with a bat in hand, but in 6½ seasons as a manager, the best he could show was a third-place finish in his first year, when he led the circuit in homers for the final time.

"Too nice a guy," was the rap against his managing, and it was that reputation that led to Leo Durocher's famous wisecrack—which was directed at Ott—that "Nice guys finish last." The Lip had been spouting his competitive philosophy (he was never a faucet that needed much turning), which endorsed kicking, scratching and brow-beating, when Ott happened to stroll out of the New York dugout and provide him with the ideal antithesis. (Leo's pungent wisdom overlooked the amiable Connie Mack, who won nine pennants with the Philadelphia Athletics.)

Ironically, when the mild-mannered Ott finally stepped aside as skipper of the Giants in July 1948, it involved perhaps the most extreme managerial shift in baseball history. Giants Owner Horace Stoneham, who had loved and respected Ott as if he were a son, replaced him with the brash, abrasive, sharp-tongued Durocher, who had worn out his welcome as manager of the Brooklyn Dodgers.

Ott's career as an active player had come to an end with four pinch-hitting appearances in 1947, a year he watched his team clout an N.L.-record 221 home runs and finish fourth.

When he retired, Ott's 511 career home runs ranked third on the all-time scroll behind Babe Ruth's 714 and Jimmie Foxx's 534. The wonderfully consistent Giant star was the N.L. record holder in home runs, RBIs, extra-base hits, walks and runs scored, and tied an N.L. mark with his 22 years of service with one club.

On a foggy November night in 1958, Ott and his wife, Mildred, were driving on a highway near Bay St. Louis, Miss., when a pair of headlights suddenly burst out of the moist darkness. The car smashed head-on into the Ott's vehicle.

Both Otts were injured, Mel critically. For seven days doctors fought to save the life of the one-time 16-year-old prodigy of the New York Giants. But on November 21, Ott died.

John McGraw had had three favorites: Mathewson, who died of tuberculosis at 47, Youngs, a victim of Bright's Disease at 30, and now the last of them, Mel Ott, dead at 49.

OTT'S CAREER RECORD

Born Mar. 2, 1909, at Gretna, La.   Died Nov. 21, 1958, New Orleans, La.
Batted left and threw righthanded.   Elected to Hall of Fame, 1951.

Year Club	League	G.	AB.	R.	H.	HR.	RBI.	B.A.
1926—New York	Nat.	35	60	7	23	0	4	.383
1927—New York	Nat.	82	163	23	46	1	19	.282
1928—New York	Nat.	124	435	69	140	18	77	.322
1929—New York	Nat.	150	545	138	179	42	151	.328
1930—New York	Nat.	148	521	122	182	25	119	.349
1931—New York	Nat.	138	497	104	145	29	115	.292
1932—New York	Nat.	●154	566	119	180	●38	123	.318
1933—New York	Nat.	152	580	98	164	23	103	.283
1934—New York	Nat.	153	582	119	190	●35	★135	.326
1935—New York	Nat.	152	593	113	191	31	114	.322
1936—New York	Nat.	150	534	120	175	★33	135	.328
1937—New York	Nat.	151	545	99	160	●31	95	.294
1938—New York	Nat.	150	527	★116	164	★36	116	.311
1939—New York	Nat.	125	396	85	122	27	80	.308
1940—New York	Nat.	151	536	89	155	19	79	.289
1941—New York	Nat.	148	525	89	150	27	90	.286
1942—New York	Nat.	152	549	★118	162	★30	93	.295
1943—New York	Nat.	125	380	65	89	18	47	.234
1944—New York	Nat.	120	399	91	115	26	82	.288
1945—New York	Nat.	135	451	73	139	21	79	.308
1946—New York	Nat.	31	68	2	5	1	4	.074
1947—New York	Nat.	4	4	0	0	0	0	.000
Major League Totals		2730	9456	1859	2876	511	1860	.304

WORLD SERIES RECORD

Year Club	League	G.	AB.	R.	H.	HR.	RBI.	B.A.
1933—New York	Nat.	5	18	3	7	2	4	.389
1936—New York	Nat.	6	23	4	7	1	3	.304
1937—New York	Nat.	5	20	1	4	1	3	.200
World Series Totals		16	61	8	18	4	10	.295

Tiger Town's Big Henry

One look at the poised sculpture that was Hank Greenberg at home plate told you all you needed to know: The towering figure, the high, cocked bat and the aura of controlled tension and self-confidence—this was a successful power hitter.

At 6-foot-4 and 215 well-proportioned pounds, he was "Big Henry," one of the most prolific fence-busters in an era that had some of the best. He came to the big leagues in 1933, when the Babe was near the end, and stayed to compete in the American League's long-ball derbies with Jimmie Foxx, Lou Gehrig, Joe DiMaggio and Ted Williams. Among such bruising company, the Detroit first baseman more than held his own, winning the home run crown four times, the Most Valuable Player award twice and four times leading the league in runs batted in. And for Greenberg, the RBI was a tastier dish than even the home run.

"Hank loved to drive those runs in," teammate Charlie Gehringer said. "If there was a man on first, he'd always say to me, 'Get him over to third, just get him over to third.' Everybody likes to drive in runs, but with Hank it was a passion. I think he got just as big a kick out of driving in a run with a single as he did with a home run."

And the big man brought himself considerable pleasure—139 RBIs in 1934, 170 in 1935, 183 in 1937, 146 in 1938, 150 in 1940, 127 in 1946.

Greenberg came in with the New Year in 1911, being born in New York on January 1. Growing up in the Bronx, he was a serious child—and most serious about athletics. He excelled in a variety of sports at James Monroe High School despite being (by his own admission) far from a natural athlete.

"I was a big, awkward, gawky kid who was always stumbling over his own two feet," he said. "Sometimes during a basketball game, I'd take a tumble and everybody would cheer—you know, a good-natured cheer, because they'd seen me do it before. But it never bothered me; things only bother you when you let them get inside you, and I'd never allow that. In the beginning, it was proba-

bly naivete. After all, here I was, the big, clumsy kid aspiring to play in the major leagues. I should have looked in the mirror and laughed, but when you're young you look in the mirror and see what you want to see. I guess I had a lot of determination. It's remarkable how that can make your dreams soar right past reality."

The dreams and determination accompanied young Henry to neighboring Crotona Park, where day after fair-weathered day he practiced his hitting and fielding. There was no problem with Greenberg's batting, at least not with his power capabilities. One thing he could always do was drive the ball a long, long way.

Hank Greenberg and the tools of his trade.

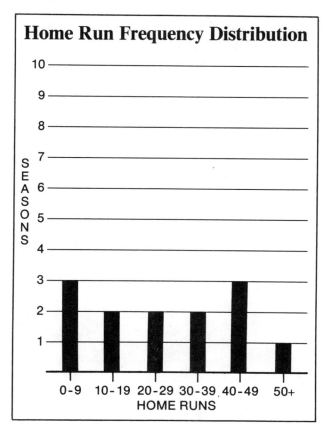

Home Run Frequency Distribution

(Bar chart: vertical axis labeled SEASONS from 1 to 10; horizontal axis labeled HOME RUNS with categories 0-9, 10-19, 20-29, 30-39, 40-49, 50+. Bars: 0-9 = 3, 10-19 = 2, 20-29 = 2, 30-39 = 2, 40-49 = 3, 50+ = 1.)

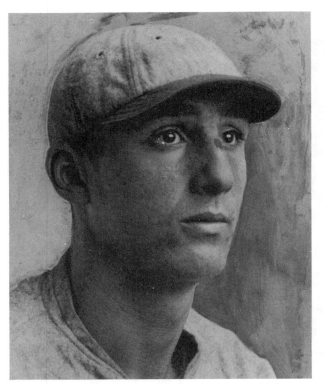

A youthful Greenberg as the star slugger of his James Monroe High School team in the Bronx.

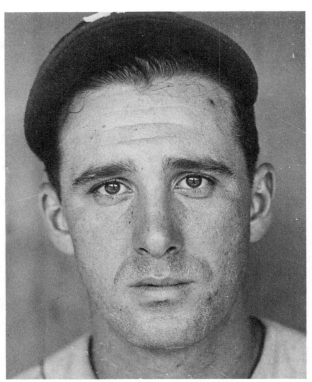

Greenberg in 1935 as the American League's Most Valuable Player.

American League big guns in 1937: (left to right) Bill Dickey, Rudy York, Greenberg, Lou Gehrig and Joe DiMaggio.

The infield that drove in 462 runs: (left to right) Greenberg, second baseman Charlie Gehringer, shortstop Billy Rogell and third baseman Marv Owen.

"He'd ask us to pitch to him," one boyhood friend recalled, "and we'd do it because he was such a nice guy, and then after awhile we'd do it because we wanted to see him hit. One of us would pitch and a couple of others would be out there shagging, and every so often he'd really rip into one and hit it so far it gave you the chills. Then we'd hit him grounders at first base, hard as we could. They'd bounce off his knees, his chest, once in awhile his noggin, but he stayed right there, very serious—you could almost feel his concentration. Looking back now, it was kind of impressive. Here was a guy trying to shape his life into something right before your very eyes. It's not something you come across very often."

That ethic didn't change, not even when Greenberg reached the big leagues.

"He made himself a great hitter through hard work and determination," Gehringer said. "When he first came up, he couldn't hit that curveball, but he learned to hang in there."

Greenberg grew up in the backyards of both the Yankees and Giants. That the Giants overlooked him is puzzling, considering John McGraw was al-

ways on the prowl for a talented Jewish player who would appeal to the large contingent of Jewish fans at the Polo Grounds.

"I did ask for a tryout with the Giants," Greenberg said. "But they said no, they had already seen me play at Monroe and didn't think I had the stuff. Sure, I was disappointed, but looking back, I think I can understand. People see what they want to see, or they don't see what they're especially looking for. Remember, in high school I was still the big, clumsy kid, kind of slow afoot and no magician with the glove. That's what they saw."

The Yankees, however, the souls of efficiency in those days, did see something special in Big Henry and pursued it. This was the summer of 1929 and Greenberg was playing sandlot ball in the Bronx, waiting to begin fall classes at New York University.

Paul Krichell, the Yankee scout who had heard the sonic booms of Lou Gehrig a half dozen years earlier, heard the clarion call of Greenberg's bat and offered the 18-year-old a contract.

Given his ambition to play baseball, given the years of relentless, devoted work to learn his craft, Greenberg would have been excused if he trampled

Greenberg (right) and Detroit pitcher Schoolboy Rowe.

Greenberg and Gehringer (right) combined to form one of the league's top slugging tandems.

Greenberg's philosophy was simple: "The most important aspect of hitting is driving in runs."

Greenberg at work: power personified.

Krichell in his haste to sign. But Greenberg, along with all his other virtues, also was a pragmatic young man. He was a first baseman and so was Gehrig.

"I'd go to Yankee Stadium," he said, "and naturally my attention was riveted by Ruth and Gehrig. I remember looking at Lou when he was on deck, sort of sizing him up. I can still remember how awed I was by the width of his shoulders and the sheer strength of him. I remember thinking, 'This man is almost as good as Babe Ruth, and he was only about 25 or 26 years old.' So, what was the point of my signing with the Yankees?"

Prudent and realistic, Greenberg knew he wasn't going to dislodge Gehrig and he believed he was too slow for the outfield, particularly that Yankee Stadium outfield, which seemed to stretch halfway to Maine. He turned his attention to three other offers he had received—from Pittsburgh, Washington and Detroit—and eventually settled with the Tigers, who signed him for a $9,000 bonus.

Greenberg started his career in 1930 with Hartford in the Eastern League (where, coincidentally, Gehrig had begun his), and made minor league stops at Raleigh (Piedmont League), Evansville (Illinois-Iowa-Indiana League) and, finally, at Beaumont in the Texas League, where he began sending out significant detonations—39 home runs and 131 RBIs in 1932, earning the league's MVP designation.

Greenberg heard plenty of cheering that season, but also scores of anti-Semitic catcalls as he toured the sun-baked diamonds of Texas.

"I listened and I let it go," he said. "I never let it get inside of me, because then it starts eating at you, and I refused to let it happen. Some of it was pretty bad, but some was the same sort of thing they yelled at Italian players or Polish or Irish. I just kept telling myself, 'The hell with it, I'm on my way to Detroit.'"

(When Jackie Robinson broke in with Brooklyn in 1947 as modern major league baseball's first black player, Greenberg, winding down his career with Pittsburgh, heard the torrents of abuse to which Robinson was subjected. Greenberg was sympathetic to his plight, offering Jackie words of support and encouragement. Robinson never forgot, and to his dying day remembered Greenberg with admiration and affection.)

Big Henry was, indeed, on his way to a ball club that was gearing up to hammer the American League into submission in 1934 and 1935 behind a menacing arsenal of bats and the strong right arms of Schoolboy Rowe, Tommy Bridges, Eldon Auker and Alvin Crowder. Greenberg would become part of Detroit's "G-Men," a hard-hitting attack that included outfielder Goose Goslin and the great second baseman Gehringer, and also featured catcher-Manager Mickey Cochrane, shortstop Billy Rogell, third baseman Marv Owen and outfielders Jo-Jo White, Gee Walker and Pete Fox.

This was a brutally methodical assault team, and the big siege gun was Greenberg, who broke in

Greenberg (left) and slugging Tiger teammate Rudy York.

**Greenberg (left) touches home plate after hitting his 53rd home run of the 1938
season. Greenberg (right) posed for this photo in 1940.**

Greenberg spent many hours working on his defensive play at first base, but his powerful bat was still his meal ticket. Greenberg (right) is greeted at the plate after hitting a three-run homer in Game 5 of the 1940 World Series.

modestly but firmly in 1933 with 12 home runs, 87 RBIs and a .301 batting average. He was now in stardom's anteroom.

In 1934, Greenberg helped drive the Tigers to their first pennant since 1909. The big first baseman hit 26 home runs, drove in 139 runs, batted .339 and slashed an eye-catching 63 doubles, four under the major league record set in 1931 by Earl Webb of the Boston Red Sox. Greenberg, though, preferred to talk about the Detroit infield's 462 RBIs, more than any other infield in history. Behind Hammerin' Hank were Gehringer with 127 RBIs, Rogell with 100 and Owen, 96.

A year later, Greenberg had piled up exactly 100 RBIs at the All-Star break as Detroit drove toward its second straight pennant. The hefty-hitting Tiger finished with a towering 170 RBIs (the league high), 36 homers (tied for the lead) and received his first A.L. MVP award. Bad luck struck in the World Series, however—not for the Tigers, who downed the Chicago Cubs to claim their first-ever Series title after losing to the St. Louis Cardinals in 1934, but for Greenberg, who missed the final four games

after suffering a fractured wrist in Game 2.

Greenberg broke the wrist again 12 games into the next season, an injury that sidelined him for the remainder of the year. Altogether, his career would be cut short by about 5½ seasons, 4½ of which were lost to military service. Despite becoming a regular at 22, he would play only nine full seasons—and average 35 homers and 132 RBIs.

As Greenberg prepared for spring training in 1937, the Tigers insisted he sign a conditional dollar-a-year contract, then prove he was fit to play before they offered a regular contract. "Of course I signed it," Greenberg said. "I had no choice if I wanted to play baseball. That's the way it was in those years—ownership held all the cards."

The Tigers need not have worried, for Big Henry went roaring through the 1937 schedule and had, in his opinion, his greatest season.

"Most people would say 1938 was my best year," Greenberg said, "when I hit 58 home runs. But I don't think so. I'd pick 1937." Naturally, since this was the year the RBI junkie drove home a league-high 183 runs, one shy of Gehrig's A.L. record, a

73

Sgt. Greenberg is off to the wars.

near miss that gnawed at him more than falling short of Ruth's home run record a year later. "The most important aspect of hitting," the practical Mr. Greenberg averred, "is driving in runs." They were more important than batting average, than home runs, "than anything."

Well, in 1937 he had a full dish of them, along with 40 home runs, a .337 batting mark and 200 hits—clearly an MVP-type year. But again this was an era of super-achievers in the American League: in 1937, DiMaggio hit 46 home runs, had 167 RBIs and batted .346; Yankee catcher Bill Dickey drove in 133 runs and batted .332; Gehrig had 159 RBIs and a .351 batting average. The award did go to another Tiger—Gehringer, who batted a league-leading .371 and drove home 96 runs.

Big Henry wasn't the MVP in 1938, either, despite a monstrous season featuring 58 home runs and 146 RBIs. The honor went instead to Foxx, the runner-up with 50 homers but the league kingpin in batting (.349) and RBIs (175). Greenberg received all the dramatic notices, however, for his assault on Ruth's 60-homer record. Foxx, helped by five homers in his last five games, had finished with 58 in 1932, but Greenberg challenged the mark more seriously, running his total to 58 with five games to play.

"I had a clear shot," he said, "but just didn't do it. Some pretty wild stories have come out of that through the years, like everybody was against me because I was Jewish, that pitchers were walking me on purpose. But that's not true. As far as I could tell, most guys were rooting *for* me. The pitchers were under a lot of pressure; they wanted to give me a chance but, at the same time, wanted me to earn it.

"I guess the most famous games came on the last day of the season. We had a doubleheader against the Indians. In the first game, we ran right up against Bob Feller at his best—he set a record by fanning 18 of us. I got a double in four at-bats. The second game was called after (seven) innings because of darkness, and that was that. I had my chances. I just ran out of gas.

By 1940, Big Henry was a left fielder, a move the Tigers made to get the big home run bat of Rudy York in the regular lineup (at first)—and a change that Greenberg, remembering the indignity of the dollar-a-year contract, approved only after receiving an extra $10,000. The Tigers' new outfielder helped bat them to another pennant with a typical season of all-around high-caliber slugging: a .340 batting average and league-leading totals in home runs (41) and RBIs (150). Greenberg earned his second MVP award, making him the first major leaguer to win the honor at different positions (a feat Stan Musial would accomplish in 1943 and 1948.)

Nineteen games into the next season, on May 7, 1941, Greenberg was inducted into the U.S. Army, not to return to the more benign wars of baseball until July 1945. World War II cut a wide swath through the heart of his career, but Big Henry had no regrets. "I was proud to have served my country

in a time of need," he said. "I have no complaints about that whatsoever."

Greenberg was, in fact, discharged on December 5, 1941, under a regulation that released draftees over the age of 28. Immediately after the attack on Pearl Harbor, however, he re-enlisted, saying, "We are in trouble and there's only one thing for me to do—return to service."

And while many big leaguers spent the war years entertaining the troops on rough-hewn baseball diamonds in remote corners of the world, Greenberg hardly saw a bat and ball for four years. He rose to the rank of captain in the Army Air Forces, serving in the China-Burma-India theater, a grim, brutal war zone that received few headlines.

Big Henry was finally mustered out in the summer of 1945, now 34 years old. Many questioned whether he could swing back to his form of 1940, but what is said about riding a bicycle must also be true about hitting a baseball—at least for Greenberg. "We need some long hits," Manager Steve O'Neill said, "and Hank is the boy who will deliver them."

Greenberg returned to the Tiger lineup on July 1, unloaded a home run to celebrate and found himself back in another war zone, this one known as a pennant race. It was a struggle fought until the final day of the season, with Detroit needing a victory to clinch the flag over the Washington Senators.

The Tigers, in St. Louis to play a doubleheader against the Browns, trailed, 3-2, as they entered the ninth inning of the opener. They loaded the bases with one out, however, bringing to the plate their leading hitter, a man who also had slugged 12 homers and drove home 56 runs in half a season's work—High Henry. Greenberg saw a pitch he liked and turned it into the most memorable of his 331 career homers, a rocket that sailed just fair into the left-field bleachers, winning the pennant for Detroit.

As he trotted around the bases, Greenberg thought about life's strange and unpredictable patterns—just a few months before, he had been stationed in India, dispatched on B-29 bombing missions to Japan, wondering when the war would end. "It was the strangest thing," he said of his home run lap. "I wasn't sure if I was awake or dreaming."

More thrills were in store in the World Series as the Tigers toppled the Cubs for their second title of the Greenberg era. The veteran smashed two home runs and collected seven RBIs, pushing his career total to 22 RBIs in 23 Series games.

For Big Henry, baseball held one more big season and one big shock. In 1946, he socked 44 home runs and drove in 127 runs, leading the American League for the fourth time in each category, though he batted just .277, the first sub-.300 season of his career. A few months later, on January 8, 1947, he was stunned by a radio report announcing he had been sold to the Pittsburgh Pirates.

"I couldn't believe it," he said. "Detroit was my team. I identified 100 percent with the Tigers. I'd

Greenberg with Pittsburgh teammate Ralph Kiner in 1947. A few tips from Big
Henry helped turn him into a dominant home run hitter.

Cleveland Indians Owner Bill Veeck (left) and the recently retired Greenberg at
the New York Baseball Writers dinner in 1948.

Greenberg's Milestone Home Runs

	Date	Place	Pitcher	Club
1	May 6, 1933	Detroit	Earl Whitehill	Washington
100	Aug. 5, 1937	Philadelphia	Eddie Smith	Philadelphia
200	Sept. 7, 1939	Cleveland	Mel Harder	Cleveland
300	Sept. 17, 1946	Detroit	Marino Pieretti	Washington
Last	Sept. 15, 1947	Pittsburgh	Charley Schanz	Philadelphia

been in the Detroit organization for 17 years . . . and here I was being dumped without even the courtesy of a phone call. I never understood it. Still don't to this day."

(New York sportswriter Dan Daniel, however, in a story that had run January 1 in The Sporting News, reported "he was in a position to say" that Greenberg would demand a pay raise (to $75,000) from the Tigers but "would like to come to the Yankees and finish his career at first base." The story was accompanied by a three-year-old photo of Greenberg (in Army livery) posing with a Yankees uniform.

(Detroit, a city that Daniel said "never took Hank unto its bosom," was shaken. The papers, according to the New York writer, "launched a violent attack on the Babe Ruth of the Bengals."

(The night before he was waived out of the league, Greenberg told the Detroit Times: "This is the bummest rap I ever have received. I've never said anything about my salary to any newspaperman. Neither have I said I would not play first base for the Tigers. No matter whether I'm in baseball or out of it, I do care about a lot of fans in Detroit. I want them to know I never would pull a stunt like this on them.")

So disheartened by what he felt was callous treatment, Greenberg announced his retirement. But the blandishments of Pirate co-Owner John Galbreath —which included a $100,000 salary—induced Big Henry to suit up for another year.

For Greenberg, it turned out to be a disappointing final season—.249, 25 home runs and 74 RBIs as the Pirates tied for last place. "I found out that I couldn't go anymore," Greenberg said. "When the legs give out on an athlete, he is through. One of my biggest regrets in baseball was that I couldn't help the Pirates."

But for Pittsburgh, it proved to be a winning investment. Greenberg patiently tutored young Ralph Kiner and helped Kiner become Pittsburgh's premier drawing card for the next half dozen years.

Upon retirement, Greenberg moved into the front-office suites. Working closely with Bill Veeck, he was part-owner and general manager of the Cleveland Indians from 1948 through 1957, then followed Veeck to the Chicago White Sox as part-owner and vice president from 1959 through 1963.

Even as an executive, Greenberg kept a close eye on his clubs' batting practice. To newcomers, the devotion provided a valuable lesson.

"Greenberg positively made a great hitter out of himself," White Sox Manager Paul Richards once observed as Greenberg, then in Cleveland, directed drills. "He did it by constant practice. He'd come out to the park as early as eight in the morning and hit for hours. He'd stay after games until darkness made him quit.

"I have heard that when Rogers Hornsby came up from the minors, he wasn't a natural hitter but became the great batsman he was by working at it."

Unlike Hornsby, however, Greenberg had been a "guess" hitter. "When I'm at bat," he once told a writer, "I can't help trying to figure out whether the pitcher is going to throw me a curveball, a fast one or a change of pace. To get power behind my swing, I've got to be set for the pitch, and the only way I can be fully set is to be confident of the kind of ball that's coming up."

And Big Henry didn't like playing the part of the fooled.

GREENBERG'S CAREER RECORD

Born Jan. 1, 1911, New York, N.Y. Died Sept. 4, 1986, Beverly Hills, Cal.
Batted and threw righthanded.   Elected to Hall of Fame, 1956.

Year	Club	League	G.	AB.	R.	H.	HR.	RBI.	B.A.
1930—Hartford		East.	17	56	10	12	2	6	.214
1930—Raleigh		Pied.	122	452	88	142	19	93	.314
1930—Detroit		Amer.	1	1	0	0	0	0	.000
1931—Evansville		I.I.I.	●126	487	88	155	15	85	.318
1931—Beaumont		Texas	3	2	0	0	0	0	.000
1932—Beaumont		Texas	154	600	★123	174	★39	131	.290
1933—Detroit		Amer.	117	449	59	135	12	87	.301
1934—Detroit		Amer.	153	593	118	201	26	139	.339
1935—Detroit		Amer.	152	619	121	203	●36	★170	.328
1936—Detroit		Amer.	12	46	10	16	1	16	.348
1937—Detroit		Amer.	154	594	137	200	40	★183	.337
1938—Detroit		Amer.	155	556	★144	175	★58	146	.315
1939—Detroit		Amer.	138	500	112	156	33	112	.312
1940—Detroit		Amer.	148	573	129	195	★41	★150	.340
1941—Detroit		Amer.	19	67	12	18	2	12	.269
1942-43-44—Detroit		Amer.			(In Military Service)				
1945—Detroit		Amer.	78	270	47	84	13	60	.311
1946—Detroit		Amer.	142	523	91	145	★44	★127	.277
1947—Pittsburgh		Nat.	125	402	71	100	25	74	.249
American League Totals			1269	4791	980	1528	306	1202	.319
National League Totals			125	402	71	100	25	74	.249
Major League Totals			1394	5193	1051	1628	331	1276	.313

WORLD SERIES RECORD

Year	Club	League	G.	AB.	R.	H.	HR.	RBI.	B.A.
1934—Detroit		Amer.	7	28	4	9	1	7	.321
1935—Detroit		Amer.	2	6	1	1	0	2	.167
1940—Detroit		Amer.	7	28	5	10	1	6	.357
1945—Detroit		Amer.	7	23	7	7	2	7	.304
World Series Totals			23	85	17	27	5	22	.318

The Great Perfectionist

The goal was simple and direct and as American as apple pie and Sunday doubleheaders. In baseball America, it was no trifling objective but as high as you could shoot.

"I wanted to be the greatest hitter that ever lived," Ted Williams said.

Well, a lot of players did. Many wanted it and felt it, but few proclaimed it and pursued it as intensely as Williams, who could probably see its aura around him whenever he looked in a mirror.

Faith and dedication were just part of it, of course. There was the cultivation of what nature had so bountifully given him—the strength, reflexes, coordination, judgment, those eyes that seemed able to pierce the very core of a baseball. But most of all, there was the hard work.

"There's no such thing as being born a great hitter," Williams steadfastly maintained. "When I was in grammar school in San Diego, I used to be down at the yard waiting for the janitor to open up in the morning so I could get a bat and get in a few licks before the school bell rang. I haven't stopped practicing since."

Bill Dickey swore he never saw Williams swing at a pitch as much as an inch off the corner. Yogi Berra said he never saw such reflexes—the trigger wrists whipping a bat that would blur as it seemingly picked balls out of his glove. Williams was the Great Perfectionist, a hitter who admitted he "asked more questions about hitting than anybody," yet one who appeared to Harry Walker "to just hit naturally. The rest of us, we have to figure and think and connive."

Few could match the ambition of Williams, who had been practicing the swing and clinging to the dream back in San Diego, sending baseballs farther and farther into the California skies—and sometimes looking there for inspiration. "I wished it on every falling star: 'Please, let me be the hitter I want to be,'" he wrote in his autobiography, "My Turn at Bat."

Ted Williams, the Boston Red Sox's Splendid Splinter.

By the time Williams finished high school, the scouts were coming around, including the New York Yankees' Bill Essick, who in 1936 offered the tall, skinny 17-year-old a $500 bonus to sign. "The story is my mother (a devoted servant of the Salvation Army) asked for $1,000 and Essick refused," Williams related.

For want of $500, baseball was deprived of having Joe DiMaggio and Williams in the same outfield. But consider the pairing of Stan Musial and Williams, "the Man" and "the Kid." The Cardinals also were interested, but Williams didn't reciprocate "because they had a huge farm system then and you could get lost."

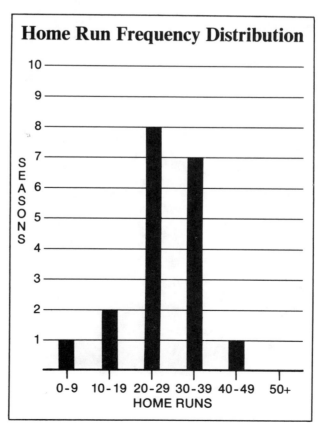

Williams was a star at San Diego's Herbert Hoover High School when he caught the attention of major league scouts.

A Red Sox rookie in 1939, Williams clung to this ambition: "I wanted to be the greatest hitter that ever lived."

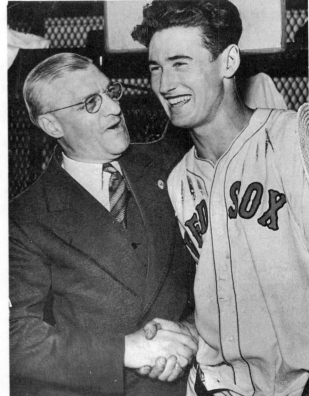

Williams' game-winning homer in the 1941 All-Star Game earned him congratulations from American League President William Harridge.

Being the best was not enough; he also had to look good doing it.

Instead, Williams signed that June with the local team, the Padres of the Pacific Coast League. It was a "civic-minded" decision, the local politicos assured him, and one that would keep him close to home, pleasing his mother. Thus, a couple of months shy of his 18th birthday, Williams broke into what was considered the fastest of the minor leagues.

Even then, he admitted, "I boiled with enthusiasm. I was always in front of mirrors with a rolled-up piece of paper or a pillow or *anything,* studying my swing. I wanted to be stylish, I wanted to look good, I wanted to *see* how I looked, how I swung at low balls, fastballs, high balls. I was forever thinking, 'I want to be able to hit *any* ball out of the park.' "

So it wasn't enough to become the greatest hitter that ever lived—he had to look good doing it, as if to lend further honor to the distinction. Ted Williams at bat was to become like no one since Babe Ruth, with fans in awe of the power, the symmetry and the dedication that made it all work.

Late that 1936 season, Boston Red Sox General Manager Eddie Collins stopped in San Diego to scout second baseman Bobby Doerr, on option to the Padres. As the club took batting practice, Collins suddenly found himself mesmerized by the swing of a tall, skinny outfielder. Now, Collins, the greatest second baseman of his time, had shared the spotlight with baseball's most exalted luminaries, including Ruth, Ty Cobb, Tris Speaker and Joe Jackson. But when he watched this Williams youngster swing, as he told Lefty Grove years later, "I said to myself, 'Uh-oh.' "

"I had my exciting experiences as a player," Collins said, "but when I saw that kid I got a terrific thrill."

The Red Sox alertly arranged an option on Williams and, after he rapped 23 homers and drove home 98 runs his first full season with San Diego in 1937, whisked him off to spring training in 1938. Williams was there only for a look, not to compete for a job with the big club, but he made a variety of impressions. He was, by his own admission, scared

The Williams shift, placing three players on the right side of the infield, was used frequently against the Boston slugger. On this occasion, he tries to foil the strategy by bunting.

Williams (left) was to make this journey 521 times. Preparing to embark on another mission (right), as a fighter pilot in World War II.

Williams signs his 1947 contract as Boston General Manager Eddie Collins, the former Philadelphia Athletics star second baseman who "discovered" him in 1936, oversees the proceedings.

and nervous, and tried to disguise it with bravado and brashness.

"Wait till you see Foxx hit," Doerr said to him.

"Wait till Foxx sees *me* hit," Williams replied. Allegedly. It remains a popular Williams anecdote, something he denied having said, but not without adding, "I suppose it wouldn't have been unlike me."

He called businesslike Manager Joe Cronin "Sport," was good-naturedly razzed by outfielders Ben Chapman, Doc Cramer and Joe Vosmik (each a .300 hitter) and responded by boasting he'd one day make more money "in this frigging game" than the three of them combined. (Which he did.)

But most of all, Williams impressed the Red Sox with that swing and graceful power.

"It was there from Day One," Cramer said. "You couldn't miss it. He hit them as far as Foxx did and his swing was perfect."

"There was no question about him," said Cronin. "But we felt he needed a year in Triple-A. Hell, he wasn't 20 years old yet. We wanted him to work on his fielding. He wasn't bad out there, but we felt he could improve. But all he wanted to do was hit. I've never seen a guy so anxious to get to the plate. And he was a great kid. He gave me more headaches than

any other player, but you had to like him. He had a dedication at home plate that I've never seen in another player. I remember saying to Collins, 'Eddie, all this kid wants to do is hit.' And Eddie said to me, 'Well, if you could swing like that, wouldn't you?' "

The Red Sox sent their prodigy to Minneapolis of the American Association, where Williams left pitchers shellshocked at every port of call. He captured the league's Triple Crown with 43 home runs, 142 runs batted in and a .366 batting average, vaulting into the American League for the 1939 season. Teams tried to get a line on the newcomer as the schedule unfolded but, by every indication, must have realized the folly of it as Williams blasted 31 homers, batted .327 and drove home a league-leading 145 runs, still the major league record for rookies.

"We had a clubhouse meeting before our first series with the Red Sox," Yankee Tommy Henrich said. "We talked about Cronin, Foxx, going down their lineup. We get around to Williams. What do we know about Williams. ... Well, the consensus was pitch him high and tight, low and away. The old words of wisdom. So we went out and played.

"The next day we're talking again. What did we learn about Williams? High and tight is ball one,

Williams with his longtime competitor, New York Yankee center fielder Joe DiMaggio.

Red Sox Manager Joe McCarthy watches closely as Williams displays his batting skills during 1949 spring training drills in Sarasota, Fla.

and low and away is ball two. Then Bill Dickey said, 'Boys, he's just a damned good hitter.' And that sizes up Ted Williams. That's what we found out, after one look. And it stuck."

Along with his power, Williams' batting eye was to become legendary. Umpires gave him the benefit of the doubt on close pitches, players said, reasoning that his judgment was superior to theirs. So acute was his sensitivity at the plate that in 1953, when he returned in midseason from the Korean War, Williams insisted to Cronin (by then the club's general manager) that the plate at Fenway Park was now slightly off line. To humor his great slugger, Cronin had the foul lines measured—and discovered the plate misaligned by a fraction.

"Everybody made a big thing of this," Williams said, "a demonstration that the Williams eye was still intact, but if you had stood at that plate as often as I had, you would know when it wasn't

right."

Following a solid second season in 1940—a .344 batting average (his lifetime mark), 23 home runs, 113 RBIs—Williams put together a masterpiece in 1941 that would become a landmark for personal achievement.

From mid-May through mid-July, the country had thrilled to the drama of Joe DiMaggio's 56-game hitting streak, but the focus soon shifted to another player's mission, this one waged by the young Boston slugger in quest of a .400 batting average. Williams had carried a .405 mark into the All-Star break, the game itself providing him with a stage for what he rated the greatest thrill of his career. His game-winning three-run homer with two out in the ninth remains one of the classic All-Star memories, as does his leaping, joyous romp around the bases.

Williams was batting .39955 as the Red Sox pre-

(From left) Williams with second baseman Bobby Doerr, center fielder Dom
DiMaggio and shortstop Vern Stephens.

Williams displays his patented swing during a game in New York's Yankee
Stadium.

pared for a season-ending doubleheader against the Athletics in Philadelphia. Cronin met with his 23-year-old left fielder, offering to sit Ted down for the day, thus ensuring his .400 average. "I don't care to be known as a .400 hitter with a lousy average of .39955," Williams said. "If I'm going to be a .400 hitter, I want to have more than my toenails on the line."

It was, as one writer has written, "not a gamble but an opportunity." And Williams took hold of it with both hands, collecting six hits in eight at-bats to finish with a .406 average, the last time a major leaguer has reached the .400 plateau. Moreover, Williams did it with power, drilling 37 home runs to win his first of four career homer titles. When he was nosed out for the MVP by DiMaggio, he shrugged off the decision by wisecracking, "All I want to be is an immortal."

Just three years into his career, Williams already *was* a colossal achiever and a study in artistry. Paul Richards, a catcher with the Tigers from 1943-46, remembered Williams' intensity at home plate.

"I've never seen such fierce concentration," Richards said. "One day in Detroit he came to bat and I was catching. I said hello to him, but he didn't answer. Now, I know that Ted wasn't unfriendly; he was, in fact, a very congenial guy. I realized that his concentration in the batter's box was so deep he didn't hear me. So the next time he came up I told myself I was going to try to break in on him, just for the hell of it. I started telling him a rather spicy anecdote about a well-known player and then stopped right at the punch line. He never acknowledged a word. There's not a man alive who wouldn't have wanted to know the end of that story; so I'm convinced he never heard a word. That's how entirely into himself he was at the plate."

Any disappointment over narrowly missing a Triple Crown in 1941 (he finished fourth with 120 RBIs, five behind the leader DiMaggio) was forgotten in 1942, when Williams won his first of two such honors with 36 homers, 137 RBIs and a .356 average. That he was runner-up to Yankee second baseman Joe Gordon (18 homers, 103 RBIs, .322) for the MVP couldn't detract from what was a magnificent send-off season to his three years in the military as a fighter pilot.

When he returned from World War II in 1946, Williams set out to prove what many people already suspected—that he was indeed the greatest of all hitters. "I'm just going to concentrate on getting base hits," he said. "The home runs will come—how many I don't know because that Fenway Park is a tough nut to crack for a lefthanded hitter."

(Had Williams played in a home park with a more inviting right-field barrier, many argued, his yearly home run totals would have soared. But Fenway, where the wall breaks sharply from the foul line to 380 feet in right-center field, offered Williams an excellent hitting background, and he hit nearly half, 248, of his 521 career homers there.)

The Great Perfectionist getting loose.

"Great hitter that Williams is," Frank Graham wrote in The Sporting News before the 1946 season, "he can't plant that long deferred pennant at Fenway Park unassisted . . . any more than he could in the four years before his departure." Yet "the guts of a ball club," as Lou Boudreau called him with simple elegance, was up to the challenge, slugging the Red Sox to their first flag since 1918 and capturing the league's MVP award. Williams' only World Series appearance was a frustrating one—five singles (one a bunt) in 25 at-bats as Boston lost a seven-game showdown to the St. Louis Cardinals.

Rookie Cardinal Manager Eddie Dyer undid Williams with a variation of the "Boudreau shift," a defensive stratagem Cleveland's shortstop-manager had introduced that season. St. Louis stacked the right side of the diamond with fielders, leaving Williams, a dead pull hitter, a clear lane 60-feet wide down the third-base line. "I foolishly tried to smash through it," Williams said, "which is just what Dyer probably figured I'd do."

The Boston slugger usually did elect to pit strength against strength, however, only rarely punching a hit into the inviting expanse in left. "I was paid to deliver the long ball," he explained. "If we need a homer to tie up the game or win it, I'll

Referring to Williams at bat, Paul Richards said, "I've never seen such fierce concentration."

Williams (left) with Johnny Pesky (center) and Dom DiMaggio.

have to go for the fences, even at the risk of having people criticize me for hitting into the packed shift in right."

Well, Williams would win another four batting titles against the shift, the first the following season, when he won his second Triple Crown with 32 homers, 114 RBIs and a .343 average. It also marked the occasion of perhaps the most disturbing snub of his career. Williams, once again, finished second in the MVP balloting, this time by one vote to DiMaggio (20 homers, 97 RBIs, .315), leading one writer to note: "Williams is the greatest of our generation and, long after we are all dead, future writers, thumbing through the records and looking at the newsreels, will wonder why some of us knocked down Williams."

Indeed, Williams was frequently torpedoed in the press because of periodic outbursts and tantrums touched off by buzzards in the stands. He trusted only "the few good" writers and had to withstand a non-stop torrent of criticism from "professional Williams wallopers. For years they have been busy figuring my 'persecution complex' instead of my batting average."

There was a league-leading .369 average in 1948, then a 1949 season of Ruthian proportions that fell just short of a third Triple Crown. Williams reached his career peak in home runs (43) and RBIs (159), both A.L. highs, but lost the batting crown by a fraction to Detroit's George Kell, .3429 to .3427. The performance earned Williams his second—and final—MVP award.

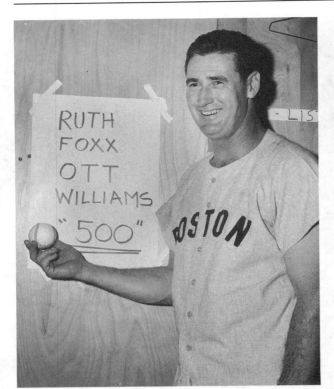

Williams (left) joined some select company when he hit his 500th career home run in 1960. By 1972, he was managing the Texas Rangers.

It began on the playgrounds of San Diego and ended in Cooperstown, N.Y. Williams (standing, left) is being inducted into baseball's Hall of Fame along with Casey Stengel (center). At the right is Commissioner William Eckert. Seated at the left, wearing dark glasses, is Ted's former manager, Joe Cronin.

Williams' Milestone Home Runs

	Date	Place	Pitcher	Club
1	April 23, 1939	Boston	Bud Thomas	Philadelphia
100	May 21, 1942	Cleveland	Joe Krakauskas	Cleveland
200	April 29, 1948	Philadelphia	Bill McCahan	Philadelphia
300	May 15, 1951	Boston	Howie Judson	Chicago
400	July 17, 1956	Boston	Tom Gorman	Kansas City
500	June 17, 1960	Cleveland	Wynn Hawkins	Cleveland
Last	Sept. 28, 1960	Boston	Jack Fisher	Baltimore

As the 1950s unfolded, Williams' playing days were cut short by two interruptions. In 1950, he suffered a broken elbow in the All-Star Game when he ran into the outfield wall at Comiskey Park. He played in only 89 games, still time enough to hit 28 homers and drive in 97 runs. Early in the 1952 season, he was recalled to serve in the Korean War, where he engaged in some pretty hot action in the air. On one mission, the Marine captain was hit by enemy ground fire and forced to land his jet with 30 feet of fire streaming from the end. "I was lucky to get it in before it blew up," he said.

Williams returned late in the 1953 season, took a few days of batting practice, then banged away at a .407 clip in 37 games. He ripped 13 home runs in 91 at-bats (a pace equal to about 75 home runs over a full season) and, according to Cronin, "set spring training back 20 years."

Despite his nearly two-year hiatus, Williams had lost none of his splendor. He batted .345, .356 and .345 over the next three seasons, and in 1957 staged an offensive exhibition that, considering he turned 39, rivaled the special niche he had carved in 1941. Williams became the oldest player to win a batting title, hitting a torrid .453 in the season's second half to finish with a magisterial .388 average. He drilled 38 home runs, second only to his 1949 season, and at one point reached base in 16 consecutive trips to the plate, a major league record.

In 1958, Williams became a 40-year-old batting titlist—this time with a more modest .328 mark—by edging past teammate Pete Runnels (.322) on the next-to-last day of the season. A year later, barely able to turn his head because of a pinched nerve in his neck, Williams batted under .300 for the only time in his career, finishing at .254 with 10 homers. His critics contended he was through, but pride would not allow this hitter to quit "on a sour note like this."

Williams returned in 1960 for his farewell season, one that would end with the most memorable valedictory swing ever taken. He had bounced back with a .316 average and 29 home runs, becoming only the fourth player to reach the 500-homer level before moving past Mel Ott into third place on the all-time list. But it was that 29th home run that would be the final brick in the towering legend of Ted Williams.

Although the Red Sox had a season-ending series scheduled in New York, Williams had decided to bow out in the team's home finale, September 28 against Baltimore. The day dawned damp and gloomy, a cold wind blowing in from Fenway's right field. The game moved uneventfully into the eighth inning when Williams, hitless in three appearances, stepped up to face righthanded Jack Fisher in what everyone sensed would be his final at-bat. To the very end, he had home run on his mind, even after missing badly on a fastball that evened the count at 1-1. When the 21-year-old Fisher, born the year Williams arrived in the major leagues, tried to pour in a second strike, Williams tagged it.

"It had a little extra on it," Williams said. "It fought the wind, and it just kept on going into right-center, toward the Red Sox bullpen. . . . It kept going and then out."

It was home run No. 521, baseball's most resounding final swing.

WILLIAMS' CAREER RECORD
Born August 30, 1918, at San Diego, Calif.
Batted left and threw righthanded.   Elected to Hall of Fame, 1966.

Year	Club	League	G.	AB.	R.	H.	HR.	RBI	B.A.
1936—San Diego		P. C.	42	107	18	29	0	11	.271
1937—San Diego		P. C.	138	454	66	132	23	98	.291
1938—Minneapolis		A. A.	148	528	*130	193	*43	*142	*.366
1939—Boston		Amer.	149	565	131	185	31	*145	.327
1940—Boston		Amer.	144	561	*134	193	23	113	.344
1941—Boston		Amer.	143	456	*135	185	*37	120	*.406
1942—Boston		Amer.	150	522	*141	186	*36	*137	*.356
1943-44-45—Boston		Amer.			(In Military Service)				
1946—Boston		Amer.	150	514	*142	176	38	123	.342
1947—Boston		Amer.	156	528	*125	181	*32	*114	.343
1948—Boston		Amer.	137	509	124	188	25	127	*.369
1949—Boston		Amer.	●155	566	*150	194	●43	●159	.343
1950—Boston		Amer.	89	334	82	106	28	97	.317
1951—Boston		Amer.	148	531	109	169	30	126	.318
1952—Boston		Amer.	6	10	2	4	1	3	.400
1953—Boston		Amer.	37	91	17	37	13	34	.407
1954—Boston		Amer.	117	386	93	133	29	89	.345
1955—Boston		Amer.	98	320	77	114	28	83	.356
1956—Boston		Amer.	136	400	71	138	24	82	.345
1957—Boston		Amer.	132	420	96	163	38	87	*.388
1958—Boston		Amer.	129	411	81	135	26	85	*.328
1959—Boston		Amer.	103	272	32	69	10	43	.254
1960—Boston		Amer.	113	310	56	98	29	72	.316
Major League Totals			2292	7706	1798	2654	521	1839	.344

WORLD SERIES RECORD

Year	Club	League	G.	AB.	R.	H.	HR.	RBI	B.A.
1946—Boston		Amer.	7	25	2	5	0	1	.200

PITCHING RECORD

Year	Club	League	G.	IP.	W.	L.	Pct.	ERA.
1936—San Diego		P. C.	1	1⅓	0	0	.000	13.50
1940—Boston		Amer.	1	2	0	0	.000	4.50

The Cadillac Of Pittsburgh

The line, "Home run hitters drive Cadillacs, singles hitters drive Fords," was uttered with Ralph Kiner in mind. For while Ted Williams was the top hitter of the day, Joe DiMaggio the best all-around player and Stan Musial the National League leader in virtually everything that a hitter could lead in, the home run belonged to Kiner. Consequently, so did the big paychecks, flashy cars and an adoring public.

In the years immediately after World War II, Kiner came to personify the home run as much as any player since Babe Ruth. The slugging Pirate left fielder not only hit more than anyone had in a long time, but also rode them for eye-pleasing distances. The classic Kiner home run soared high into the air and then, as if fitted with a booster rocket, seemed to pick up velocity and height and distance.

"Against Kiner," teammate Ernie Bonham mused, "the other clubs aren't playing their out-fielders high enough."

"A lot of people never realized how hard Ralph used to hit the ball," Cincinnati first baseman Ted Kluszewski said, "because it would go so high so quickly. Guys like Mays, Aaron, Banks, they would hit these high line drives that just took off and two seconds later would be in the bleachers. But nobody hit them quite like Ralph, except Williams. They would get that ball to a height where you finally found yourself wondering if it was ever going to come down."

And Kiner fully understood the symbolic significance of his art form.

"People enjoy the big pass play in football," he said, "the heavy punchers in boxing and the home run in baseball, but not simply the home run—they want to see that ball go a long, long distance. When people talk about home run hitters, the landmark names are Babe Ruth, Jimmie Foxx, Mickey Mantle, Ted Williams—the men who could put that ball out there a long way. Ironically, you don't often hear mentioned the name of Hank Aaron, and the reason for that is simple: Hank, as a rule, did not hit

Ralph Kiner, Pittsburgh's muscle man.

for tremendous distance; he hit steadily and well, but it's that long ball, that 500-foot clout, which seems to capture the imagination of the fans."

With Kiner unloading in Forbes Field, fans came flocking to his preserve. Despite being, save for one season, a struggling second-division club, the Pirates drew more than 1 million fans per year from 1947 through 1950 and shattered their single-season club attendance record (869,720) set in 1927. Lured there by Kiner, crowds also frequently left in droves after he batted in the late innings.

For Kiner, that kind of crowd-pleasing power was a gift he remembered having even back in his childhood, when he was always "able to hit the ball

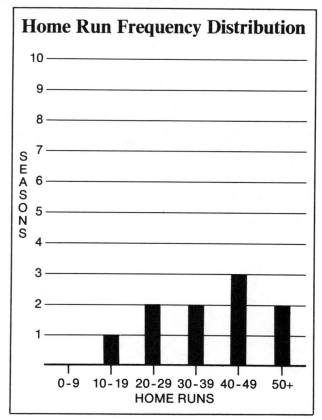

Home Run Frequency Distribution

Pirate pitcher Rip Sewell (left) is looking for the source of all that home run power.

Kiner, weapons in hand (left), hit them often and hit them far. So did Ted Williams (left, right photo), Kiner's American League slugging counterpart.

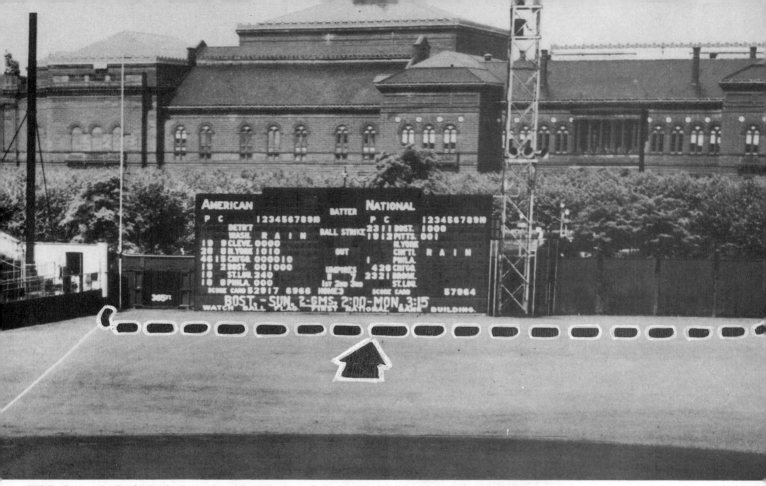

With the arrival of Hank Greenberg in Pittsburgh in 1947, the Pirates moved in the distant
left-field fence at Forbes Field. The area behind the new fence (positioned as the above
diagram shows) was dubbed "Greenberg Gardens" and later renamed "Kiner's Korner."

Greenberg, Kiner's 1947 slugging mate.

farther than anyone of comparable age." And at that early age, this ability determined his approach to hitting. "I always set myself up to go for the long ball," he said. "This was my style."

Kiner became the first—and only—major leaguer to win or share home run titles in each of his first seven seasons. Beginning with his second season, he hit at least 40 homers for five consecutive years, an N.L. record later equaled by Brooklyn's Duke Snider. In the 16 seasons prior to '47, only one National Leaguer had reached the 40-homer mark, Johnny Mize, with 43 in 1940.

A versatile athlete, Ralph's dreams set their course with the changing seasons while he was growing up in Southern California. "I wanted to be whatever the sport in season was," he said. "When the football season started, I wanted to be a football player; same thing with basketball. During the Olympic Games of 1932, I wanted to be an Olympic track star. I went with the tide."

By the time Kiner reached high school, the big-league scouts were zeroing in, attracted by those long, high fly balls which were like signals being emitted forth into the stratosphere of baseball. Pirate scout Hollis Thurston, a former major league pitcher nicknamed "Sloppy" because, Kiner noted, "he was always impeccably dressed and indeed was a high-class man," secured the young slugger for what became one of the best bargains in baseball—

Kiner with Brooklyn Dodgers first baseman Gil Hodges (left).

"I always set myself up to go for the long ball," said Pittsburgh's strongman, the National League's home run champion for seven straight years.

$3,000 to sign and another $5,000 if he made it to the major leagues.

As much as Kiner respected Thurston, the first time he saw Forbes Field, "I wanted to wring Hollis Thurston's neck." For a righthanded hitter whose forte was the long ball, the ball park was close to being a graveyard: 365 feet down the left-field line and 457 in left-center. "I was really downhearted," Kiner said.

But in his first year of professional ball, with Albany of the Eastern League in 1941, Kiner hit in parks that were nearly as roomy. As an 18-year-old fleet-footed center fielder (Kiner was always proud late in his career when teammates referred to his one-time speed afoot), he hit 11 homers, but managed 14 the next season to lead the league. In 1943, the Pirates promoted him to Toronto in the International League, where his manager was the old spitball pitcher Burleigh Grimes.

"He was a wild swinger in those days," Grimes said. "It was a good swing, but he was putting too much into it. When you swing too hard you're taking your eye off the ball. I tried to get him to ease

up a little and get a harness on it. But he wasn't around that long. We were in the war, and it seemed that nobody was around for very long, except for old duffers like myself."

After 43 games with Toronto, Kiner entered the Navy Air Corps, where he learned to pilot a patrol bomber that flew anti-submarine missions in the Pacific. He was discharged in December 1945, 20 pounds heavier (now 190 pounds on his 6-foot-2 frame) but stronger and more confident, even when he heard he was being ticketed for the Hollywood Stars of the Pacific Coast League. "I was confident I could make the big team and had made up my mind that I just wasn't going to let them send me back to the minors," he said.

Joining the Pirates at their California spring training camp, Kiner began swinging and connecting and never stopped, putting on an explosive power show that caught the attention of baseball people everywhere.

"I had such a tremendous spring," Kiner said, "that I think I even surprised myself a little. I hit at least a dozen home runs, some of them for real

The well-spoken Kiner always enjoyed his status as the toast of Pittsburgh.

Kiner preferred to trot across the plate, but that was not always possible. He slides home safely (above) against the New York Giants and catcher Wes Westrum at the Polo Grounds.

distance, knocked in a ton of runs and won a job that nobody ever expected me to win. I opened the 1946 season in center field for the Pirates and that was the start of my major league career."

Kiner led the league with 23 home runs (though Mize, the runner-up with 22, missed the last month and a half to injury), becoming the first—and last—N.L. rookie to lead in four-baggers since Brooklyn's Tim Jordan in 1906. For Kiner, who moved to left field in August, it was the first of those remarkable seven straight home run titles.

The following year, the Pirates made what was to be for Kiner a "priceless" addition. In a stunning move, the Detroit Tigers sold 36-year-old slugger Hank Greenberg out of the American League to the Pirates. With Greenberg, the A.L. leader with 44 home runs in 1946, the Pirates now had the distinction of having both of the majors' long-ball leaders

in their 1947 lineup.

Always a serious-minded player, young Kiner was taken with the veteran Greenberg's tireless work habits.

"During spring training," Kiner said, "he used to spend a lot of time taking extra batting practice after the day's session was over. I was impressed by the fact that this great star, who certainly didn't have to prove anything to anybody, was working that hard. I asked him if I could join him, and I ended up shagging balls for him and he'd shag balls for me."

It was the beginning of a friendship that lasted until Greenberg's death in 1986, a friendship that was to prove decisive for young Kiner's career.

Despite leading in home runs in 1946, Kiner had struck out a league-high 109 times and batted only .247. Greenberg, though, recognized a powerhouse

Kiner with the Chicago Cubs in 1953.

of untapped potential and tutored his willing pupil throughout spring camp and into the opening weeks of the season.

"Hank got me in a better position in the batter's box," Kiner said, "right on top of the plate, which enabled me to start pulling outside pitches for home runs. I changed my stance and my whole approach to hitting. Those were the right changes for me to make but they were also very tough to adapt to.

"I got off to a horrendous start in 1947 and for a month and a half I was really struggling. By the end of May, my record was still dismal (three home runs). I was confident I'd straighten out in due time, but the ball club was beginning to have its doubts."

Kiner said he heard rumblings that he was about to be returned to the minors but Greenberg interceded. "He asked (club President Frank) McKinney not to send me out," Kiner said. "Hank told him I had a good swing, I was working very hard, I was determined and that I was going to make it."

The Pirates, a hopeless club that would finish tied for last, could afford to extend their patience with Kiner. "It was a close call," Kiner said, but the decision was a wise one, for the combination of Greenberg's patient tutelage and Kiner's gritty determination suddenly began paying huge dividends.

Kiner began unleashing thunderbolts at an incredible pace, piling up 48 homers from June 1 until the end of the season for a final total of 51, tying him for the league lead with Mize. They became the first National Leaguers to clear the 50-homer mark since Chicago's Hack Wilson set the league standard with 56 in 1930. Kiner wound up second in the league with 127 runs batted in and posted a career-best .313 batting average.

Greenberg also provided, albeit indirectly, another big boost for Kiner's career. With Big Henry's addition, the Pirates reduced those imposing left-field dimensions by 30 feet to take advantage of his righthanded power. The bullpen was moved from foul territory into the former playing area behind a new left-field fence, creating an enclosure christened "Greenberg Gardens" in anticipation of the veteran slugger's long ones. Greenberg, however, hit only 25 home runs in what was to be his final season, and when his young protege began hammering them out in wholesale numbers, the "Garden" became "Kiner's Korner"—even though most of Kiner's blows cleared *everything.* The name followed Ralph into his broadcasting days with the New York Mets, becoming the title of his postgame interview show.

Kiner had the knack for hitting home runs in dramatic clusters (he contended they had to be hit this way, that no one could hit the long ball consistently), and on September 10, 11 and 12 of 1947 set a major league record by slamming eight homers, in four consecutive games. (A month earlier, he had tied the record with seven blasts in four straight games.) Ten times he hit at least two homers in a

Kiner with the Cleveland Indians in 1955.

game to set a single-season N.L. record, but he rated his 50th homer, September 18 off Dodger rookie Jack Banta, as his biggest thrill. "So few players hit 50 in a season, I thought I really became a man that day," said Kiner, only the fifth man to reach the plateau.

He was young, bright, handsome and suddenly sitting atop the world of baseball after just his sec-

Cleveland rookie lefthander Herb Score (left) with Kiner (center) and Manager Al Lopez.

Kiner, interviewing New York Mets Roger Craig (left) and Elio Chacon in 1962, successfully extended his baseball career into the broadcast booth.

Kiner's Milestone Home Runs

	Date	Place	Pitcher	Club
1	April 18, 1946	St. Louis	Howie Pollet	St. Louis
100	July 18, 1948	Pittsburgh	Vern Bickford	Boston
200	Aug. 13, 1950	Pittsburgh	Johnny Schmitz	Chicago
300	May 25, 1953	Pittsburgh	Al Corwin	New York
Last	Sept. 10, 1955	Boston	Ellis Kinder	Boston

ond season, not just a star, but as a charismatic home run hitter—a star of stars. Poised and level-headed, he handled the acclaim with ease and grace.

"Frankly," he said, "I kind of liked it. I'm sort of a gregarious person anyway. I wasn't like a country boy suddenly hitting it big in the city. Bing Crosby had bought into the Pirates in 1946, and through Bing's interest in the club and in baseball I had gotten to meet a lot of Hollywood celebrities. (I) played golf with Bing and Bob Hope and people like that. So when I made my own way into the limelight, I wasn't a total stranger to it and that helped a lot."

Saddled throughout his career in Pittsburgh with woeful clubs, he soon became virtually the sole reason for going to Forbes Field. Kiner kept bringing them out with the home runs, pounding 40 in 1948 to again tie Mize for the lead, then a career-high 54 one-way blasts in 1954, the second-highest total in N.L. history. He batted .310 and led the league with 127 runs batted in.

"Kiner could be a good, steady .330 hitter if he stopped uppercutting the ball and leveled his swing," Thurston had said. "But, hell, he wouldn't be Kiner then."

Kiner might have achieved even greater heights had the hapless Pirates provided him with "protection" in the lineup. Outside of outfielder Wally Westlake, who had a few decent years for the Pirates, Kiner was pretty much the lone long-ball threat in the Pittsburgh offense.

Nevertheless, Kiner kept swinging, claiming the home run crown with 47 blasts in 1950, 42 in 1951 and 37 in 1952, when he shared his third title, this time with Chicago's Hank Sauer. The next season, in a deal that stunned and dismayed the city of Pittsburgh, he was traded to the Cubs in a 10-player deal on June 4.

"When Branch Rickey took over as general manager (before the 1951 season)," Kiner said, "I knew I was gone. He had a reputation for not having high-salaried ball players; he also had a reputation for trading players whom he felt had reached their peak and might begin to decline. I fit into both categories, so it seemed a foregone conclusion that I would be traded."

Playing for the Pirates and Cubs in 1953, Kiner hit 35 home runs, a respectable total but, for the first time in his career, not good enough to lead the league. Kiner was, in fact, fifth, behind Eddie Mathews, Snider, Roy Campanella and Kluszewski, all 40-homer men.

In 1954, Kiner slipped to 22 home runs, continuing a decline from his peak of 54 in 1949. The drop-off had been modest from one year to the next, but it had been steady: 54, 47, 42, 37, 35, 22. After the season, he was traded to Cleveland, where Greenberg now served as the Indians' general manager.

The Indians finished second in 1955, three games behind the Yankees. It was the best finish for any club on which Kiner had played (the Pirates had been fourth in 1948) and the closest he came to fulfilling the dream he shared with every other player: participating in a World Series.

"That's the one big regret I took out of baseball," he said, "not playing in a World Series. But I guess I have pretty good company—Ernie Banks, Ted Lyons, Luke Appling, George Sisler, guys of that caliber."

Bothered by back trouble, Kiner batted .243 for the Indians and hit 18 home runs. At the age of 33, he retired, leaving behind 369 lifetime home runs (sixth on the all-time list at the time) and an impressive array of long-ball records.

"I could have played a few years longer than I did," he said, "but I had a bad back, and when I couldn't reach the performance level I was used to, the high standards I always set for myself, I didn't feel it was right to continue...."

KINER'S CAREER RECORD

Born October 27, 1922, at Santa Rita, N.M.

Batted and threw righthanded. Elected to Hall of Fame, 1975.

Year Club	League	G.	AB.	R.	H.	HR.	RBI.	B.A.
1941—Albany	East.	●141	509	94	142	11	66	.279
1942—Albany	East.	*141	483	84	124	*14	75	.257
1943—Toronto	Int.	43	144	22	34	2	13	.236
1943-44-45—Pittsburgh	Nat.	(In Military Service)						
1946—Pittsburgh	Nat.	144	502	63	124	*23	81	.247
1947—Pittsburgh	Nat.	152	565	118	177	●51	127	.313
1948—Pittsburgh	Nat.	●156	555	104	147	●40	123	.265
1949—Pittsburgh	Nat.	152	549	116	170	*54	*127	.310
1950—Pittsburgh	Nat.	150	547	112	149	*47	118	.272
1951—Pittsburgh	Nat.	151	531	●124	164	*42	109	.309
1952—Pittsburgh	Nat.	149	516	90	126	●37	87	.244
1953—Pitts.-Chi.	Nat.	*158	562	100	157	35	116	.279
1954—Chicago	Nat.	147	557	88	159	22	73	.285
1955—Cleveland	Amer.	113	321	56	73	18	54	.243
National League Totals		1359	4884	915	1373	351	961	.281
American League Totals		113	321	56	78	18	54	.243
Major League Totals		1472	5205	971	1451	369	1015	.279

The Mick

"You have to wonder," someone said in the mid-1950s, "how many kids had to be deprived of base-ball talent for the good Lord to have made one Mickey Mantle."

He was as abundantly gifted as any man who ever played America's national game—gifts that were not just diverse, but spectacular in their dimensions. And above all else, there was that hitting power that fairly destroyed the pastime's time-honored standards.

On April 17, 1953, the 21-year-old New York Yankee fired the first salvo in what was to become the legend of Mickey Mantle. Batting righthanded, he caught hold of a delivery from Washington Sen-ators lefthander Chuck Stobbs and sent it rocketing toward Griffith Stadium's left-center field bleach-ers, 391 feet away. This ball kept carrying, however, as if it would fly forever, soaring beyond the back of the bleachers (460 feet away) and caroming off a beer sign as it left the park. Five hundred sixty-five feet from home plate, in the backyard of a tenement house across the street from the stadium, the ball returned to earth.

Witnesses called it the longest homer ever hit, longer than any of Babe Ruth's fabled drives, a blow that bordered on the unthinkable. "I've never seen a ball hit farther," Yankee Manager Casey Stengel said. "I've seen a lot of home runs, I saw

Mickey Mantle, as a youngster playing for Joplin (above) in 1950 and later (left) as a feared slugger for the New York Yankees.

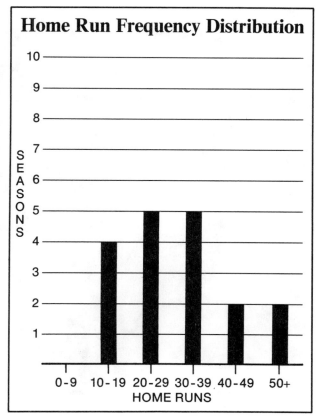

Home Run Frequency Distribution

SEASONS / HOME RUNS

0-9, 10-19, 20-29, 30-39, 40-49, 50+

Mantle as a Yankee rookie in 1951.

The youngster with some pretty flashy company: Joe DiMaggio (left) and Ted Williams (right).

Yankee center fielder DiMaggio, the man Mantle soon would replace, stands over the fallen rookie in Game 2 of the 1951 World Series (left photo). Mantle caught his spikes on a drainage outlet and suffered the first of several career knee injuries.

Ruth. . . . But I've never seen anything like it by a righthander or a lefthander."

Only eight days earlier, Mantle had fired a warning shot, whaling a drive over the right-field roof of Pittsburgh's Forbes Field in a preseason exhibition game. Mantle, swinging lefthanded, duplicated a feat accomplished by only two other players: the Babe and Pirate Ted Beard.

"That's what I can't figure," Stengel had said in the spring of 1951, the first time he saw Mantle. "He can unload them like cannon shots from either side of the plate. Nobody ever did that before."

But this wasn't the extent of the youngster's enchantments. He possessed a track man's speed, more speed than a man who hit baseballs 500 feet was entitled to have. Dashing from home to first, he could stop a watch in 3.1 seconds. It just didn't figure, Stengel kept saying in that revelatory spring of 1951. "Nothing he does figures." He had watched Ruth and Cobb, and therefore believed he had seen it all—the power and the speed. But now he was seeing it again, only this time compacted in one man.

And there was more. "An arm like a cannon," Tommy Henrich said. And the ultimate gift, especially if this kid was going to star in New York City after Ruth, Lou Gehrig and Joe DiMaggio: charisma. Grace under pressure.

And it was that titanic home run in Washington that assured the faithful that Yankee tradition would be carried forward, an assurance that proved unsettling for the rest of the American League.

"You know what was scary about that home run,

don't you?" offered Paul Richards, manager of the Chicago White Sox at the time. "It was the fact that it was a Yankee that hit it. Hell, DiMaggio had just retired a year earlier and the Yankees never stopped winning pennants. Then came this shot by Mantle. Man, that was a bad omen."

The Yankees would win 12 pennants and seven World Series titles during Mantle's 18 seasons, including nine of 10 A.L. crowns from 1955 through 1964. Among Series participants, Mantle stands alone for career slugging devastation, holding World Series records for home runs (18) and runs batted in (40), as well as setting the standard for runs scored, total bases and walks.

This bountiful package of baseball merchandise, born in Oklahoma during the Great Depression, was named after his father's favorite player, Mickey Cochrane, the former fighting, scrapping catcher of the Philadelphia Athletics and Detroit Tigers. Elvin (Mutt) Mantle had a dream for his eldest son, a dream he took with him each workday several hundred feet underground into the region's lead and zinc mines. His was the fate of many men and boys of Commerce, Okla., one he did not want to befall Mickey.

Mutt Mantle put the dream into serious, dedicated motion, working at the molding and shaping of a ball player. Most important, Mickey would be a switch-hitter. Mutt, a righthander, pitched to the small lefthanded hitter; Mickey's grandfather, a lefty, pitched to him when he swung from the right side (his natural side). This was a family undertaking, and with them nature had conspired, binding

Mantle making some noise at home plate in the 1956 World Series. The catcher is Brooklyn's Roy Campanella.

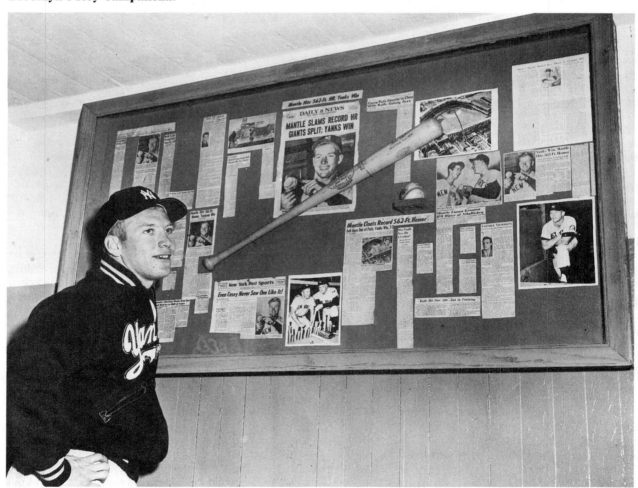

The bulletin board is covered with newspaper accounts of Mantle's monstrous home run against Washington in 1953.

Mantle and Milwaukee Braves contemporary Eddie Mathews.

into the boy a network of muscles and reflexes that no dream, no matter how ardent, could have achieved alone.

By the time Mantle turned 17, his home run shots were traveling through the skies like news on a crackling telegraph wire. Yankee scout Tom Greenwade, a tall, laconic Missourian who plied the back roads of the dust bowl, spotted the youngster in Baxter Springs, Kan., where Mantle traveled to play for the town's entry in the Ban Johnson League. Just days after he graduated high school, Mantle was snapped up by Greenwade and the Yankees—for a bonus of $1,100.

Mantle was a shortstop then, and by general agreement, not a very good one. His arm was strong but inaccurate—he made 47 errors (mostly throwing) in 89 games during his first season with Independence (Mo.) of the Class-D Kansas-Oklahoma-Missouri League. Of greater interest to the organization was his hitting: seven homers, 63 RBIs and a .313 average.

Time and again during that summer of 1949, Greenwade trekked to the simple ball yards of the K-O-M League to monitor his discovery's progress. He was pleased initially, then impressed, and by season's end, he was in awe. "I know just how (Paul) Krichell felt the first time he saw Gehrig," Greenwade said. "Krichell said that as a scout, he knew he'd never have another moment like it. I felt the same way when I first saw Mickey Mantle. He's

going to be one of the all-time greats."

A report filed by Independence Manager Harry Craft, the former Cincinnati Reds outfielder, corroborated the scout's judgment. "Can be a great hitter," Craft wrote. "Exceptional speed. Attitude excellent. Will go all the way. He has everything to make a great ball player."

The forecasts were even more prescient after Mantle's second season, when he batted a league-high .383, rapped 26 homers and drove in 136 runs for Joplin (Mo.) of the Class-C Western Association. Still at short, he committed 55 errors, proof positive that his future would be at another position. But that didn't worry the Yanks, whose regular shortstop, Phil Rizzuto, was voted the A.L. Most Valuable Player that season.

The Yankees decided to invite Mantle to spring training in 1951, work him out with the big club, then send him along to the minors, most likely the Class-A Eastern League, where he might earn a promotion to the Class-AAA level. But under the hot, dry Phoenix sun, the shy 19-year-old Oklahoman abruptly made the baseball earth shudder.

"He wowed 'em," said Henrich, who had retired after the 1950 season and was now serving as coach. "They assigned him to me for outfield instruction. He was a little wobbly on ground balls, and I helped him with that. I also drilled him on how to get a fast break on a ball. But there was nothing I could teach him about throwing or running. What

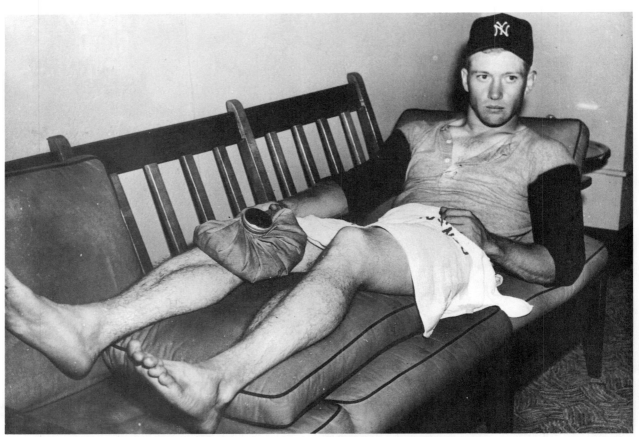

Injuries are almost as big a part of the Mantle story as home runs. This one was only a muscle strain in 1953.

Billy Martin (left) and Mantle.

Mantle taking in the scene at Yankee Stadium.

Mantle with Bobby Richardson (center) and close friend Whitey Ford (right) after a game in the 1960 World Series.

speed, and what an arm! There was nobody in camp who could outrun him. Nobody even came close, and we had some pretty fast guys there."

The first time Mantle ran with a group, he outdistanced his teammates by such a margin that coaches ordered the sprint run a second time, certain that the others must have stumbled at the start.

But it was at home plate that Mantle truly dazzled everyone.

"He hit them 500 feet righthanded and he hit them 500 feet lefthanded," Henrich said.

Stengel had never seen anything like it; nobody had. The pack of sportswriters from New York, where nearly 10 major dailies served the city, fired off sensational stories to whet the appetites of baseball-starved readers back home.

"By the time spring training was over," Herald-Tribune staffer Red Smith said, "the people of New York must have thought somebody from the planet Krypton had landed in Phoenix and put on a Yankee uniform."

By now, even a brief stopover at Class-AAA Kansas City was scratched for the barreling Mantle express.

"He should have spent that year in Triple-A," Stengel said. "But the writers had blown him up so much we had no choice but to bring him in with us."

Thus, on a riptide of publicity and into a fever of high expectations, Mantle jumped to New York, all the way from Class-C ball, to join the two-time Series champion Yankees. On opening day, he was in right field, next to the irreplaceable center fielder he was supposed to one day replace: the great DiMaggio, who was beginning what would be his final season. To many Yankee fans, the idea of the shy kid from Oklahoma displacing baseball's sleekest ship of state was presumptuous as well as flagrantly premature.

When Mantle was less than spectacular over the first few months, some grumbling was heard. The youngster showed some power and was leading the team in RBIs, but he was also striking out a lot. And Yankee standards were exacting. In mid-July, he was sent to Kansas City.

"You know Mantle was down in Joplin with a lot of young fellows like himself," Stengel said. "Young pitchers—fast, curves maybe, wild. But few screwballs, knucklers, sliders. They don't know how to throw them yet. Up here they do.

"Now he'll see them at Kansas City. He'll be back —and he'll be great."

Mantle's exile did not last long. He ripped American Association pitching for a .361 average, 11 home runs and 50 RBIs in 40 games and was back in New York before the end of August. He boosted

Mantle (left), a Triple Crown winner in 1956, gets together with Yankee Manager Casey Stengel (right).

The veteran center fielder blasted away in 1961 but had to share headlines with teammate Roger Maris (right, right photo). The M & M boys combined for 115 homers.

Mantle greeting Maris after one of his record 61 home runs.

his final rookie totals to 13 homers, 65 RBIs and a .267 batting average, helping the Yankees overtake the Cleveland Indians and win their third straight pennant.

Mantle's career was to be notable for many things, among them a haunting string of injuries. In the second game of the 1951 World Series, he suffered the first of several serious knee injuries when, in pursuit of a ball hit to right-center by the New York Giants' Willie Mays, he caught his spikes on the cover of a drainage outlet. His right knee buckled, tearing the ligaments and finishing him for the Series.

In 1952, DiMaggio had retired and Mantle made the transition to center field. He was steadily productive, though not sensationally so, over the next three seasons, batting .311, .295 and .300, with home run totals of 23, 21 and 27 and a high of 102 RBIs in 1954. That handiwork and his hard-driving style of play earned him the respect of teammates and opponents alike, but Mantle continued to be vexed by the extravagance of those early press clippings.

"He was doing fine," Stengel said, "he was doing great, but they seemed upset that he wasn't batting .800."

"They" were certain Yankee fans, a vocal segment that showered the young center fielder with cascades of boos.

"It wasn't fair," said pitcher Whitey Ford, Man-

tle's close friend. "He was doing his job out there, hitting the ball and hustling all the time. He was getting a raw deal from the loudmouths, but he never complained."

That was one of the hallmarks of the Mantle personality: stoicism. He never snapped, nor did he bemoan the injuries that befell him, playing through pain as few ever had.

In 1955, Mantle broke loose to lead the American League in home runs for the first time, hitting 37, while tying teammate Andy Carey for the lead with 11 triples (the first time an A.L. player had led in both categories). It was a solid season, but it proved to be but a tuneup for one of the staggering individual slugging spectacles of the postwar era: 1956, the year Mickey Mantle made the leap to superstardom, when all the forecasts and expectations were stamped "paid."

The 24-year-old Mantle did something that neither Ruth nor DiMaggio could do, that only Gehrig and seven other men ever had—win a Triple Crown. He did it with bruising authority, too: 52 home runs (the most ever by a major league batting champion), 130 RBIs and a .353 batting average. The onslaught earned Mantle his first of three A.L. MVP awards.

Mantle had enjoyed a torrid start, belting 20 home runs even before the end of May. And upon the occasion of No. 20, struck May 30 off Washing-

His presence was commanding, even in the on-deck circle.

Mantle was a natural righthanded hitter; his father taught him to switch-hit.

Mickey and The Man—St. Louis Cardinal star Stan Musial.

ton's Pedro Ramos at Yankee Stadium, Mantle "came so close to making history that he made it," wrote Robert Creamer.

This was a blow that was nearly the first ever hit fair out of the big Bronx ball yard, a towering shot that rose higher and higher in defiance of the gravity that strove to drag it down. The ball bounced off the filigreed facade above the right-field grandstand's third tier, an estimated 18 inches short of leaving the stadium. Mantle had added another punctuation mark to his burgeoning career.

In 1957, he pushed his batting average to a career-high .365, only to be upstaged by Ted Williams' .388 mark. The rest of the league did find a way to keep his home run and RBI counts within reason (34 homers, 94 RBIs), using a tactic as old as the game itself.

"I saw no point in pitching to him with men on base and the game still up for grabs," Boston Red Sox Manager Pinky Higgins said. "He was just too strong and he swung from both sides of the plate, which meant the pitcher had no advantage at all. And anyway, the pitchers—the sensible ones—were afraid of him. They just didn't want to come near the plate on him."

As a consequence, Mantle was walked 146 times (only Ruth, Williams and Eddie Yost, who coaxed them out of pitchers, ever drew more in the American League) yet was accorded MVP honors for the

second straight season, narrowly beating out Williams in a controversial vote.

Mantle claimed his third home run title in 1958, rapping 42 homers, and his final crown two seasons later with 40 four-baggers. Ironically, when he staged the biggest and most dramatic home run blitz of his career, Mantle failed to lead the league.

The 1961 season will be forever remembered in baseball annals for the achievement of Roger Maris and the home run duel he waged with Mantle. Playing in just his second season as a Yankee, Maris started hitting home runs at a pace no one ever had, driving threateningly toward Ruth's single-season record of 60. And just as remarkable, there was Mantle, batting cleanup behind Maris and hitting the ball out almost as frequently.

"I hope Roger hits 80 home runs," Mantle admitted, "and I hope I hit 81."

The M & M boys kept clocking the long ball at a furious pace, bearing down not only on the Babe's individual mark, but also the two-man record of 107 homers set by Ruth and Gehrig in 1927. Noting Gehrig's 47 homers after he hit his 48th on August 31, Mantle pulled Maris aside and remarked, "Well, I beat my man, now it's up to you."

Hobbled by a hip abscess in September, Mantle couldn't keep pace with his teammate, who pulled away and smashed his record 61st homer off Boston's Tracy Stallard in the season finale. Mantle fin-

Mickey Mantle Day at Yankee Stadium, June 8, 1969.

Mantle's Milestone Home Runs

	Date	Place	Pitcher	Club
1	May 1, 1951	Chicago	Randy Gumpert	Chicago
100	June 19, 1955	New York	Sandy Consuegra	Chicago
200	July 26, 1957	New York	Jim Bunning	Detroit
300	July 4, 1960	Washington	Hal Woodeshick	Washington
400	Sept. 10, 1962	Detroit	Hank Aguirre	Detroit
500	May 14, 1967	New York	Stu Miller	Baltimore
Last	Sept. 20, 1968	New York	Jim Lonborg	Boston

ished with 54 homers, the standing record for a runner-up, and the Yankees set the major league team mark with 240 homers overall.

In an interesting twist to the home run derby, Mantle emerged more popular with New York fans than ever before. Maris, a private man, had been uncomfortable with the ceaseless pressure and attention that built around him. He began snapping at the press, which, in turn, began to paint unflattering portraits of this relative newcomer who had no business breaking Ruth's hallowed record. If anyone should be making the assault, this reasoning went, it should be Mantle, the established Yankee, who had already qualified for the challenge by hitting 52 home runs in 1956. Consequently, those Yankee fans who had never fully accepted Mantle now became his advocates. No longer would he be slighted when compared with Yankee greats of the past. Instead, his popularity in New York would remain at sublime heights, through the rest of his career and into retirement.

Mantle had a couple of productive years remaining as the 1960s unfolded, winning the MVP for the third time in 1962 at 30, then hammering 35 homers with 111 RBIs in 1964, his best season post-1961.

By 1965, however, the myriad of injuries Mantle had suffered had begun to erode his superb talent. His medical case history was spattered with knee injuries, broken bones and surgeries, as well as pulled muscles, tears and sprains.

"He was always pulling a muscle," Stengel said, "because he had so many of them."

One of Mantle's "problems" was his own determination to play through pain and injury. Managers, fascinated by his enormous talent, also were reluctant to sit him down to allow proper healing time. In 1967 and 1968, Mantle's final two seasons, the club did move him to first base, hoping to reduce the wear and tear on his legs.

"I never got used to seeing him at first base," one Yankee fan said. "It just didn't look right. It made the whole field look out of sync."

"He was like a lion in a cage," Red Smith said. "You knew he was just aching to break loose and run, but he had nowhere to go."

In those final two years, Mantle batted .245 and .237, dropping his career average below .300, but he totaled 40 home runs and finished his career with 536, third at the time behind Ruth and Mays. Pitchers still regarded him warily, as if he were an old heavyweight who still possessed his haymaker swing, walking him more than 100 times each year.

At the start of spring training in 1969, Mantle's aching body and wounded pride prevailed upon him to call it a career. "I just can't play anymore and I know it," he said. "I can't go from first to third when I want to. I can't steal second when I want to, and I can't score from second on a hit anymore. It really breaks me up to feel I can't do those things. . . ."

Things that, for the previous 18 seasons, he had done like no one else could, combining devastating power from either side of the plate and speed that, in the early years, enabled him to outrun any man on the field. "All I have," he would offer shyly, "is natural ability."

MANTLE'S CAREER RECORD

Born October 20, 1931, at Spavinaw, Okla.
Batted both and threw righthanded.   Elected to Hall of Fame, 1974.

Year Club	League	G.	AB.	R.	H.	HR.	RBI.	B.A.
1949—Independence.....	K-O-M	89	323	54	101	7	63	.313
1950—Joplin...................	W. A.	137	519	*141	*199	26	136	*.383
1951—New York............	Amer.	96	341	61	91	13	65	.267
1951—Kansas City.........	A. A.	40	166	32	60	11	50	.361
1952—New York............	Amer.	142	549	94	171	23	87	.311
1953—New York............	Amer.	127	461	105	136	21	92	.295
1954—New York............	Amer.	146	543	*129	163	27	102	.300
1955—New York............	Amer.	147	517	121	158	*37	99	.306
1956—New York............	Amer.	150	533	*132	188	*52	*130	*.353
1957—New York............	Amer.	144	474	*121	173	34	94	.365
1958—New York............	Amer.	150	519	*127	158	*42	97	.304
1959—New York............	Amer.	144	541	104	154	31	75	.285
1960—New York............	Amer.	153	527	*119	145	*40	94	.275
1961—New York............	Amer.	153	514	●132	163	54	128	.317
1962—New York............	Amer.	123	377	96	121	30	89	.321
1963—New York............	Amer.	65	172	40	54	15	35	.314
1964—New York............	Amer.	143	465	92	141	35	111	.303
1965—New York............	Amer.	122	361	44	92	19	46	.255
1966—New York............	Amer.	108	333	40	96	23	56	.288
1967—New York............	Amer.	144	440	63	108	22	55	.245
1968—New York............	Amer.	144	435	57	103	18	54	.237
Major League Totals............		2401	8102	1677	2415	536	1509	.298

WORLD SERIES RECORD

Year Club	League	G.	AB.	R.	H.	HR.	RBI.	B.A.
1951—New York............	Amer.	2	5	1	1	0	0	.200
1952—New York............	Amer.	7	29	5	10	2	3	.345
1953—New York............	Amer.	6	24	3	5	2	7	.208
1955—New York............	Amer.	3	10	1	2	1	1	.200
1956—New York............	Amer.	7	24	6	6	3	4	.250
1957—New York............	Amer.	6	10	3	5	1	2	.263
1958—New York............	Amer.	7	24	4	6	2	3	.250
1960—New York............	Amer.	7	25	8	10	3	11	.400
1961—New York............	Amer.	2	6	0	1	0	0	.167
1962—New York............	Amer.	7	25	2	3	0	0	.120
1963—New York............	Amer.	4	15	1	2	1	1	.133
1964—New York............	Amer.	7	24	8	8	3	8	.333
World Series Totals..............		65	230	42	59	18	40	.257

A Baseball Masterpiece

Birmingham, Ala., was long billed as the steel center of the South, an area rich in such natural resources as iron, coal and limestone. It also produced one of baseball's greatest natural resources on the outskirts of town: Willie Mays.

Leo Durocher, Mays' first big-league manager with the New York Giants in 1951, portrayed his multitalented young center fielder as "Joe Louis, Jascha Heifetz, Sammy Davis and Nashua rolled into one." Indeed, Mays was the perfect image of power, artistry, entertainment and speed, and like all virtuosos, he had a captivating style all his own. "He played every game like a kid who was trying to make the team," one writer said simply. Where Joe DiMaggio (whose superb arsenal of abilities Mays most approximated) exuded grace on the field, Willie's aura was one of unbridled joy.

When he was 16 years old, Mays already was good enough to be playing for the Birmingham Black Barons in the Negro National League, a great league bound for extinction because of something just and heroic happening in Brooklyn that summer of 1947: the shattering of baseball's color barrier by Jackie Robinson. For the next few years, black talent would be like an open gold mine, its nuggets—sizable and otherwise—had for the picking by major league clubs quick to break their ties with a segregated past. And standing in the outfield in Birmingham's Rickwood Field was one of baseball's landmark talents, waiting to be discovered.

In the spring of 1950, the Giants dispatched scout Eddie Montague to Birmingham to check out the Black Barons' big first baseman, Alonzo Perry. "In search of a candle," it has been written, Montague became the man who "discovered sunrise instead."

"My eyes almost popped out of my head during batting practice when I saw a young Negro swing the bat with great speed and power," he said. "Remember how Joe Louis hit a man so fast in succession you couldn't count the punches? Mays swung that quickly at a baseball." And that wasn't all. The youngster could field and run and throw, and do it

The pride of Birmingham, Willie Mays.

all so wondrously well that Montague came to the conclusion that the Barons' center fielder was "the greatest ball player I had ever seen in my life."

The Giants went to work, aware that the Boston Braves had been scouting Mays for the last year and a half. The Braves, however, had just "given up the ship" (in the words of scout Bill Maughn, who knew better) and New York landed the 19-year-old prospect for $15,000, two-thirds of which the Barons took as "compensation."

The Giants sent Mays to their minor league affiliate in Trenton, N.J., where he became the first black to play in the Class-B Inter-state League. He batted a robust .353 in 81 games for Trenton, but flashed his

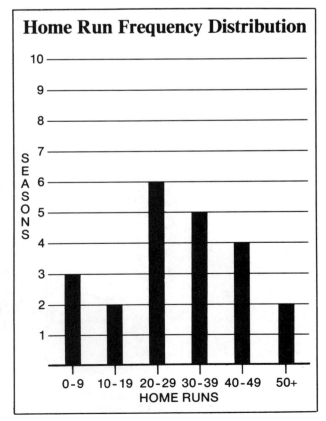

Mays was a rising star with the Minneapolis Millers (left) in the spring of 1951. A few weeks later, he was wearing a New York Giants uniform.

Brooklyn's Roy Campanella tagging Mays out at home plate during action at New York's Polo Grounds. The umpire is Al Barlick.

 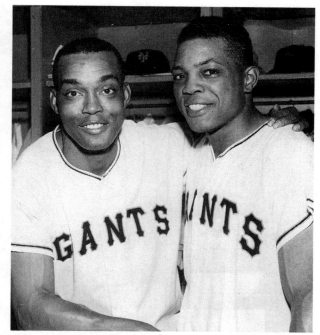

Giants Owner Horace Stoneham (left, left photo), Bobby Thomson (center) and Manager
Leo Durocher embrace moments after Thomson's pennant-winning home run in 1951. Two
other key members of that team were Mays (right, right photo) and Monte Irvin.

home run power only on occasion (as evidenced by
his total of four homers).

"We started hearing about him late that summer," said Giants outfielder Monte Irvin. "Somebody said he was a line-drive hitter, but somebody
else said, 'Yeah, but those line drives go into the
outfield like he's hitting them off of a golf tee.'"

If Willie was hitting bristling line drives, his
throws from center were nothing short of bullet-
fast. Despite playing just over half of the schedule,
he ranked third in the circuit with 17 assists. "I
never knew a peg could come in so fast from the
outfield," a Trenton infielder attested. "He could
throw a ball 200 feet and make your hand sting. His
pegs came at you like pitches—right on the money
and humming."

In 1951, Mays was assigned to the Minneapolis
Millers of the Class-AAA American Association. It
was a sizable promotion, but one the Giants were
confident he could handle. And Willie not only
handled the American Association, he took possession of it.

Mays loved American Association pitching, and
Minneapolis loved Mays. After 35 games, he had a
batting average straight out of the torrid zone—
.477. He was fielding and running and throwing
with the same zest and skill that would soon capti-
vate New York, and radiating those sparkling intangibles of his effervescent personality that bub-
bled like freshly opened champagne.

The Giants decided to send scout Hank DeBerry
to Minneapolis to see if .477 meant what it said.
DeBerry had been a catcher for the Brooklyn
Dodgers in the 1920s, the favorite of Dazzy Vance,
and was regarded as a wise old owl when it came to

baseball and evaluating the talent that made it go.
He also leaned to the conservative side when he
passed judgment, and when his report on Mays
began "Sensational," ears perked up. The report
went on:

*Is the outstanding player on the Minne-
apolis club and probably in all the
minor leagues for that matter. . . . Hits
all pitches and hits to all fields. . . .
Everything he does is sensational. He
has made the most spectacular catches.
Runs and throws with the best of
them. . . . When he starts somewhere,
he means to get there, hell bent for election. Slides hard, plays hard. He is a
sensation and just about as popular
with locals as he can be—a real favorite.
This player is the best prospect in
America. It was a banner day for the
Giants when this boy was signed!*

Scouting report? This read more like a ticket to
the Hall of Fame. Cooperstown would have to wait,
however, while Willie put in his 22-year career.

If everything about Mays the ball player suggested the theatrical, so did the circumstances of his
entry into the major leagues. The Giants, picked to
contend for the 1951 National League pennant,
were fighting to escape the second division after suffering an 11-game losing streak shortly after opening day. Before May was out, the call went out for
Mays.

But even the storybook career of Willie Mays did
not begin with the new man as instant elixir; in fact,

The vast center-field area at the Polo Grounds was Mays' hunting ground.

Willie gets a playful tug from Giants Manager Leo Durocher after a May 28, 1952, game against Brooklyn. Mays reported for military duty the next day.

Mays and another classy New York center fielder — Brooklyn's Duke Snider.

he dropped into the major leagues like someone whose parachute had not opened. He joined the team in Philadelphia on May 25 (after Giants Owner Horace Stoneham took out an ad in the Minneapolis papers, apologizing for calling up Mays) and proceeded to go 1-for-26 in his first seven games. Embarrassed and frustrated, he broke down crying in the clubhouse, fearful he was headed back to Minneapolis. Durocher came over and delivered a message: "Willie, see what is printed across my

jersey? It says 'Giants.' And as long as I'm the manager of the Giants, you are my center fielder. Period."

That first hit, in Mays' first at-bat at the Polo Grounds, had at least provided a respite. Mays announced his presence with a majestic home run onto the left-field roof, connecting against one of the all-time princes of the pitching mound, Warren Spahn. "I'll never forgive myself," the Braves' left-hander said, wryly. "We might have gotten rid of

Mays' catch against Vic Wertz and the Cleveland Indians in Game 1 of the 1954 World Series.

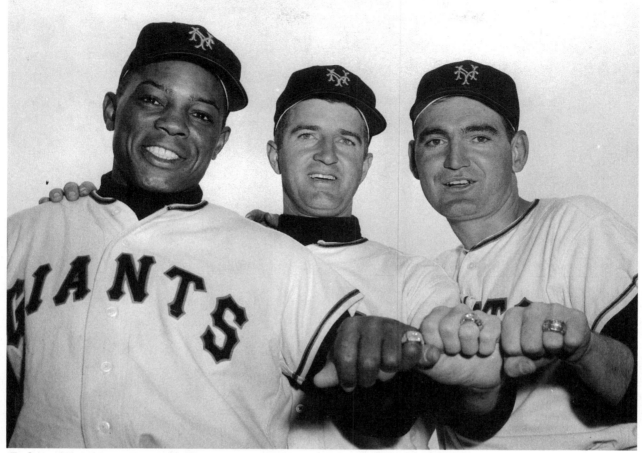

(Left to right) Mays, Don Mueller and Dusty Rhodes showing off their World Series rings.

Willie forever if I'd only struck him out." Asked what kind of pitch Mays had hit, Spahn replied, "All I know is that for 60 feet, it was a hell of a pitch."

Durocher's encouragement proved to be the turning point for Mays. By the end of June, he was batting .300 and the rejuvenated Giants were steadily turning around their season. In mid-August, trailing Brooklyn by 13½ games, New York launched an incredible comeback that culminated with Bobby Thomson's fabled home run in the bottom of the ninth inning of the final game of a three-game pennant playoff with the Dodgers. Thomson, now installed at third, had been the Giants' center fielder until Mays arrived.

The romance between Mays and the New York fans was immediate and lasting. According to Red Smith: "I don't think any ball player ever related to the fans as quickly as Willie. Maybe Giant fans were more trusting, but they seemed to believe from the very beginning that he was the real article, that he bypassed 'promise' and 'potential' and showed up in full arrival."

Of course, it didn't hurt that he was constantly lionized by Leo, who declared him "the best rookie I've seen in 25 years in baseball.

"There are only five things you can do to be great in baseball: hit, hit with power, run, field and throw," Durocher said. "And the minute I laid eyes on Willie, I knew he could do them all."

On paper, Mays' offensive contributions to the "Miracle" pennant (the Giants' first since 1937) seem modest—20 home runs, 68 runs batted in and a .274 batting average. But add to this his brilliant defense and the infectious spirit he brought into the clubhouse and you have the man who, by unanimous agreement, made the difference. Durocher made that clear early the next season under some unfortunate circumstances—after 34 games, Mays was drafted into the Army, not to return until 1954.

"We'll miss him as a ball player but we'll miss him more as a person," the Giants' skipper professed. "The Giants without Willie would be like our old Gas House Gang without Pepper Martin. He's the fellow you play with and kid. He's always laughing and good-natured, the heart and soul of the ball club."

Mays spent the better part of two seasons in military service, a fact often overlooked by those same baseball romanticists who dwell wistfully on the "lost years" of Bob Feller and Ted Williams. In Mays' case, the dim recollection is probably due to the fact that he lost time at the beginning of his career, when he had no panoply of glittering statis-

Willie also was devastating with his glove. He takes a home run away from Ted Williams (left) in the 1955 All-Star Game and goes high for a catch at Chicago's Wrigley Field (right).

Mays hitting one of his four home runs in a 1961 game against Milwaukee.

Mays, who appeared in a record 24 consecutive All-Star Games, joins Yankees Roger Maris (left) and Mickey Mantle (right) before an early 1960s All-Star contest.

tics after playing only part of one season. Yet, accepting 30 home runs as his average per lost season (probably a conservative figure, considering he smoked 41 in 1954, his first full season, after that 20-homer rookie campaign), Mays would have hit close to 720 career homers and, in 1972 or 1973, eclipsed Babe Ruth's lifetime home run count even before Hank Aaron.

These, however, are speculations for fantasy land; the real Mays is fantastic enough, and his return to the Giants in 1954 sparked sumptuous expectations. "There he is, there's the pennant," club vice president Chub Feeney said only half-jokingly in spring camp. Willie Howard Mays Jr. was the second coming of himself—exceptionally good in 1951, surpassingly great in 1954.

Mays did drive the Giants to the flag that year and made his breathtaking over-the-shoulder catch on Vic Wertz in Game 1 of a four-game sweep of Cleveland in the World Series ("Had it all the way," he told Irvin, the left fielder, as they trotted in after the inning). Mays was voted the N.L. Most Valuable Player and captured his lone batting crown with a .345 mark.

In 1955, Willie established his long-ball credentials with thunder and lightning. Until that season, only three N.L. hitters had reached the half-century mark in home runs—Hack Wilson, Johnny Mize

and Ralph Kiner (twice)—but Mays rifled 51, good enough to take his first of four home run titles.

Mays' home run style was the sudden shot—the high, quickly disappearing drive that was ticketed "home run" from the moment of impact. In his book "The American Diamond," Branch Rickey provided a vivid description of a signature Mays belt:

> *The memory of Willie . . . propelling the ball in one electric flash off the Polo Grounds scoreboard on the face of the upper deck in left field for a home run is a cherished image. The ball got up there so fast it was incredible. Like a pistol shot, it would crash off the tin and fall to the grass below. He would still have the knob of the bat in his huge hand and be but leaning in the direction of first base.*

Mays' home run kick, according to Rickey, lay in the ferocity of his bat speed. "If there was a machine to measure each swing of a bat," he said, "it would be proven that Mays swings with more power and bat speed, pitch for pitch, than any other player."

Given this full, powerful effort behind every rip, it is evidence of Mays' exceptional talent that he was not an easy strikeout. Where recklessness marked

Always a dangerous baserunner, Mays hustles back to third base as Yankee Clete Boyer awaits the throw in 1962 World Series action.

The San Francisco veteran with New York Mets ace Tom Seaver.

Willie's lifetime total of 660 home runs is topped only by Hank Aaron and Babe Ruth.

the boom-or-bust swings of most home run hitters, Mays possessed bat control, striking out only 60 times when he hit 51 home runs and more than 100 times in a season just once—1971, when he was 40 years old. Consequently, Mays was more of a threat to reach base—and always a threat to steal when he did. He led the National League in stolen bases for four straight years beginning in 1956 and was the first N.L. player to hit 30 homers and steal 30 bases in a season, which he accomplished in 1956 and 1957. In 1955, he had become the first major leaguer to hit 50 home runs and steal 20 bases in one year.

After the 1957 season, the Giants moved to San Francisco, where Mays dug in to play the bulk of his career. Playing his first two years on the West Coast in Seals Stadium, Mays batted a career-high .347 in 1958, then posted his first of eight consecutive 100-RBI campaigns (an N.L. record he shares with fellow Giant Mel Ott) in 1959.

From 1961 through 1965, Mays turned on the long-ball juice in earnest. He averaged 45 home runs per season, leading the league with 49 homers in 1962 as the Giants won the pennant, 47 in 1964 and 52 in 1965, when he was named the N.L. MVP and joined an elite slugging class that had crashed the half-century mark in home runs more than once: Ruth (four times), Jimmie Foxx, Kiner and Mickey Mantle (twice each). The exclusivity of this club is even more evident when one considers that top bangers such as Lou Gehrig, Hank Aaron, Ernie Banks and Harmon Killebrew failed to hit 50 even once.

Mays with the Mets in 1973, his final season as an active player.

Mays' Milestone Home Runs

	Date	Place	Pitcher	Club
1	May 28, 1951	New York	Warren Spahn	Boston
100	Aug. 7, 1955	Cincinnati	Joe Nuxhall	Cincinnati
200	May 23, 1958	Milwaukee	Warren Spahn	Milwaukee
300	July 4, 1961	Chicago	Jack Curtis	Chicago
400	Aug. 27, 1963	San Francisco	Curt Simmons	St. Louis
500	Sept. 13, 1965	Houston	Don Nottebart	Houston
600	Sept. 22, 1969	San Diego	Mike Corkins	San Diego
Last	Aug. 17, 1973	New York	Don Gullett	Cincinnati

Mays' single greatest day at the plate came against the Milwaukee Braves on April 30, 1961, when he etched his name onto the scrolls of still another exclusive club by belting four home runs in one game. He became the third N.L. player since 1900 to accomplish the feat in a nine-inning game (Brooklyn's Gil Hodges had done it in 1950 and Milwaukee's Joe Adcock in 1954, both at Ebbets Field).

Mays followed up his 52-homer campaign with 37 homers in 1966, a year in which he became the National League's reigning home run king. In a May 4 game against the rival Dodgers, he slugged No. 512 of his career to surpass Ott. At season's end, he had moved past Ted Williams and Foxx, and was second only to Ruth with a total of 542 home runs. At this point, however, Mays began a long, slow decline, one painful to witness at the end. He had seven years remaining in the major leagues, but save for one surge of 28 home runs in 1970, his long-ball totals ceased to be impressive.

Mays had been a remarkably durable player, playing more than 150 games in 13 consecutive seasons (1954-1966). But there is an inevitable pause in the legend of a great player, that stage after the creation and tenure of the legend, those thrilling early years, and before the final stage, the apotheosis of retirement, when one remembers all that was great. For Mays, the painful second stage, when the talent erodes and the quickness ebbs, was to be enacted in the same city where it had all begun.

In May 1972, the attendance-starved Giants released themselves of Mays' salary (estimated to be $165,000) by trading him to the New York Mets, whose ownership had no illusions about the 41-year-old but certainly a lot of sentiment. "We have always wanted Willie ever since the Mets were formed," said Donald Grant, the club's chairman of the board.

In 1973, his farewell season, Mays played 45 games in center field for the pennant-winning Mets and, tellingly, 17 at first base. The quickness was gone—at bat, in the field and on the bases—and he batted .211 with six home runs, the last of his 660.

When the Mets engaged the Oakland Athletics in a seven-game World Series, Mays spent the last four games on the bench. But what is a legend without some poignancy? At any rate, Mays had announced his retirement a few weeks before the end of the regular season.

"When you're 42 years old and hitting .211, it's no fun," said Willie, who fended off questions over whether he'd manage or coach. "Managing is hard work and I don't want that. And I don't want to be a coach and just stand out there like an Indian."

Standing around wasn't for Willie Mays, with those flashing instincts for knowing just what to do on a ball field. "I believed that when I went out on that field," he said, "that I was on a stage."

And everybody stuck around for the whole show.

"I'm not sure I know just what the hell charisma is," Ted Kluszewski had said, "but I get the feeling it's Willie Mays."

MAYS' CAREER RECORD

Born May 6, 1931, at Westfield, Ala.
Batted and threw righthanded.   Elected to Hall of Fame, 1979.

Year	Club	League	G.	AB.	R.	H.	HR.	RBI.	B.A.
1950—Trenton		Int. St.	81	306	50	108	4	55	.353
1951—Minneapolis		A. A.	35	149	38	71	8	30	.477
1951—New York		Nat.	121	464	59	127	20	68	.274
1952—New York		Nat.	34	127	17	30	4	23	.236
1953—New York		Nat.			(In Military Service)				
1954—New York		Nat.	151	565	119	195	41	110	★.345
1955—New York		Nat.	152	580	123	185	★51	127	.319
1956—New York		Nat.	152	578	101	171	36	84	.296
1957—New York		Nat.	152	585	112	195	35	97	.333
1958—San Francisco		Nat.	152	600	★121	208	29	96	.347
1959—San Francisco		Nat.	151	575	125	180	34	104	.313
1960—San Francisco		Nat.	153	595	107	★190	29	103	.319
1961—San Francisco		Nat.	154	572	★129	176	40	123	.308
1962—San Francisco		Nat.	162	621	130	189	★49	141	.304
1963—San Francisco		Nat.	157	596	115	187	38	103	.314
1964—San Francisco		Nat.	157	578	121	171	★47	111	.296
1965—San Francisco		Nat.	157	558	118	177	★52	112	.317
1966—San Francisco		Nat.	152	552	99	159	37	103	.288
1967—San Francisco		Nat.	141	486	83	128	22	70	.263
1968—San Francisco		Nat.	148	498	84	144	23	79	.289
1969—San Francisco		Nat.	117	403	64	114	13	58	.283
1970—San Francisco		Nat.	139	478	94	139	28	83	.291
1971—San Francisco		Nat.	136	417	82	113	18	61	.271
1972—S. F.-N. Y.		Nat.	88	244	35	61	8	22	.250
1973—New York		Nat.	66	209	24	44	6	25	.211
Major League Totals			2992	10881	2062	3283	660	1903	.302

CHAMPIONSHIP SERIES RECORD

Year	Club	League	G.	AB.	R.	H.	HR.	RBI.	B.A.
1971—San Francisco		Nat.	4	15	2	4	1	3	.267
1973—New York		Nat.	1	3	1	1	0	1	.333
LCS Totals			5	18	3	5	1	4	.278

WORLD SERIES RECORD

Year	Club	League	G.	AB.	R.	H.	HR.	RBI.	B.A.
1951—New York		Nat.	6	22	1	4	0	1	.182
1954—New York		Nat.	4	14	4	4	0	3	.286
1962—San Francisco		Nat.	7	28	3	7	0	1	.250
1973—New York		Nat.	3	7	1	2	0	1	.286
World Series Totals			20	71	9	17	0	6	.239

Steady Eddie

"Rookies come and go," remembered Robin Roberts, the Philadelphia Phillies' ace righthander. "You don't pay too much attention—at least I never did. I was always in deep concentration on the mound, so deep that sometimes I didn't even know who was up there. But one day I noticed this kid standing at the plate and looking out at me, and I remember thinking, 'This guy looks pretty serious. He means business.' That was Eddie Mathews."

Mathews' no-nonsense personality was, indeed, danger incarnate at home plate. There was nothing flashy about him as he waited for a pitch, no wasted motion. His lefthanded stance was straight up and down, feet wide apart, front foot pointing toward right-center field, bat held high and steady. He attacked the pitch with a short stride, whipping the bat around with terrific wrist action.

"He could wait on a pitch as well as anybody," Brooklyn Dodgers catcher Roy Campanella said. "He hit balls that, I swear, were almost in my glove."

Mathews was big, strong, handsome and a man you wanted on your side when the benches cleared.

"Tough kid," said Charlie Grimm, his manager at Milwaukee in the mid-1950s. "Anytime there was a scrap out on the field, there was Eddie, beating a path right through the middle of it with his fists. He never started a fight—he only finished them."

Mathews was born in Texarkana, Tex., on October 13, 1931, one week before the birth of Mickey Mantle and just months after a couple of newborns named Ernie Banks and Willie Mays inaugurated baseball's distinguished Class of '31. Eddie was 6 years old when the family moved to Santa Barbara, Calif., where his father, a telegrapher for Western Union, sought to realize in his only child the baseball ambitions he had once upon a time entertained for himself. Taking advantage of the temperate California climate, the family would trek to a nearby playground after the evening meal, Eddie's father serving him pitch after pitch while the boy's mother shagged his modest pop flies.

Milwaukee's no-nonsense Eddie Mathews.

By the time Mathews reached high school, his name was popping up in some significant athletic circles. Clarence Schutte, his baseball and football coach and a former grid star at Minnesota, likened Eddie to "a ring-tailed wildcat" at fullback, something that wasn't lost on college scouts all down the Pacific Coast. On the diamond, his slugging exploits were resounding enough to attract scouts from virtually every big-league club. Eddie, however, had made up his mind to sign with the Boston Braves before listening to any offers.

"I had always played third," Mathews said, "even when I was a little kid, and now I knew I was going to sign with a big-league club. One night after din-

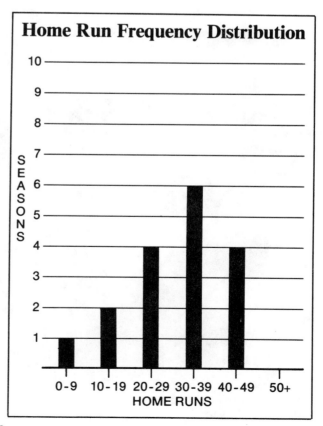

Mathews was a rookie third baseman for the Boston Braves in 1952.

The youngster belted 25 home runs in his rookie season and was an immediate hit with the Boston fans.

Mathews was ready for prime time when the Braves moved to Milwaukee in 1953.

He approached the game seriously and meant business whenever he stepped on the field.

ner, Dad and I sat down and studied the rosters of all the major league clubs. We decided that we'd go with the club which had the oldest third baseman. That happened to be Bob Elliott, then with the Braves. So we picked them."

Mathews proved to be one of the most nattily attired signees in baseball history, if not the first to sign his professional contract in a tuxedo. While Eddie was indeed properly respectful of the occasion, there happened to be another memorable event that night—his high school graduation dance. Since baseball law forbade the signing of a player until his class had graduated, Eddie had to wait until the clock struck midnight.

"Three scouts showed up at the graduation dance," Mathews recalled, "so I waltzed my girl outside at 11:30. We jumped in my car and drove to the Barbara Hotel down State Street, where (Braves scout Johnny) Moore was staying. There were only four of us in the room, with the shades pulled down. I was only 17, so my dad had to sign the contract, too. That was at 12:05. Then we went back to the dance. The scouts were gone—tipped off by the grapevine, I guess. An hour later, there wasn't one of them left in town."

That summer, the Braves sent Mathews to High Point-Thomasville in the Class-D North Carolina State League and the young man went right to work. Getting into 63 games, he batted .363, hit 17 homers and drove in 56 runs. After that, his progress was rapid. In 1950, as an 18-year-old playing a pretty fast brand of ball for Atlanta in the Class-AA Southern Association, Eddie clouted 32 homers and drove in 106 runs to lead the Crackers to a pennant. It wasn't just the frequency of his homers that attracted the Braves' front office, it was

(Left to right) Mathews and outfielders Bill Bruton and Sid Gordon in 1953, the Braves' first season in Milwaukee.

Back-to-back in the same lineup for 13 seasons: Mathews (left) and Hank Aaron.

Mathews owned the home run records for third basemen until Mike Schmidt came along.

also the distance some of them traveled. "When he gets to a pitch," said his manager, Dixie Walker, "he drives it as far as anybody I've ever seen." That was a rather heady statement, coming from a man who had played with or against Ruth, Gehrig, Foxx and Greenberg.

After the 1950 season, Mathews signed up for a four-year hitch in the Navy, just in time for the Korean War. After a few months in bell-bottoms, however, Eddie received word that his father had fallen ill with tuberculosis and was unable to work. As the family's sole source of support now, Mathews was discharged from the service and returned to baseball. He played parts of the season with Atlanta and Milwaukee, then an American Association club (and each a city where he would one day play with the Braves. In club history, Mathews is the only man to play with the Braves in Boston, Milwaukee and Atlanta).

Limited to just 49 minor league games in 1951,

Mathews hit the ball hard enough to warrant an invitation to the Boston Braves' spring training camp in 1952. He showed enough there to persuade the club to deal Elliott, who, despite three 100-RBI seasons in the last five years, was 35 now and deemed too old to play third base regularly—just as Eddie and his father had suspected when mapping out the boy's future.

"He'll hit," said Manager Tommy Holmes, the most interested observer among the crowd that gathered around the batting cage every day to watch the young phenom with the trigger wrists. "With that swing, he'll move the ball."

Mathews belted 25 home runs in his rookie year, including three against the Dodgers at Ebbets Field on the next-to-last day of the season to set a National League single-game record for a rookie. Despite his .242 batting average, his league-high 115 strikeouts and some shakiness in the field, the Braves were more than pleased with their new third base-

Mathews receives an enthusiastic greeting after hitting a two-run, 10th-inning home run against the Yankees in Game 4 of the 1957 World Series.

man.

"From the first day he reported to the Braves' spring training camp in 1952, you knew he belonged," one writer said. "He let you know; not by anything he said—he didn't say much—but by the way he played and by the way he carried himself, and by the way he looked at you—he had a stare that was deadly serious. It made you forget how young he was."

After Mathews' rookie season, the Braves packed up and made big-league baseball's first franchise shift in half a century, moving to Milwaukee. There, Mathews made the astonishing "overnight" leap from promising rookie to superstar—an often misused delineation, but in this case an apt one. When the Braves assembled for the rites of spring, Mathews' increased voltage at home plate was quite apparent.

"We were sitting around the clubhouse after a game in St. Pete when some old guy, a newspaperman, walked in," Grimm remembered. " 'Who's that kid?' he asked. I knew damn well who he was talking about—Eddie had hit one about three miles; it landed on a highway beyond the fence in right field.

" 'What kid?' I asked.

" 'Mathews,' he said. 'Who is Mathews?'

"This guy had been covering baseball in St. Pete for decades, back when the field was known as Waterfront Park, and he said he hadn't seen a ball hit that far since Ruth and Gehrig had been there. I told him to stick around, that the kid hadn't really loosened up yet."

Mathews and Milwaukee formed one of the most fortuitous of baseball pairings. The people of Milwaukee were anxiously awaiting big-league baseball but, at the same time, had to be realistic—the Braves were a woeful, seventh-place team in 1952, and other than lefthander Warren Spahn, were without a major star. Nevertheless, the fans came pouring into County Stadium, bringing musical instruments, cowbells and the loudest vocal encouragement outside of Ebbets Field ("At least in Ebbets Field," a bemused Grimm said, "they don't cheer foul balls."). Willing to settle just for baseball, more than 1.8 million Milwaukee partisans set an N.L. attendance record and, to their delighted surprise, witnessed the sudden skyrocketing of "a young Babe Ruth."

Mathews hit thunderously and beyond all expectations, leading the league with a franchise-record 47 home runs, driving in 135 and batting .302. Those home run and RBI totals would prove to be his career highs, but to say that Mathews far exceeded himself in 1953 would be misleading: He hit 40 homers in 1954, 41 in 1955, a league-leading 46 in 1959, as well as more than 30 in six other seasons. Before he turned 23, he already had hit 112 homers.

Mathews, the runner-up to Campanella in the 1953 Most Valuable Player balloting, became the idol of Milwaukee. A walk through the business district would draw crowds and snarl traffic; he

Mathews hit 512 big-league home runs, but lost in the shuffle was his reputation as a steady gloveman.

could not enjoy a meal in a restaurant without being besieged by autograph hunters. Milwaukee had a genuine national figure in its midst and, perhaps inevitably, everything about him became exaggerated: If Mathews frowned at a reporter or gave terse answers to a question, he was called "spoiled" or "arrogant"; if he was seen having a few beers in a lounge, it was a binge by the time the papers came out; if he was seen with a young woman, it sparked rumors of imminent marriage.

"A lot of baloney got into the papers those first few years," Grimm said. "But I don't think it bothered him. He was a very mature guy, and considering what a star he was at such an early age, he handled it very well. After the 1953 season, some people were even saying he was the one who might break Ruth's record. Listen, when a guy hits 47 homers before his 22nd birthday, people go a little nuts."

But Mathews' swing was, indeed, something to behold, much like Ted Williams' because of the terrific wrist action, but with the extra power of a

Third-base action in the 1958 World Series between the Braves and Yankees. Mathews is taking the throw too late to get New York's Norm Siebern. No. 2 is Yankee coach Frank Crosetti.

Aaron and Mathews in 1964: The sign in the background says it all.

Foxx. "He can get a piece of the ball and send it as far as some guys can with all the wood," St. Louis Cardinals Manager Eddie Stanky pointed out early in the 1953 season.

By 1956, the Braves were contending with an aging Dodger team for the pennant. It was the first of four exciting years for Milwaukee baseball, when the hands of the clock froze at high noon. The Braves had assembled an exceptionally strong team, led by the one-two punch of Mathews and Hank Aaron, who would combine for 863 career home runs as teammates, more than even Ruth and Gehrig. They were ably supported by fellow long-baller Joe Adcock, catcher Del Crandall, shortstop Johnny Logan and some excellent front-rank pitching in Spahn, Lew Burdette and Bob Buhl. Although the Braves would lose the pennant to Brooklyn on the final day of the season, they won handily in 1957, by eight games over the Cardinals, and headed into the World Series against a heavily favored New York Yankee team that had claimed six world championships in the last eight years.

Mathews, though limited to only five hits in 22 at-bats, proved to be the key man in the October festivities.

His two-run homer in the bottom of the 10th in-

ning of Game 4 gave the Braves a 7-5 win and enabled them to even the Series. In Game 5, Mathews beat out a chopper to second in the bottom of the sixth and came around on hits by Aaron and Adcock to score the only run in Burdette's 1-0 victory over Whitey Ford. "We all thought he was merely a fair runner," said Yankees shortstop Gil McDougald, "but the truth is that there aren't many who can beat him getting down to first."

In Game 7, at Yankee Stadium, Mathews' double in the third drove in the game's first two runs. It was in the bottom of the ninth inning, however, that Mathews had what is probably his most memorable moment on the diamond. Ironically, it came not with a swing of the bat but with the swipe of a glove.

Trailing 5-0, the Yankees loaded the bases with two out when Bill Skowron lashed a hot smash down the third-base line. Just when the ball appeared to be sprouting extra-base wings, Mathews —who had developed from a mediocre to good fielder—dove to his right, made a dazzling stab, then jumped on third with both feet to dramatically end the Series and give the Braves their first world championship since 1914.

To many, the big hero was Burdette, who hurled

When Mathews moved to Detroit midway through the 1967 season, he hooked up
with another pretty fair slugger—Tiger Norm Cash (left).

A brief stop in Houston in 1967.

Manager of the Braves in 1974.

Mathews' Milestone Home Runs

	Date	Place	Pitcher	Club
1	April 19, 1952	Philadelphia	Ken Heintzelman	Philadelphia
100	Aug. 1, 1954	Brooklyn	Clem Labine	Brooklyn
200	June 12, 1957	Brooklyn	Ed Roebuck	Brooklyn
300	April 17, 1960	Philadelphia	Robin Roberts	Philadelphia
400	April 16, 1963	Milwaukee	Jack Hamilton	Philadelphia
500	July 14, 1967	San Francisco	Juan Marichal	San Francisco
Last	May 27, 1968	California	Sammy Ellis	California

three complete-game victories. But several Yankees singled out Mathews as "the guy who really killed us."

"Without him in that Milwaukee lineup, it would have been a different Series," Yankees Manager Casey Stengel said.

"Before the Series started, we all knew he could take you out of the game with one shot. Just in case we didn't know it, he reminded us with that homer that beat us in the fourth game. But I'm not talkin' so much about his hittin'. Where he really opened our eyes was in the field. Why, he plays a great third base."

Said Ford: "My impression of him (had been) that he was a wild swinger. I thought he went for the fences all the time. But he's got as good an idea of the strike zone as any hitter I've ever pitched to. The only guy with a better eye is Ted Williams."

Guided by the home run bats of Mathews and Aaron and the 20-victory arms of Spahn and Burdette, the Braves repeated in 1958, but this time lost a seven-game Series to the Yankees, who rebounded after trailing three games to one. Milwaukee suffered another heartbreaking setback in 1959, ending the season in a first-place deadlock with the Dodgers (now in Los Angeles), but losing a best-of-three playoff, two games to none. It had been a smashing year for Mathews, who led the league with 46 home runs, drove in 114 runs and batted a career-high .306. It was the fourth and last of his 40-homer seasons.

In 1966, the 34-year-old Mathews moved with the Braves to Atlanta, where he played just one year, hitting only 16 home runs, half of his output in '65.

"He still had that beautiful swing," Dodgers Manager Walter Alston said, "but now he was just a fraction late on the fastball. You still didn't like to see him come up there in a close game, but he wasn't hurting you as much as he once had."

After the season, Mathews' long association with the Braves came to an end (though he would later manage the club) when he was traded to the Houston Astros. In July 1967, the Astros dealt him out of the league to Detroit, where he filled in at third and first through the 1968 season, swinging a rather sluggish bat. Mathews did, however, end his playing career on a winning note as the Tigers downed the Cardinals in the 1968 World Series. He retired with

512 home runs, sixth on the all-time list at the time. His 503 N.L. homers ranked second to Mel Ott's 511 among N.L. lefthanded hitters.

The young Eddie Mathews had come to the big leagues with a serious, hard-working attitude, and it never changed. Billy Herman, the Hall of Fame second baseman and a coach for the Braves in 1958 and 1959, remembered that ethic during the glory years:

"I'll tell you something interesting about that team, and I think you can apply it to most any team. There were three leaders there—Spahn, Burdette and Mathews. All the other players followed those three guys. They were going to set the standard, no matter what it was going to be. Well, it so happened that those three guys went out every day and worked their tails off. Spahn and Burdette would run and run and run, and Mathews would always be a-fieldin' and a-hittin' and in a pepper game. They were stars and they set a great example. That makes it a hell of a lot easier for a manager."

MATHEWS' CAREER RECORD
Born October 13, 1931, at Texarkana, Tex.
Batted left and threw righthanded.   Elected to Hall of Fame, 1978.

Year Club	League	G.	AB.	R.	H.	HR.	RBI.	B.A.
1949—H. Point-Th'ville	N.C. St.	63	240	62	87	17	56	.363
1950—Atlanta	South.	146	552	103	158	32	106	.286
1951—Atlanta	South.	37	128	23	37	6	29	.289
1951—Milwaukee	A. A.	12	9	2	3	1	5	.333
1952—Boston	Nat.	145	528	80	128	25	58	.242
1953—Milwaukee	Nat.	157	579	110	175	*47	135	.302
1954—Milwaukee	Nat.	138	476	96	138	40	103	.290
1955—Milwaukee	Nat.	141	499	108	144	41	101	.289
1956—Milwaukee	Nat.	151	552	103	150	37	95	.272
1957—Milwaukee	Nat.	148	572	109	167	32	94	.292
1958—Milwaukee	Nat.	149	546	97	137	31	77	.251
1959—Milwaukee	Nat.	148	594	118	182	*46	114	.306
1960—Milwaukee	Nat.	153	548	108	152	39	124	.277
1961—Milwaukee	Nat.	152	572	103	175	32	91	.306
1962—Milwaukee	Nat.	152	536	106	142	29	90	.265
1963—Milwaukee	Nat.	158	547	82	144	23	84	.263
1964—Milwaukee	Nat.	141	502	83	117	23	74	.233
1965—Milwaukee	Nat.	156	546	77	137	32	95	.251
1966—Atlanta	Nat.	134	452	72	113	16	53	.250
1967—Houston	Nat.	101	328	39	78	10	38	.238
1967—Detroit	Amer.	36	108	14	25	6	19	.231
1968—Detroit	Amer.	31	52	4	11	3	8	.212
National League Totals		2324	8377	1491	2279	503	1426	.272
American League Totals		67	160	18	36	9	27	.225
Major League Totals		2391	8537	1509	2315	512	1453	.271

WORLD SERIES RECORD

Year Club	League	G.	AB.	R.	H.	HR.	RBI.	B.A.
1957—Milwaukee	Nat.	7	22	4	5	1	4	.227
1958—Milwaukee	Nat.	7	25	3	4	0	3	.160
1968—Detroit	Amer.	2	3	0	1	0	0	.333
World Series Totals		16	50	7	10	1	7	.200

Mr. Cub

A shortstop who hits 45 home runs, drives in 143, bats .304 and, just to top it off, makes only 12 errors all year to set a single-season fielding record for the position? You could call him Superman, one supposes, but in 1959 you would have called him Ernie Banks, the National League's Most Valuable Player for the second straight year.

Beginning in 1957, Banks bombarded the league with the heaviest gunning ever done by a big-league shortstop: four consecutive seasons with more than 40 home runs and 100 runs batted in. Shortstops weren't supposed to hit like that—none ever had—but here was Banks, pounding the ball with thundering regularity and bringing zest to the also-ran Chicago Cub teams he was fated to play with throughout a major league career that spanned 19 seasons.

Winning back-to-back MVP awards in the National League was a pretty mean feat in the late 1950s, perhaps the most star-studded era in league history. In Milwaukee, there were Eddie Mathews, Hank Aaron and Warren Spahn. Stan Musial graced St. Louis; Frank Robinson, Cincinnati. The Giants had Willie Mays; the Dodgers, Duke Snider.

Each moved in a distinct atmosphere, driven to greatness by something within. For Robinson, it was an unrelenting aggressiveness; for Aaron, a deceptive reticence; for Mays, uninhibited exuberance. With Banks, it was a sunniness of disposition, a congeniality that weathered all storms and disappointments. Reporters never tired of hearing Ernie sing, "Isn't it a great day for a ball game? Let's play two today." And for a man whose club was usually stumbling through the gloomy airs of the second division, those sentiments displayed a good deal of character.

"Do you know of a better way to earn a living than playing baseball?" Banks reasoned. "Baseball isn't work to me. It's a game. If I was with the Yankees I couldn't play any more innings than I do for the Cubs."

Banks, however, lacked that burning desire to

Ernie Banks with that ever-present smile.

play the game that animated the boyhood years of so many future Hall of Famers. His interests leaned toward softball, football, basketball or track, and it was in these areas that he concentrated his best efforts. Nevertheless, Ernie's father, a former semipro player in their hometown of Dallas, encouraged the boy to cultivate a deeper interest in baseball.

"He never insisted I play ball," Banks said. "But I loved my father and I knew that it made him happy when I played, so naturally I did. He never pushed me, but he had his way of getting me out there."

First, he bought the boy a baseball glove, a prized possession for any athletic-minded youngster, but especially so during the lean times of the Depres-

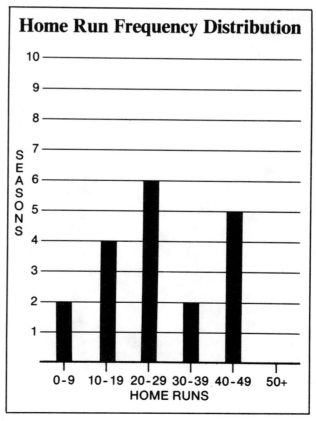

Banks: slim, trim and powerful.

Jackie Robinson, the man who broke baseball's color barrier. He was one of Banks' predecessors at shortstop for the Kansas City Monarchs. He is pictured here in 1945, at about the time the Brooklyn Dodgers were secretly scouting him.

Banks as a 22-year-old rookie in 1953.

The National League's Most Valuable Player in 1959 receives his plaque from league President Warren Giles.

sion. "Also," Ernie recalled with a laugh, "he'd give me a couple of nickels to go out and play catch with him. So maybe you could say he bribed me into it."

Before long, talent becomes its own motivation, a source of energy and pride, and Banks was recruited to tour with a black semipro team during his high school summer vacations. Upon graduating, he was signed by the Kansas City Monarchs, arguably the greatest club in Negro league history, a team whose demanding standards had been set by players like Satchel Paige and Jackie Robinson. Monarchs Owner Tom Baird regarded Banks as a "sure-fire" major leaguer when he first reported to the club, some heady praise the youngster would prove was justified in his two seasons with the club.

"Ernie didn't have a very high batting average with the Monarchs," Baird said, "but he continually hit the long ball and he was brilliant in the infield."

Banks was a rocket about to be launched, and Baird sat him down for a talk as Kansas City wound down its 1953 schedule. "I don't think you know this," he began, "but you're going to wind up in the major leagues. The Chicago White Sox are interested in you."

"That news almost floored me," Banks recalled. "I sat tight, and as it turned out, the Cubs and not the Sox were the ones interested."

The White Sox, according to John Rigney, their farm director at the time, "could never pin Baird down to naming a price for Ernie." And after watching Banks in an uneventful all-star game in Comiskey Park, "We didn't think there was anything to get excited about."

The Cubs, however, were convinced Banks was headed straight for the top—and the top is where he began. Purchased without delay, he was deemed a finished product and flown straight to Chicago. On

A shortstop who hit 45 home runs, drove in 143 runs and made just 12 errors all season—that was Banks in 1959.

Five happy Chicago Cubs. (Left to right) catcher Del Rice, left fielder Walt Moryn, pitcher Don Cardwell, Banks and second baseman Jerry Kindall. Banks had contributed a homer to Cardwell's May 15, 1960, no-hitter against the St. Louis Cardinals.

September 17, 1953, with 22-year-old Ernie in the starting lineup at shortstop, the Cubs became the eighth major league club to field a black player (hardly a record for social progress, considering Robinson had integrated big-league baseball in 1947).

Banks played in the Cubs' final 10 games that September, hit his first two home runs and batted .314. That the Cubs were satisfied is unmistakable, for Banks played in 424 consecutive games from the start of his career, more than any player in major league history.

By 1955, Banks' skills must have seemed otherworldly. Playing in just his second full season, he set the standard for shortstops with a record 44

home runs and led the National League in fielding at his position. It was a historic season all around, featuring another home-run feat that had eluded all of the game's greatest sluggers: five grand slams. The record did not come easily for Banks, who had tied the major league record shared by 10 others when he nailed his fourth slam on August 2.

"After that I had about three or four chances and I failed," Banks said. "Every time I went to the plate, I was saying to myself, 'This is my chance to get Number 5.'"

On September 19, however, he rifled one into the stands off St. Louis Cardinals rookie Lindy McDaniel, who was making his first major league start. After the game, Banks explained why he had been

Eddie Banks (right), the proud father of "Mr. Cub."

First baseman Banks (right) with (left to right) third baseman Ron Santo, shortstop Don Kessinger and second baseman Glenn Beckert.

Banks (center) with two long-ball Giants—San Francisco sluggers Willie McCovey (left) and Orlando Cepeda.

successful, articulating a credo that most home run hitters have subscribed to.

"I wasn't thinking home run at all," he said. "All I wanted to do was hit the ball. You get home runs when you're not really trying for them."

Always on the hunt for new heroes, the media took to the 24-year-old slugger. They found a warm, well-adjusted young man, one who was modest, amiable, optimistic—a man who was one of the best-liked players in the league. They also learned he had a sly sense of humor. In a June game against Pittsburgh, Banks was taking some heavy razzing by teammates after being hit in the nose by a pitch. Hank Sauer, a man whose schnozzle could have been a landmark, suggested that Ernie quit sticking his nose where it didn't belong. "True enough,"

Banks replied, "but if it had hit *you* in the nose, it would have been a solid single."

Physically, Banks was a lean 6-foot-1, 180 pounds —far from the home run hitters' classic mold. "He may look thin up on top," Philadelphia Phillies ace Robin Roberts said, "but from the elbows down he's got the muscles of a 230-pounder." Indeed, it was the strength in his wrists that gave Banks his terrific power. His swing was short and quick and lethal, just like his home runs, which moved to their destination as fast as anybody's. Like Aaron, Banks did not muscle a ball out of the park; he *rifled* it out with a snap of those powerful wrists.

Asked how he had been able to leap from 19 home runs (in 1954) to 44 in only a year, Banks revealed he had switched to a lighter bat. At the end

Ernie was not the only talented shortstop in Chicago. Luis Aparicio (left) was a favorite of White Sox fans.

Banks played 19 seasons in Chicago's Wrigley Field, but was never a member of a National League pennant-winner.

Banks tips his cap to Wrigley Field fans after hitting career home run No. 500 in 1970.

"You never hit home runs when you're really trying for them," the Cubs' shortstop-first baseman discovered with experience.

of the 1954 season, his 34-ounce bat had begun to "feel like a telephone pole." When he picked up a 31-ounce model one day, "it felt like I was swishing a broomstick." It enabled him to wait longer on a pitch and get around faster. The impact it made on his career was stunning.

Banks' success with a lighter bat did not go unnoticed in that most intercommunicative of fraternities, baseball. Other heavy hitters began switching to lighter bats, veering away from an old baseball doctrine, promulgated by Babe Ruth, among others, that contended it was the weight of the bat that drove the ball a great distance. A new reality set in: the momentum with which a ball was dispatched at impact was a combination of bat weight *and* speed, and with lighter bats being whipped more quickly, balls were being hit harder and farther. (Hillerich and Bradsby, the supplier of Louisville Sluggers to the big leagues, found that in 1949, only 14 percent of the bats used in the majors weighed 32 ounces or less; by 1959, the number had increased to nearly 70 percent.)

Bringing his lively bat to the lively ball, Banks settled in as one of the preeminent sluggers of all time. In 1957, he cleared the 40-homer mark for the first of four consecutive years, and in 1958 and 1959, became the first National Leaguer to win back-to-back MVP awards.

Banks earned the MVP distinction with scintillat-

Banks kicks up his heels before the 1977 season after learning of his election to baseball's Hall of Fame.

Banks' Milestone Home Runs

	Date	Place	Pitcher	Club
1	Sept. 20, 1953	St. Louis	Gerry Staley	St. Louis
100	June 9, 1957	Philadelphia	Robin Roberts	Philadelphia
200	June 14, 1959	Chicago	Carlton Willey	Milwaukee
300	April 18, 1962	Chicago	Dick Farrell	Houston
400	Sept. 2, 1965	Chicago	Curt Simmons	St. Louis
500	May 12, 1970	Chicago	Pat Jarvis	Atlanta
Last	Aug. 24, 1971	Chicago	Jim McGlothlin	Cincinnati

ing displays of power: in 1958, a league-high 47 homers, the standing major league record for shortstops (along with a league-leading 129 RBIs and a career-best .313 batting mark), and in 1959, 143 RBIs, the most in the league since 1937 (along with 45 homers and a .304 average). And with a league-best 41 homers in 1960, Ernie became only the third hitter in N.L. annals to post five 40-homer seasons (joining Duke Snider and Ralph Kiner).

Almost lost in the dazzling array of slugging feats is Banks' lone Gold Glove in 1960, when he led the league's shortstops in fielding for the second straight year. Regarded as a hitter first, Banks was nevertheless a solid fielder, blessed with good range and great hands.

"Ernie has tremendously quick hands and sharp reflexes," said Stan Hack, the Cubs' manager from 1954 through 1956. "That's why you hear people say that there is no such thing as a bad hop to Ernie Banks."

Some fans may have knocked Banks' arm, but those closest to the game didn't agree. "There may be some shortstops with arms that are a little stronger," allowed Cubs first baseman Dale Long, "but none of them can be any more accurate."

Banks' style was just one of consummate ease.

"You're never conscious of him making a great throw, but he always gets his man," Phillies Manager Mayo Smith pointed out.

Beginning in 1962, however, Banks was a first baseman, a move that was necessary to ensure his playing future. He had wrenched cartilage loose in his weak left knee during the 1961 season, making it difficult to pivot quickly to his left and right. In his nine seasons at short, he left behind 277 home runs, still the major league record for the position.

"First base presents many problems," Banks said with a straight face, "not the least of which is what to do with my feet. Sometimes I have too many and sometimes not enough."

Banks aged gracefully at first, averaging 25 home runs and 91 RBIs as the regular there from 1962 through 1969, but never was able to see an N.L. pennant raised over Wrigley Field. He remained the eternal optimist, however, picking the Cubs to win the flag whenever he reported to spring camp.

"I always felt we had a chance," he said. "Most of the Cubs felt the same way. Did you ever hear of a baseball team that conceded the pennant in spring training?"

In 1969, the Cubs made their only serious pennant run in Ernie's career, only to collapse in September and allow the "Amazin' Mets" to sweep past for the N.L. East title. The 38-year-old Banks was amazing himself, driving in 106 runs, the eighth time he had cleared the century mark, in what would be his last year as a regular. Early the next season, on May 12, he hit his 500th career homer, capturing the moment as only Ernie Banks could. "The riches of the game are in the thrills," he said, "not the money."

Banks' great hitting, along with his endearing personality, earned him the sobriquet, "Mr. Cub." His popularity reached such proportions that, paradoxically, there was once a movement among certain Cub fans to have Banks traded—just so he might play with a contender.

Ernie retired a Cub, however, after the 1971 season. "I always like to think a baseball player dies twice," he had said. "He dies a natural death and he dies when he has to quit baseball."

Banks thus became one of those baseball legends whose long careers were destined never to be crowned with a World Series appearance. But the ever-sanguine Cub voiced no regrets. "I had my moments," he said. Most assuredly, and they included 512 lifetime home runs.

BANKS' CAREER RECORD
Born January 31, 1931, at Dallas, Tex.
Batted and threw righthanded.   Elected to Hall of Fame, 1977.

Year	Club	League	G.	AB.	R.	H.	HR.	RBI.	B.A.
1953—Chicago		Nat.	10	35	3	11	2	6	.314
1954—Chicago		Nat.	●154	593	70	163	19	79	.275
1955—Chicago		Nat.	●154	596	98	176	44	117	.295
1956—Chicago		Nat.	139	538	82	160	28	85	.297
1957—Chicago		Nat.	●156	594	113	169	43	102	.285
1958—Chicago		Nat.	★154	★617	119	193	★47	★129	.313
1959—Chicago		Nat.	●155	589	97	179	45	★143	.304
1960—Chicago		Nat.	★156	597	94	162	★41	117	.271
1961—Chicago		Nat.	138	511	75	142	29	80	.278
1962—Chicago		Nat.	154	610	87	164	37	104	.269
1963—Chicago		Nat.	130	432	41	98	18	64	.227
1964—Chicago		Nat.	157	591	67	156	23	95	.264
1965—Chicago		Nat.	163	612	79	162	28	106	.265
1966—Chicago		Nat.	141	511	52	139	15	75	.272
1967—Chicago		Nat.	151	573	68	158	23	95	.276
1968—Chicago		Nat.	150	552	71	136	32	83	.246
1969—Chicago		Nat.	155	565	60	143	23	106	.253
1970—Chicago		Nat.	72	222	25	56	12	44	.252
1971—Chicago		Nat.	39	83	4	16	3	6	.193
Major League Totals			2528	9421	1305	2583	512	1636	.274

Hammerin' Hank

"We had just brought up this kid pitcher," long-time Dodger Manager Walter Alston recalled. "Good arm, good stuff. We went into Milwaukee and I was sitting on the bench with him, talking about their hitters. We got to Hank Aaron.

" 'I know how to pitch to Aaron,' he said.

" 'You do?' I asked. I didn't press him on it, and we went on down the rest of the hitters.

"Well, in about the middle of the game the Braves had a couple of guys on and our pitcher was through. So I brought in the new kid. Aaron was the batter. The kid threw two pitches; the second one Aaron lined like a dart into left-center, scoring two runs. After the inning was over the kid came off the mound and sat down on the bench. I glanced over at him and found him looking at me.

" 'I said I knew how to pitch to him,' he said. 'I didn't say I'd get him out.'

"I had to laugh," Alston said. "But that was the truth. I never heard anybody say they could get Hank Aaron out."

Oh, they tried, all right. And for at least part of Aaron's first season, most pitchers probably liked their chances against this hitter who appeared to spell anything but danger. As a 20-year-old rookie in 1954, Henry Louis Aaron entered the big leagues in an atmosphere of calm that 23 major league seasons would not shatter.

There was no wasted motion; most observers concluded he moved only as fast as a situation warranted. "A long time ago my father told me, 'Henry, never hurry unless you have to,' " he was quoted as saying. "I've remembered that ever since and here I am, playing in the majors."

There was that easy, loping stride that inspired an early nickname, "Snowshoes," among some teammates because of the way he pushed himself along. There was the calm that bordered on nonchalance as he stepped into the batter's box, not a taut muscle in his body. He waved the bat before he set himself, enveloped in serenity. "He's the only man I know of who can go to sleep between pitches and wake up

in time to hit the next one," Robin Roberts supposedly said.

If it had been an act, Aaron could be congratulated for being sly like a fox. But sharp observers detected right from the start that he was deep in concentration, his eyes fixed on the pitcher. "Throwing a fastball by Henry Aaron," said Curt Simmons, "would be like trying to sneak the sun past a rooster."

That was part of the allure of Aaron, that calm manner and effortless grace. And not long after he began flicking those powerful wrists around National League parks, the baseball public realized that there might be more to Hank Aaron than

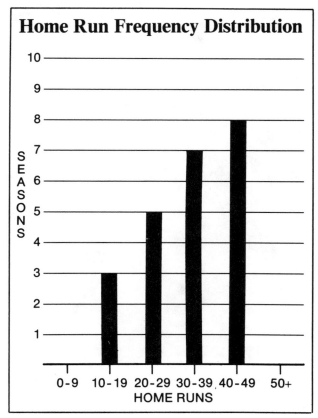

Home Run Frequency Distribution

Hammerin' Hank Aaron.

Milwaukee's rising young star with veteran Boston Red Sox slugger Ted Williams.

Aaron (left) was a hopeful young second baseman with Jacksonville in 1953, his second year of professional baseball. A year later, he was playing the outfield and beginning to terrorize National League pitchers.

amazing grace.

"He was the kind of player that a scout takes one look at and says, 'That's it. Here's a ball player.'" said Bobby Bragan, who managed Aaron at both Milwaukee and Atlanta. "Henry was always that good, that complete. He didn't light up a field the way a Mays or a Clemente did, but he was their equal. You look at his record. Henry Aaron played for 23 years, and for the first 20 of those years he was a star. In his 20th year, he hit 40 home runs. Willie got all the attention—and he deserved it—but Henry did it longer. And in the opinion of a lot of people, he did it just as well if not better."

When Aaron was born in Mobile, Ala., on February 5, 1934, George Herman Ruth was preparing to head south for what would be his final spring camp as a Yankee. Fourteen years later, when the nation was mourning the Babe's death, Aaron had not yet even played organized baseball. Henry got his early experience playing softball in the playground leagues around Mobile, learning what he could on his own.

"All I can remember," he said, "is that some guy told me, 'Always throw overhand.' I never thought I'd get anywhere."

Before long, his reputation grew as a dangerous righthanded hitter (albeit a crosshanded hitter), and he was recruited to play shortstop for the Mobile Black Bears, a Sunday sandlot team. One summer afternoon in 1951, the Indianapolis Clowns of the Negro American League stopped in Mobile to take on the Bears in an exhibition. "Before they left, their traveling secretary said they'd send me a contract the next year," Aaron said. "I said that would be fine, figuring I'd never see this guy again."

The following spring, Aaron was a member of the Clowns. Now under the tutelage of professionals, Aaron thrived. The batting grip was no longer crosshanded, but the batting average was above .400. "They wanted me to change my grip, so I did it in the middle of the game," he related. "No problem. But if I got two strikes on me and my back was to the dugout, sometimes I'd sneak the left hand up on top."

Clowns Owner Syd Pollock was a close friend of Boston Braves farm director John Mullen and frequently recommended prospects he spotted around the Negro leagues. At the end of one such letter to Mullen early in 1952 was an intriguing postscript: "Incidentally, I've got an 18-year-old shortstop batting fourth on my club and hitting over .400 by the name of Henry Aaron."

"That's all he said," Mullen recalled. "Nothing more."

Dewey Griggs, one of Boston's top scouts, caught up with Aaron in Buffalo and sent back a glowing report. "I don't know what it would take to get this guy," he concluded, "but I'd pay it out of my own pocket." The Braves secured on option on Aaron, just about the time the New York Giants sent him a contract.

"I had the contract in my hand," Aaron said.

Aaron "was a dream to manage," said Braves skipper Bobby Bragan. "Just a dream—on and off the field."

"but the Braves offered $50 more a month to play at Eau Claire in the Class-C Northern League than the Giants offered at Sioux City in the Class-A Western League.

"That's the only thing that kept Willie Mays and me from being teammates—$50."

Aaron reported to Eau Claire that summer and ripped apart the league's pitching. In 87 games, he batted .336, drove in 61 runs and hit nine homers, a rampage that earned him the league's top rookie honors. Billy Southworth, now a Braves scout after concluding a managing career marked by four N.L. pennants, was sent to Eau Claire to see if Aaron was for real.

"Aaron has all the qualities of a major league shortstop," he wrote in his report. "He is a line-drive hitter although he has hit a couple of balls out of the park for home runs. . . .

"Aaron told me that he had turned 18 years of age last February. Consequently, I like his chances of becoming a major league player far more than I do either Gene Baker, shortstop of Los Angeles, or James Pendleton of Montreal, first because of the differences in ages. Then, too, I think he has better hands than either Baker or Pendleton. He has proven his ability in the short time he has been here.

The big guns of Milwaukee's 1957 and '58 pennant winners: (left to right) Aaron, first baseman Joe Adcock and third baseman Eddie Mathews.

The Aaron swing.

"Baker and Pendleton are faster men, but this boy will outplay them in all departments of the game when he has more experience. . . ."

Promoted to Jacksonville in the Class-A South Atlantic League in 1953, Aaron turned in another torrid year. "Henry just stood up there flicking those great wrists of his and simply overpowered the pitching," Manager Ben Geraghty said.

"Overpowered" was putting it conservatively. Aaron (one of the first blacks in the league) led the circuit "in everything but hotel accommodations," one writer said. He ranked first with a .362 batting mark, 208 hits, 125 runs batted in, 36 doubles, 115 runs scored and was second with 14 triples and 22 home runs. Now playing second base, he also committed 36 errors, the league high at his position (and one more than he'd committed at shortstop in 1952).

Although Aaron was at the top of the Braves' list of prospects for 1954, club officials doubted his qualifications as an infielder. By general agreement, they decided to work him in the outfield when spring training convened, not a desperation move, considering that Manager Charlie Grimm was seeking a hard-hitting outfielder to bat fourth behind Eddie Mathews, his 22-year-old third baseman who had led the National League with 47 homers the previous season, the Braves' first in Milwaukee.

"There are several guys around, like Bobby Thomson of the Giants, Frank Thomas of the Pirates and Del Ennis of the Phillies," Grimm said, "but we won't bust up our club by giving up one of our best pitchers to get any of these fellows."

The Braves did acquire Thomson, who busted himself up by fracturing an ankle in spring training. Because baseball is forever a game of actions and reactions, of accidents and opportunities, 20-year-old Hank Aaron got his chance—a home run legend-to-be replacing the man who had hit baseball's single most dramatic homer.

Installed in left field in 1954, Aaron batted .280 and stroked 13 homers before suffering a broken ankle himself, sliding into third base in a September 5 game against Cincinnati. It was the only serious injury in the long career of Aaron, who would play in no fewer than 145 games in each of the next 16 seasons.

It was the perfect career—no injuries, no time lost to military service, home parks in Milwaukee and Atlanta that were congenial to his righthanded power. Provided the opportunity to show exactly what he could achieve, an opportunity denied for various reasons to Ted Williams, Mickey Mantle and others, Aaron made the most of it, totaling more career home runs and RBIs than any player in major league history and ranking only behind Pete Rose and Ty Cobb in career hits. In baseball annals, only Rose and Carl Yastrzemski played in more games.

"I was impressed the first time I saw him," Alston said. "He held the bat up and far away from his body, but he hit the ball sharply, which told me he

Aaron "was the kind of player that a scout takes one look at and says, 'That's it. Here's a ball player.' "

Aaron (left) with Cardinals ace righthander Bob Gibson.

Aaron "didn't light up a field the way a Mays or Clemente did, but he was their equal."

Aaron and Willie Mays (right), now in the twilight of their careers.

The Hammer is greeted by happy teammates after hitting home run No. 500 in 1968.

had exceptionally strong wrists. To tell you the truth, I never thought he'd be the home run hitter he became. He'd pop them all right, but they never went any farther than they had to; it was like he'd measured off the distance he needed before the game and that's how far he'd hit them."

Aaron developed a reputation as a bad-ball hitter in his early years, to the extent that Grimm described his strike zone as "a general area ranging from the top of his head to the tips of his toes." He hacked away at anything within reach ("I go to the plate looking for one thing—the baseball," he said) but "got more hits off bad balls than most hitters got off good ones," Pirate righthander Bob Friend said.

And hits were what mattered to Aaron, who figured he had a decided advantage in the duel between pitcher and batter: "All he has is a ball; I have a bat." He insisted he was no home run hitter at this point, but cracked 27 homers with 106 RBIs in his second season, then 26 home runs in 1956, when he captured the N.L. batting championship with a .328 mark.

In 1957, Aaron rose to new heights in his development as a slugger, leading the league with both 44 home runs and 132 RBIs as the Braves brought an N.L. pennant to Milwaukee. Fittingly, Aaron—a .322 hitter to boot—slammed a two-run 11th-inning homer that clinched the flag in a 4-2 victory over the second-place St. Louis Cardinals on September

23. Voted the N.L. Most Valuable Player, he led the Braves' offense in the World Series, belting three more home runs in their seven-game decision over the New York Yankees. The only Milwaukee regular to hit .300 in the Series, Aaron batted .393 with seven RBIs, hitting safely in each game to tie a World Series record.

The Braves repeated as N.L. champions in 1958, with Henry again providing much of the spark—30 homers, 95 RBIs and a .326 average. In what would be his final World Series appearance, he bowed out admirably, batting .333, although the Braves squandered a three-games-to-one lead and fell to the Yanks in seven games.

At this stage, Aaron was exhibiting the maturity and all-around talent that Southworth had foretold of in his 1952 report. He had his wings in the outfield now (stationed mainly in right field), playing well enough to earn his first of three consecutive Gold Glove awards in 1958. Over the next five seasons, he averaged 40 home runs and 125 RBIs per year, launching the offensive in 1959 with a career-high 223 hits and .355 average, good for a second N.L. batting title. In 1963, he became only the third "30-30" man in major league history by rapping 44 homers (tied for the league lead) and stealing 31 bases. For good measure, he drove in a league-high 130 runs.

As Aaron's legend grew so, too, did his character. There were no outbursts, no tantrums. He waged

Aaron responds to the crowd after hitting homer No. 700 in 1973.

By the end of 1973, Aaron had reached nail-biting time. One homer to tie Babe Ruth, two more to become king.

his assault on enemy pitching with dignity. Like Joe DiMaggio, he gradually became a quiet leader through performance and strength of character.

"Unless you watch him over a long period of time," one Braves official said, "you don't realize what a strong, deep influence he has." Aaron was attentive to the young players, answering their questions and laughing at their jokes. "He creates a family mood," the man said, "which is especially valuable when things aren't going so well." Both on and off the field, Aaron maintained "a consistently high standard of conduct."

Consistently high standard. Therein is the story of Aaron's ultimate achievement. He was a long-distance runner who never broke stride, a mountain climber who never slipped in his quest for the summit.

For 20 consecutive seasons, from 1955 through 1974, Aaron hit 20 or more home runs, a major league record. Fifteen times he hit at least 30 homers, another all-time mark, and eight times cracked 40 or more, second only to Ruth. He scored 100 or more runs in 15 seasons, a major league record, and drove in more than 100 runs on 11 occasions, an N.L. mark.

But as records fell and others were threatened, Aaron had only one burning ambition: to collect 3,000 hits. "That has always been my goal," he said. "If I can do that, I feel like the rest of the things will fall together—the home runs, the RBIs the other things. But you have to hit the ball before you set records."

On May 17, 1970, Aaron became the ninth player to reach the 3,000-hit plateau when he beat out an infield single in the second game of a doubleheader at Cincinnati's Crosley Field. And though eight others had come before him, Aaron's place in the club was exclusive—he was the only member to crash it with 500 home runs (a feat matched later that season when Mays collected hit No. 3,000).

With the relocating of the Braves' franchise to Atlanta in 1966, Aaron provided most of the baseball excitement for a club destined to wrestle with mediocrity. In his first two seasons in Atlanta, he won back-to-back home run titles, and in 1968, knocked out his 500th career homer in front of the hometowm fans (July 14, off the San Francisco Giants' Mike McCormick).

The Braves forgot all about destiny in 1969, celebrating baseball's centennial season and introduction of divisional play by marching to the N.L. West title. Winners of 17 of 20 games down the stretch, the Braves were anchored by the big bats of Orlando Cepeda, Rico Carty and Aaron, who whaled exactly 44 home runs for the fourth time in his career (and, for the first time, failed to claim a share of the home run title in doing so). Aaron rekindled memories of his epic hitting for Milwaukee in the World Series when he bashed home runs in all three games of the League Championship Series against the New York Mets, who, nevertheless, made short shrift of Atlanta to add another amazin'

chapter to their storybook season.

It was clear by now that Ruth's career home run record was no longer secure in its vault, and Aaron closed in unrelentingly. In 1971, he reached his single-season peak with 47 homers, collecting career homer No. 600 on April 27 off the Giants' Gaylord Perry at Atlanta Stadium. The following season, he took over the all-time N.L. home run lead from Mays, who by now was but a shadow of himself and resolved to accept that the Babe's mark was out of his reach.

"Guys kept writing about Willie's chances all those years, but I was always wondering about mine," Aaron cracked. "Truthfully though, the first time I really thought I might (challenge Ruth) was in 1971. I had expected my homer production to slow down, but when I hit 47 that year I knew I had a chance."

Still the same hitter fundamentally—popping the ball deep by snapping those wrists—Aaron was, in his mind, "stronger and more selective. I don't swing at anything anymore."

What lent added dignity to Aaron's quest for the most sacred of baseball records was that he pursued it vigorously, not as a player hanging on, prolonging a fading career for the sake of a record. In 1973, at the age of 39, he ripped 40 home runs, ending the season with 713, one tantalizing swing short of Ruth's mark. "I think I'll be 39 again next season," mused Henry, who joined with teammates Davey Johnson (43 homers) and Darrell Evans (41) to form the only 40-homer trio in major league history.

So it was inevitable now—sometime in April 1974, Ruth's 714, once looked upon as absolutely inviolate, would fall.

Aaron prepared for the start of the 1974 season amid unprecedented fanfare. The media crunch could have broken a man many times over, but Aaron remained cooperative, patiently answering the same questions over and over: "When did he think he'd hit The Homer?" "Did he feel pressured?" "How did he feel about replacing the Babe at the top?" It was as if he were preparing to undergo a coronation, and in a sense he was, for being king of the home run hitters was no small throne to occupy in baseball America.

But as he moved toward the most celebrated conquest in sports history, Aaron also experienced—along with the exhilaration of the pursuit—racist hate mail, death threats and derogatory comparisons with Ruth. Even a plea from the Babe's widow went unheeded by this malicious sect. "The Babe loved baseball so very much," Mrs. Ruth said, "I know he would have been pulling for Hank Aaron to break his record."

Aaron admitted he had been the target of "hatred and resentment" since the start of the 1973 season, "but I decided that the best way to shut up these people was to have a good year. . . .

"Put it this way, the more they push me, the more I want the record."

Aaron watches the flight of home run No. 715 in the Braves' 1974 home opener against the Los Angeles Dodgers.

Atlanta fans were ready to celebrate as their hero challenged the record.

Aside from this abuse, Aaron kept his cool in the face of suggestions that some teams had begun to groove the ball to help his chances. When several pitchers said on the record that they would serve up home run No. 715 when the time came, baseball Commissioner Bowie Kuhn announced that "suspension will follow where anyone intentionally fails to give his best efforts."

"I might add," he said, "that nothing will be permitted which would tarnish the achievements of a truly great player such as Henry Aaron."

Aaron found humor in this episode, noting, "I haven't seen a pitch down the middle in 20 years and I don't expect to see one now."

But before Aaron could take those historic rips at home plate, one last sideshow was destined to be staged. The idea of one of his players going for the record hoisted dollar signs before the eyes of Braves Owner Bill Bartholomay. There were profits to be made, and with the Braves opening the 1974 season in Cincinnati, Bartholomay announced that Aaron would sit out the three-game series so that he would have his first attempts to hit the landmark home runs in Atlanta. Kuhn intervened, declaring that if Aaron was fit to play, play he must.

Aaron wasted little time in recording his record-tying homer. Number 714 was perfectly in character—there was no fuss, no mounting drama. On April 4, in his first at-bat in the first inning of the season's first game, Aaron hit a home run on his first swing, lashing a 3-1 pitch from Reds righthander Jack Billingham over the left-field wall. "It wasn't a bad pitch," Billingham said, "but it wasn't good enough against Hank Aaron.

Tied with the Babe now (with the benefit of 2,890 additional at-bats, his detractors intoned) Aaron sat out the Braves' second game before going hitless in three at-bats in the series finale. He headed home for Atlanta, where a baseball-crazed city awaited the coronation.

By itself, a home opener was a festive occasion, but on April 8, 1974, Atlanta Stadium swelled with pomp and circumstance. A record crowd of 53,775 packed the stands as writers, photographers and network TV cameramen jammed the press areas. There were baseball dignitaries, luminaries from the entertainment world and the inevitable politicians, including Georgia Gov. Jimmy Carter. They had all come to celebrate home run No. 715, as if it would be struck just as sure as their being there.

With his natural showmanship, Ruth would have reveled in the scene. But Aaron was a different cut. He confided to a couple of teammates, "I'll get it over with tonight. I promise." It was a private remark, not a grand forecast or gesture. There was no pointing or not pointing to the bleachers. Henry was an original in his own way.

Lefthander Al Downing, the starting pitcher for the visiting Los Angeles Dodgers, had not been one of the pitchers to intimate he'd serve up a fat delivery for the privilege of lifetime membership on the game's trivia scrolls. When Aaron first batted in the second inning, Downing walked him on five pitches. When he came to the plate again in the fourth inning, Downing issued ball one just as quickly. The overflow crowd was on edge, its anticipation by now a palpable presence in the ball park.

Downing fired again, a fastball, intending it to

Aaron is back in Milwaukee, this time with the Brewers. The year is 1975.

Aaron's Milestone Home Runs

	Date	Place	Pitcher	Club
1	April 23, 1954	St. Louis	Vic Raschi	St. Louis
100	Aug. 15, 1957	Cincinnati	Don Gross	Cincinnati
200	July 3, 1960	St. Louis	Ron Kline	St. Louis
300	April 19, 1963	New York	Roger Craig	New York
400	April 20, 1966	Philadelphia	Bo Belinsky	Philadelphia
500	July 14, 1968	Atlanta	Mike McCormick	San Francisco
600	April 27, 1971	Atlanta	Gaylord Perry	San Francisco
700	July 21, 1973	Atlanta	Ken Brett	Philadelphia
Last	July 20, 1976	Milwaukee	Dick Drago	California

break down and away. But it didn't. For more than 20 years, this had been the meat and potatoes for Aaron, a prey wandering a few inches too close to the snare. His bat whipped forward, those iron wrists rolled and snapped once again and the ball sailed high into the Atlanta night. Dodger left fielder Bill Buckner waited at the fence, believing he had a chance to make a catch. He timed his jump and left his feet, glove raised high.

"It was as if an unseen force sort of lifted the ball out of the park," Buckner said. "I really believed 54,000 people prayed that ball over the fence."

The new record-holder trotted around the bases, head down, completing the journey for the 715th time, more than any player ever had.

It had seemed so easy.

Seemed easy. Maybe even *looked* easy. But think about it. Not only had Aaron pursued the most revered record in all of baseball, but the holder of that record was the most popular and fabled athlete of all time, a Barnum and Bailey act who had been credited with saving the game at its bleakest moment. To some, it was as if a sanctum sanctorum was to be invaded. Added to this was the fact that Aaron was black, something that disturbed certain benighted people to begin with and even more so under these circumstances.

In his favor, Aaron had his even temperament, his self-confidence, his self-discipline, his superb talent and, unlike Roger Maris in 1961, had not been swinging against a calendar. As Aaron approached the record, it became obvious that he would eventually break it. And when he did, Henry was completely in character—there was no long, dramatic buildup but instead a couple of decisive swings as the season began. It was a conclusive demonstration of a great hitter going about his business, getting the job done, taking those cuts as if he were in serene isolation, insulated from all challenges except that old, direct and uncomplicated one that issued from the pitching mound.

Like Ruth, who had returned "home" to Boston to conclude his playing career, Aaron was sent back to his Milwaukee roots after the 1974 season, traded on November 2 to the Brewers for outfielder Dave May and a player to be named (pitcher Roger Alexander). In 21 seasons in a Braves uniform, he left behind 733 home runs.

"Milwaukee was the city that allowed me respect when I was growing up and stood by me as a kid," Aaron said. "I wanted to end my career there."

Forty-one years old now, taking on a new assignment (as a designated hitter) in a new league, Aaron hit 12 homers in 1975, then another 10 in 1976 to push his career total to 755. And though he had already announced his retirement before the end of the 1976 season, the memories were destined to live on.

Perhaps regrettably, one thing that will remain as vivid as home run No. 715 itself is the hysteria, hype and controversy that crowded the assault on the record. Aaron, however, cut through it all with one simple statement: "I'm not trying to make anyone forget the Babe, but only to remember Hank Aaron."

AARON'S CAREER RECORD

Born February 5, 1934, at Mobile, Ala.
Batted and threw righthanded.   Elected to Hall of Fame, 1982.

Year Club	League	G.	AB.	R.	H.	HR.	RBI.	B.A.
1952—Eau Claire	North.	87	345	79	116	9	61	.336
1953—Jacksonville.......	Sally	137	574	*115	*208	22	*125	*.362
1954—Milwaukee...........	Nat.	122	468	58	131	13	69	.280
1955—Milwaukee...........	Nat.	153	602	105	189	27	106	.314
1956—Milwaukee...........	Nat.	153	609	106	*200	26	92	*.328
1957—Milwaukee...........	Nat.	151	615	*118	198	*44	*132	.322
1958—Milwaukee...........	Nat.	153	601	109	196	30	95	.326
1959—Milwaukee...........	Nat.	154	629	116	*223	39	123	*.355
1960—Milwaukee...........	Nat.	153	590	102	172	40	*126	.292
1961—Milwaukee...........	Nat.	*155	603	115	197	34	120	.327
1962—Milwaukee...........	Nat.	156	592	127	191	45	128	.323
1963—Milwaukee...........	Nat.	161	631	*121	201	●44	*130	.319
1964—Milwaukee...........	Nat.	145	570	103	187	24	95	.328
1965—Milwaukee...........	Nat.	150	570	109	181	32	89	.318
1966—Atlanta	Nat.	158	603	117	168	*44	*127	.279
1967—Atlanta	Nat.	155	600	●113	184	*39	109	.307
1968—Atlanta	Nat.	160	606	84	174	29	86	.287
1969—Atlanta	Nat.	147	547	100	164	44	97	.300
1970—Atlanta	Nat.	150	516	103	154	38	118	.298
1971—Atlanta	Nat.	139	495	95	162	47	118	.327
1972—Atlanta	Nat.	129	449	75	119	34	77	.265
1973—Atlanta	Nat.	120	392	84	118	40	96	.301
1974—Atlanta	Nat.	112	340	47	91	20	69	.268
1975—Milwaukee...........	Amer.	137	465	45	109	12	60	.234
1976—Milwaukee...........	Amer.	85	271	22	62	10	35	.229
American League Totals....		222	736	67	171	22	95	.232
National League Totals.......		3076	11628	2107	3620	733	2202	.310
Major League Totals...........		3298	12364	2174	3771	755	2297	.305

CHAMPIONSHIP SERIES RECORD

Year Club	League	G.	AB.	R.	H.	HR.	RBI.	B.A.
1969—Atlanta	Nat.	3	14	3	5	3	7	.357

WORLD SERIES RECORD

Year Club	League	G.	AB.	R.	H.	HR.	RBI.	B.A.
1957—Milwaukee...........	Nat.	7	28	5	11	3	7	.393
1958—Milwaukee...........	Nat.	7	27	3	9	0	2	.333
World Series Totals..............		14	55	8	20	3	9	.364

A Killer Instinct

If ever anyone wielded a blunt instrument at home plate, it was Harmon Killebrew. There was nothing subtle about the Idaho strongboy: it was always his intention to mash a pitched ball as hard and as far as he could. "I didn't have *evil* intentions," he would explain, "but I guess I did have power."

The focus on what Killebrew could do was always precise, because what he did best, many believed, was close to being all he could do on a ball field. Built like half a tank, he did not run well and spent his career on a carrousel between third base, first base and left field. Yet when he concluded his career 22 years after donning a big-league uniform, Killebrew had earned All-Star Game berths at each position and, what really mattered, hit 573 home runs.

Killebrew was raised in the small farming community of Payette, Idaho, just miles down the road from that prominent bump on the relief map of baseball: Weiser, Idaho. It was there, in 1907, that a traveling salesman reported an awesome sighting to the Washington Senators—a young unknown pitcher named Walter Johnson. Well, an indelible part of the Killebrew saga is how he, too, was recommended to Washington, also by a scout of amateur standing, but one who was otherwise quite notable—Idaho's U.S. Senator Herman Welker, a baseball zealot and close friend of Senators Owner Clark Griffith.

"The senator was a great fan of ours," Griffith acknowledged, "but he had given Vern Law to Bing Crosby for the Pirates and I insisted that he owed us a prospect."

Killebrew, a 6-foot, 195-pound T-formation quarterback in high school, was good enough to attract an athletic scholarship from the University of Oregon ("He was so damned strong," one high school opponent recalled, "that it was like tackling a tree trunk."), but it was his long-ball-hitting feats that rang loudest across the otherwise quiet Idaho landscape. When the senator saw how far his muscular

Minnesota Twins masher Harmon Killebrew.

young constituent-to-be was hammering baseballs, he tipped off Griffith, who sent farm director Ossie Bluege out to Idaho to investigate in that summer of 1954. "Inasmuch as I expect to be in Washington a few more years," Welker said, "I want to see him play in Griffith Stadium as well."

Bluege had played third base for most of his 18 years with the Senators and later managed the club for five, so he knew the difference between a ball player and a lamppost. He was also a serious man, but when he saw Killebrew rip a pitch 435 feet into a beet field beyond the left-field fence, his all-business heart was warmed by a glow.

"He hit line drives that put the opposition in

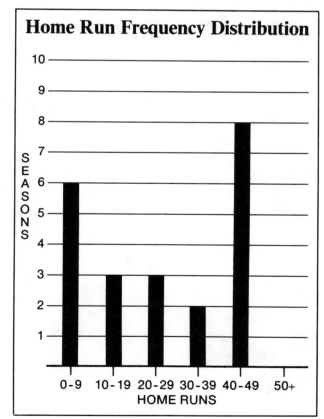

Home Run Frequency Distribution

Killebrew, Washington's 18-year-old bonus baby, with Sen. Herman Welker, the Idaho politician who "discovered" the youngster.

Killebrew and young Cleveland slugger Rocky Colavito (left).

jeopardy," Bluege said, "and I don't mean infielders, I mean outfielders. And when he put one high in the air, it went so far you almost lost track of it. I had traveled clear across the continent to see him and it was worth it. How often can you say that about a young ball player?"

Bluege could hardly report back fast enough. "I wired Mr. Griffith that the sky was the limit in signing him. When I visited his home, I saw a dozen Ted Williams bats in a corner and I knew I had to work fast against the Red Sox."

Heads turned when the notoriously tight-fisted Griff parted with a $30,000 bonus—the first ever offered by Washington—to land the 17-year-old bale of muscles. Under the existing baseball rules, however, a bonus player had to remain on the big-league roster for two years. When Killebrew reported to the Senators in June 1954, he was, in effect, given a two-year reserved seat on the pine.

Killebrew watched and tried to learn while he sat—but what he saw could not have been inspiring. The Senators lost 88 games in 1954 and 101 in 1955, using their bonus baby in a total of only 47 games over both seasons. Sen. Welker, who took a paternal interest in his discovery, often shouted into the Washington dugout from his box seat, asking Charlie Dressen (the manager in 1955) why he wasn't playing "my boy." Dressen, who had gone through the baseball wars with such boisterous characters as Leo Durocher and Larry MacPhail, wasn't about to take advice from a mere U.S. senator, and one night had to be restrained from leaping out of the dugout and telling Welker to go take a flying filibuster.

His bonus "sentence" ended, Killebrew split the 1956 season between Washington and Charlotte in the Class-A South Atlantic League but was assigned to Chattanooga of the Class-AA Southern Association when the Senators broke camp in 1957.

"He has power and he has guts," said coach Cookie Lavagetto, who had watched Killebrew bomb nine homers in his rare batting opportunities. "He can hit a ball a mile, but he has to get out and play and get experience."

Playing 142 games at Chattanooga, Killebrew led the league with 29 home runs—and committed a league-high 31 errors at third base. His fielding wasn't much better in stops at Class-AAA Indianapolis (11 errors in 38 games) and Chattanooga (12 errors) in 1958. Confident nevertheless, Washington decided the 22-year-old Killebrew was ready for 1959 and traded longtime third baseman Eddie Yost to Detroit. The Senators had no illusions about what they expected Harmon to do; Lavagetto, now the manager, was quite direct about it: "He pays his way with his bat."

In May alone, Killebrew yielded a bonanza. He unloaded 15 home runs for the month, one under Mickey Mantle's major league record for May, and the word was passed along the pitchers' grapevine, that most sensitive of communications systems: "Killebrew is for real."

Given the Senators' third-base job in 1959, Killebrew cracked 42 homers.

"Naturally, we'd always spend a lot of time on him in pregame meetings," one pitcher said. "It was a waste of time, but it was part of the drill. How do we pitch 'The Fat Kid?' That's what we called him, but believe me, it was always said respectfully. Pitch him high? No, somebody would say, that's the one that goes into the seats. Pitch him away? No, because he'll go to right field with it. Pitch him low? Crazy, because he'd take your leg off. So the final wisdom was, pitch around him. That's the way it always went."

"You could fool him, he struck out a lot, and he never hit for average," Baltimore Orioles Manager Paul Richards said, "but, dammit, he could wreck you with one swing. Some pitchers will tell you they like to see those free-swinging power hitters up there because they can be pitched to. But I can tell

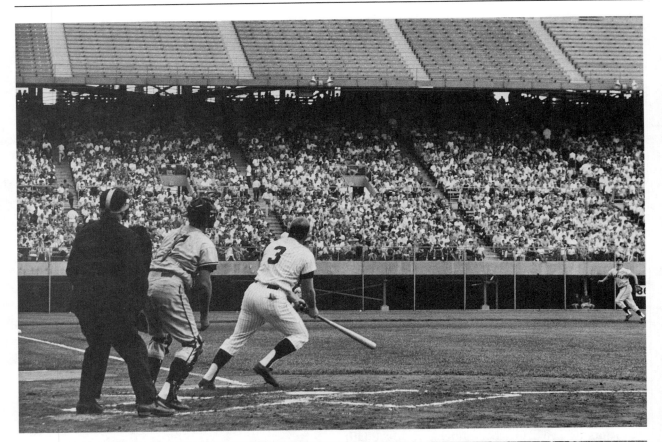

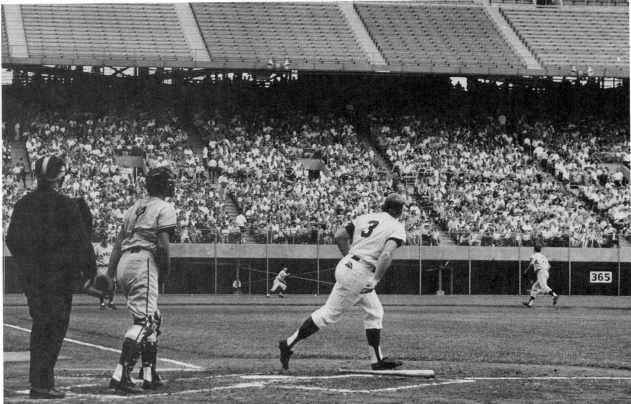

Minnesota's big No. 3 checks out his long drive (top) against the California
Angels and then begins his home run trot (bottom) as the ball disappears into the
crowd and the left fielder runs out of room.

**Never known as a great fielder, Killebrew played third base (above), first base
and the outfield while relying heavily on his powerful bat.**

you, a manager doesn't particularly enjoy the experience, because I've never yet seen a pitcher who can hit his spot every time. And if you miss with a guy like Killebrew, well, a few seconds later they're putting a new ball in play."

Hitting tape-measure drives with consistency, Killebrew became one of the league's riveting figures at home plate. He stood deep in the box, bat held high, and went to work with a minimum of fuss—just one or two practice strokes before he set himself. When he laid into a pitch, the mild-mannered youngster's seemingly inappropriate nickname made sudden sense—he was, indeed, a "Killer."

"He seems to hit everything as though there is a 10-story building where second base should be and that somehow he must get the ball over it," one man would write.

"You thought you had him out when he pumped those pitches high out into the sky," an opposing pitcher noted," but somehow they reached the seats —and deep."

On the final day of the 1959 season, Killebrew connected for his 42nd home run to tie Cleveland's

Rocky Colavito for the league leadership. Just turned 23, he became only the second Senator (next to Roy Sievers in 1957) to top the circuit in homers and posted a team-high 105 runs batted in.

Host though it was to the giants of the land, Washington, D.C., had never been heavily populated with baseball heroes. But suddenly it had one, and he promised to be the biggest since the heyday of Walter Johnson. Some writers compared the Senators' new blockbuster with Joe Hardy, the long-ball hitter of the popular musical of the time, "Damn Yankees." Killebrew, called upon to speak to a group one evening after he had fanned three times that afternoon, made note of the comparison with modest charm. "Some people have compared me to Joe Hardy," he began. "Well, today I looked more like Andy Hardy."

One writer suggested that next to President Dwight Eisenhower (who came out to Griffith Stadium to meet the man he described as "my grandson's greatest hero"), Killebrew was the most popular man in Washington. Even the secretary of defense asked Harmon to the Pentagon for a social

This mild-looking man was nicknamed "Killer."

Killebrew lies near first base after pulling a hamstring in the 1968 All-Star Game, an injury that almost ended his career.

chat, a meeting that afforded the local baseball wags an opportunity to exercise their wit. Killebrew, they said, was the last man the secretary should be discussing defense with.

Though his glove sometimes resembled something that had been quarried, Killebrew was selected the American League's starting third baseman in the first game of baseball's first All-Star double-feature. As Lavagetto pointed out, "We all knew he was a threat whenever he swung the bat."

So, too, were many of the other Senators, who, despite finishing in last place in 1959, were a long-ball terror all season. With the likes of Killebrew, Jim Lemon (33 homers), A.L. Rookie of the Year Bob Allison (30) and Sievers (21), Washington tattooed 163 home runs, second in the league to Cleveland's 167.

The labor pains of stardom now were over for

Killebrew, who banged 31 homers in 1960 as the Senators broke their three-year stranglehold on last place and finished fifth. Finally showing signs of life, the club packed up after the season and moved to Minnesota as part of the westward expansion of the American League in 1961.

Financially, the early years were lean for the transplanted franchise. "He kept us in business," longtime club President Calvin Griffith said of Killebrew. "When we first arrived, Harmon and Bob Allison were our stars and our gate attractions. Everyone likes long-ball hitters, and with them we had a home run derby. They drew the fans for us. Especially Killebrew."

The Killer busted loose for 46 homers in 1961, setting the stage for his three consecutive home run crowns from 1962-64, the longest reign in the league since Babe Ruth ruled the A.L. roost from 1926

Part of the robust lineup that helped Minnesota reach the 1965 World Series.
(Left to right) third baseman Rich Rollins, Killebrew, outfielder Bob Allison, first
baseman Don Mincher and outfielders Jimmie Hall and Tony Oliva.

Killebrew being presented the 1969 Most Valuable Player award by American
League President Joe Cronin.

The Killebrew cut on career homer No. 534.

through 1931. Killebrew boomed 48 homers in 1962, 45 in 1963 and 49 in 1964, giving him an average of 44 homers per season in his first six years as a big-league regular.

Steadily, the Twins gained respect around the league, winning 91 games in both 1962 and 1963 to finish second and third, respectively. Though they slipped to four games under .500 in 1964, they looked for big things in '65 and looked to Killebrew as the big man to lead them.

"This team without Killebrew is like dressing up for a formal affair with white tie and tails and then wearing muddy shoes," catcher Earl Battey mused before the season. "Harmon puts us all in bigger shoes and adds a sparkle of polish. We feel like we are among the best with him in the lineup, because one of the best is one of us."

As August unfolded, the first-place Twins were the class of the loop and Killebrew was tied for the league lead with 22 home runs and leading with 70 RBIs. "He has given so much to this club . . . you just can't imagine," Manager Sam Mele said.

On August 2, however, Killebrew suffered a dislocated elbow, an injury that shelved him for the next seven weeks. The Twins never faltered, though, winning a club-record 102 games to capture the franchise's first pennant since 1933. Killebrew returned in time to play in his only World Series, hitting one homer in a seven-game drama Minnesota lost to the Los Angeles Dodgers.

In 1967, Killebrew moved past such long-ball immortals as Jimmie Foxx, Hank Greenberg, Ted Williams and Mickey Mantle when he claimed his fifth home run crown. The co-leader with 44 home runs that season, he surged past those elite hitters who had been tied for second in the A.L. hierarchy with four titles apiece, still far behind the Babe, a 12-time leader. The following season, Killebrew added his

Killebrew batting during his last major league season with the Kansas City Royals.

Killebrew's Milestone Home Runs

	Date	Place	Pitcher	Club
1	June 24, 1955	Washington	Billy Hoeft	Detroit
100	June 16, 1961	Chicago	Early Wynn	Chicago
200	July 19, 1963	Minnesota	Jim Duckworth	Washington
300	May 21, 1966	New York	Bob Friend	New York
400	April 27, 1969	Chicago	Gary Peters	Chicago
500	Aug. 10, 1971	Minnesota	Mike Cuellar	Baltimore
Last	Sept. 18, 1975	Minnesota	Ed Bane	Minnesota

name to another distinguished list, one no player necessarily wanted to join—the All-Star Game casualty list.

In 1937, there was Dizzy Dean's broken toe. In 1950, Ted Williams' fractured elbow. And in 1968, there was Harmon Killebrew's ruptured hamstring, an injury that nearly ended the career of the Minnesota slugger. Playing first base, he slipped when he stretched for a low throw in the third inning, severely injuring his left hamstring muscle when he collapsed into the splits. "To tell the truth, I wasn't sure I'd play again," he said.

Killebrew bounced back spectacularly though, playing in all 162 games in 1969 as he led Minnesota to the A.L. West title in baseball's first year of divisional play. The Twins' slugger rapped a league-leading 49 homers to tie his career high (and claim his sixth title) and set a club record with a league-best 140 RBIs. Voted the A.L. Most Valuable Player, he also stole eight bases, one more than he had swiped in his entire career.

Never confused with the speed kings of baseball, Killebrew didn't ring up the high batting averages, either, recording his personal best with a .288 mark in 1961. He is one of only three players (along with Detroit's Darrell Evans and the Milwaukee Brewers' Gorman Thomas) to hit 40 or more home runs while batting under .250 in the same season—and he did it twice. In 1959, he had 42 homers and a .242 batting average, and in 1962, 48 homers and a .243 mark.

"I didn't think much about batting average when I was playing," Killebrew admitted. "I would have been capable of hitting for a higher average, but it might have cost me some power. I found out early in life I could hit a baseball farther than most players, and that's what I tried to do."

He did that better than just about everyone else who played the game. With a career total of 573 home runs, Killebrew holds the A.L. record for homers by a righthanded batter and ranks fifth overall on the all-time list.

Killebrew posted his last monstrous slugging season in 1970, leading the Twins to a second straight division title with 41 homers and 113 RBIs. After two strong seasons in 1971 (28 home runs and a league-high 119 RBIs) and 1972 (26 homers), he played less frequently for Minnesota, serving main-

ly as a part-time designated hitter. Released after the 1974 campaign, he played his final big-league season with the Kansas City Royals in 1975.

Upon his election to the Hall of Fame, Harmon speculated on what might have been if Idahoans hadn't sent a baseball-minded senator to Washington some 30 years earlier. "When we had the real good hitting teams in Minnesota in the early '60s, we used to go into Boston and tattoo the wall," he said. "You would hit a couple of fly-ball home runs there over the weekend, and when you left town, you would be saying, 'Maybe I should have taken a little less money and signed with the Red Sox.'"

And while Killebrew reflected on what might have been, Calvin Griffith and the Minnesota populace reveled in what was. "He was," said Griffith, "the backbone of the franchise."

KILLEBREW'S CAREER RECORD

Born June 29, 1936, at Payette, Idaho
Batted and threw righthanded.   Elected to Hall of Fame, 1984.

Year	Club	League	G.	AB.	R.	H.	HR.	RBI.	B.A.
1954—Washington		Amer.	9	13	1	4	0	3	.308
1955—Washington		Amer.	38	80	12	16	4	7	.200
1956—Washington		Amer.	44	99	10	22	5	13	.222
1956—Charlotte		Sally	70	249	61	81	15	63	.325
1957—Chattanooga		South.	142	519	90	145	*29	101	.279
1957—Washington		Amer.	9	31	4	9	2	5	.290
1958—Washington		Amer.	13	31	2	6	0	2	.194
1958—Indianapolis		A. A.	38	121	14	26	2	10	.215
1958—Chattanooga		South.	86	299	58	92	17	54	.308
1959—Washington		Amer.	153	546	98	132	●42	105	.242
1960—Washington		Amer.	124	442	84	122	31	80	.276
1961—Minnesota		Amer.	150	541	94	156	46	122	.288
1962—Minnesota		Amer.	155	552	85	134	*48	*126	.243
1963—Minnesota		Amer.	142	515	88	133	*45	96	.258
1964—Minnesota		Amer.	158	577	95	156	*49	111	.270
1965—Minnesota		Amer.	113	401	78	108	25	75	.269
1966—Minnesota		Amer.	162	569	89	160	39	110	.281
1967—Minnesota		Amer.	163	547	105	147	●44	113	.269
1968—Minnesota		Amer.	100	295	40	62	17	40	.210
1969—Minnesota		Amer.	●162	555	106	153	*49	*140	.276
1970—Minnesota		Amer.	157	527	96	143	41	113	.271
1971—Minnesota		Amer.	147	500	61	127	28	*119	.254
1972—Minnesota		Amer.	139	433	53	100	26	74	.231
1973—Minnesota		Amer.	69	248	29	60	5	32	.242
1974—Minnesota		Amer.	122	333	28	74	13	54	.222
1975—Kansas City		Amer.	106	312	25	62	14	44	.199
Major League Totals			2435	8147	1283	2086	573	1584	.256

CHAMPIONSHIP SERIES RECORD

Year	Club	League	G.	AB.	R.	H.	HR.	RBI.	B.A.
1969—Minnesota		Amer.	3	8	2	1	0	0	.125
1970—Minnesota		Amer.	3	11	2	3	2	4	.273
LCS Totals			6	19	4	4	2	4	.211

WORLD SERIES RECORD

Year	Club	League	G.	AB.	R.	H.	HR.	RBI.	B.A.
1965—Minnesota		Amer.	7	21	2	6	1	2	.286

The Fearless Leader

"You had to play with Frank Robinson to appreciate him," recalled Eddie Kasko, a shortstop-third baseman for 10 major league seasons. "I played two years against him before coming to the Reds and I hated him. I don't really know what it was. He just had the attitude of a guy you want to beat.

"He challenges you all the time. He slides tough to break up the double play. When a pitcher knocked down (Vada) Pinson and Robinson was in the on-deck circle, Frank would yell at the pitcher. That's the kind of opponent you want to beat. But play with Robinson and you realize everything he does is predicated on winning."

You hear about the inspirational leaders in baseball. The performances are always dynamic, their personalities ignited by some underlying spark. Blended together, these attributes create a motivating aura that is almost spiritual. Talent is, of course, a necessity, but these players must be daring, aggressive, virtually immune to pain. They need not be particularly voluble, for they are most effective when leading by example.

Frank Robinson was the most widely acknowledged leader of his time, and most particularly during his years with the Baltimore Orioles. Paul Richards, one of the keenest of all managerial minds, once was asked about leadership in general and Robinson in particular.

"A ball player who can drive his teammates to better performances is very rare," Richards said. "I would say Joe DiMaggio probably did it with his own pride. Seeing this great player taking nothing for granted out there, striving to be at his peak, certainly had to affect his teammates. Mickey Mantle was a stoic—he punished himself day in and day out by playing with pain and injuries and never complaining.

"Frank Robinson is a different case. He played as relentlessly and as aggressively as any player I've ever seen. Being black was no doubt part of it; we can only guess at what anger had been instilled in him early on in life."

Frank Robinson, the relentless leader.

Robinson played with such uncompromising fervor that he may well have created an unconscious fear in his teammates—a fear of not giving their utmost because he was always giving so much.

"I was with the White Sox when Frank came into the league and he was the finest competitor I've ever played against," said Don Buford, who joined the Orioles in 1968. "We were known as the Go-Go Sox, always running hard and taking the second baseman out. We used to really get Davey Johnson, who was the Orioles' second baseman. Frank decided to do something about it.

"In a 1967 game, Frank was running toward second and our guy, Al Weis, was on the left side of the

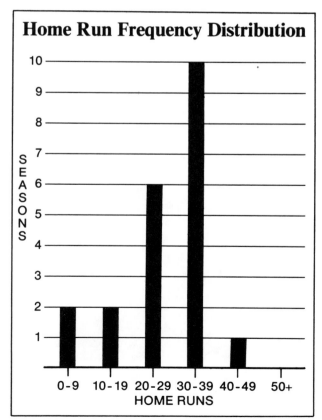

Home Run Frequency Distribution

The uncompromising Robinson played as aggressively as any player in baseball.

Robinson as a Cincinnati rookie in 1956 (left) and receiving his 1961 Most Valuable Player award from National League President Warren Giles (right).

Robinson stood virtually on top of the plate when he batted; consequently, he spent a lot of time dodging brush-back pitches.

bag. Frank shifted his body and was off-balance when he went for Weis. He hit his head on Weis' knee and suffered a concussion that left him with double vision for more than a year.

"That showed me what a great competitor Frank is. He sacrificed himself for the team. By 1969, Frank was healthy again and we won three straight division championships."

Seldom has a player displayed the sustained drive of Robinson. He was on a crusade out on the field, much like Jackie Robinson had been. That he earned this reputation when he joined the Orioles is no coincidence. Traded by Cincinnati after the 1965 season, he had been stung by Reds President Bill DeWitt's remark that while Robinson was only 30 years old, he was "an old 30." He never forgot that put-down; he took it all the way to the Hall of Fame.

Growing up in Oakland, the future terror of big-league basepaths had a life that focused on baseball "from morning to night." Other sports held his interest, too, including basketball and football, but it was the baseball player that attracted the Reds, who had been watching since Robinson was 14 and playing American Legion ball. As soon as he had graduated high school, Robinson signed with Cincinnati.

The Reds assigned their young discovery to Ogden, Utah, of the Class-C Pioneer League in 1953. Robinson batted .348, hit 17 homers and drove in 83 runs in 72 games, an auspicious and appropriate

beginning for a future Hall of Famer. After two seasons with Columbia, S.C., in the Class-A South Atlantic League, Robinson broke in with the Reds in 1956 as a 20-year-old rookie.

"He had an unusual stance," teammate Ted Kluszewski remembered. "He really crowded the plate. Sometimes he leaned right out over it. Naturally, he was thrown at a lot; he was forever getting hit or going down. But it never bothered him. He'd get right back up and dig right back in.

"I say it didn't bother him, but it must have made him mad, because a lot of times he'd really drive the ball after they threw at him. I heard that at one point, Gene Mauch, who was managing the Phillies (in the 1960s), had an automatic 50-dollar fine for any of his pitchers who knocked Frank down. Frank was a quiet kid in those years, sometimes moody, but he had a fire in him, right from the beginning."

And right from the beginning he was a hitter. There was no gradual breaking in for Robinson, no need for those dubious labels "promise" or "potential." He established himself that first year, batting .290, driving in 83 runs and tying Wally Berger's major league record for rookies with a team-high 38 home runs (a mark that stood until 1987, when Oakland rookie Mark McGwire slugged 49 homers). Leading the club in home runs was no small task, either, considering the presence of Wally Post (36 homers), Kluszewski (35), Gus Bell (29), Ed

The American League Triple Crown winner in 1966 with Pittsburgh Pirates star Roberto Clemente (left).

The heart of the lineup that brought the Orioles four pennants in six years: (left to right) first baseman Boog Powell, third baseman Brooks Robinson and Frank Robinson.

Bailey (28) and Ray Jablonski (15), a bash brigade that helped the Reds tie the 1947 New York Giants' single-season big-league record of 221 homers.

A unanimous choice as the 1956 N.L. Rookie of the Year, Robinson lost none of his touch in 1957, earning his second straight starting assignment in left field for the N.L. All-Star squad during the course of a 29-homer, .322 season. Still, those early days were for Robinson "the dark side of baseball." Moody, wary, perhaps insecure in spite of his success, "I was in a shell," he said, "and I didn't have a friend on the club."

"What a lot of people forgot about Frank," Kluszewski said, "was how young he was. Hell, he was just 20 years old when he came up, and he was a star. Some people said he was cold and aloof, but I never got the feeling. To me, he was being careful, like a guy testing the ground before putting his foot down. When he became a superstar he knew just how to handle it."

By the end of the 1959 season, Robinson was a star on par with Hank Aaron and Willie Mays. Asked to make a transition to first base that year, he had responded with 36 homers and 125 runs batted in. He was out of the "shell" now and showing some flash. Robinson admitted he "changed cars like people change shirts" and walked around with a bankroll the size of a baseball. He also had something else in his pocket one February night in 1961, and it got him some unwanted headlines.

Robinson and two companions were in a Cincinnati restaurant when they became involved in a dispute with several men, including the chef. According to one account, the chef grabbed a butcher knife and advanced on Robinson, who stopped the man cold by drawing a .25-caliber pistol. Police arrived and arrested Robinson on a charge of carrying a concealed weapon and held him overnight in a detention cell. He later pleaded guilty, explaining he kept the weapon as "protection," and was fined $250. DeWitt, who had been named the club's general manager three months earlier, was deeply disturbed by the incident (he had stayed in bed when called to post bail for Robinson) and, some people say, never forgave Robinson.

Robinson called the episode "the turning point in my life," a time he would prove to everyone "that I was more mature as a ball player, and as a man."

Dugout wits gave "Pistol Packin' Frank" a going-over that summer, but it only helped spur him on to a breakthrough season. Driving the Reds to their first pennant since 1940, Robinson batted .323, hit

Robinson after hitting grand slams in consecutive innings of a 1970 game.

Robinson (left) spent his last season with the Orioles in 1971 and then continued his home run siege with the Los Angeles Dodgers in 1972.

37 home runs, drove in 124 and was voted the N.L. Most Valuable Player. "I've never seen such a dramatic change in one player," reliever Jim Brosnan said. "Frank became the club's leader that year."

Always a hard-nosed player, he became even more aggressive, diving into the stands if he had a remote chance to snare a foul fly, sliding ferociously into second to break up double plays. "You don't play halfway," he said. "You're not deliberately trying to hurt someone, you're just doing your damndest to try and win."

At one point, Robinson believed the Cincinnati staff had turned soft, thus allowing pitchers to throw at the Reds without fear of retaliation. He called a team meeting and demanded that the staff answer in kind, a suggestion met with murmurous agreement.

When a Reds batter was plunked a few days later, the seething Robinson took his position in right field and awaited the response. It was not immediately forthcoming, and third baseman Gene Freese recalled what happened next:

"I looked over my shoulder and here comes Robinson. He's trotting in from right field to pop our pitcher right there on the mound. I hollered over, 'Here he comes! Here he comes!' The pitcher turned around, pretending to be rubbing up the ball, and waved Robinson back. He was nodding at Frank,

'OK, OK.' " The batter took a shot in the ribs on the next pitch.

Robinson's most satisfying act of revenge probably had occurred a year earlier against Milwaukee. In the opening game of a doubleheader, he slid hard into Braves third baseman Eddie Mathews, who took exception by throwing a hard right to Frank's left eye during an ensuing argument. Robinson, his eye swollen shut, insisted on playing the second game and clobbered a home run and double to key a Cincinnati victory.

Late in the game, when Mathews lashed a screaming liner toward the left-field corner, Robinson raced to the line and speared the ball before tumbling headfirst into the stands. "He got even with me the good way," Mathews remarked.

Robinson followed up his MVP season with an even bigger one, statistically, in 1962: a .342 average (his personal high), 39 home runs, 136 RBIs and a third straight slugging title (.624) while almost single-handedly leading the third-place Reds to 98 victories.

Despite a series of nagging injuries in 1963, he took over the Reds' career home run leadership from Kluszewski, who had poled 251 homers in not quite 10 seasons with the club. Robinson had pushed his total to 324 homers by the end of his 10th year in 1965, good for an average of 32 clouts

Baseball's first black pilot is greeted by John Lowenstein after hitting a
first-inning home run for Cleveland in his managing debut in 1975.

Robinson as a player for the California Angels in 1973 (left) and as manager of the San Francisco Giants in 1981 (right).

per year. RBIs? An average of 101. That winter, however, DeWitt—an accomplished baseball man—made the biggest blunder of his career.

On December 9, 1965, Robinson was dealt to Baltimore for righthander Milt Pappas and two lesser lights. DeWitt's rationale was that Cincinnati needed pitching (which it did) and Robinson, "an old 30," was due to fall off precipitously before long. The deal stunned the baseball community. Pappas was a solid pitcher, one who averaged 14 wins per season in his eight years in the Orioles' rotation, but not a player who could compensate for the loss of a Frank Robinson. The Reds, with Robinson, had won in 1961, finished 3½ games back in '62, one back in '64, and stayed in the race until the final week of the 1965 season; in the three seasons after his departure, they finished no closer than 14 games back. (Pappas, in fact, was with Cincinnati only until June 1968, when he was traded to Atlanta following 12- and 16-victory seasons.)

The Orioles had been contenders in 1964 and 1965, finishing in third place each season, but lacked the intimidating force so vital to any championship team—that force within the ranks who despised losing so intensely that the fear of losing became even more powerful than the thrill of winning. What they needed was Frank Robinson.

Robinson, in turn, needed no provocation to play harder, but had one anyway—DeWitt's "old 30" remark, which, one writer noted, "was like waving a red flag in his face every morning." Robinson tore through the league with gale-force velocity, galvanizing the two-time contenders into world champions. Fresh off his Triple Crown performance (49 homers, 122 RBIs, .316) during the regular season, Robby started and ended the World Series scoring with home runs, keying a four-game sweep of the Los Angeles Dodgers. Voted the Series MVP, Robinson also was accorded A.L. MVP honors, becoming the only player to receive the award in both major leagues.

It was, indeed, Robinson's pinnacle year, for achievement and probably for personal satisfaction. "I've never played with a better hitter, a better all-around player and a better competitor than Frank Robinson," declared Baltimore third baseman Brooks Robinson.

Teaming with his namesake third baseman, slugging first baseman Boog Powell and a superb pitching staff headed by righthander Jim Palmer and lefthanders Dave McNally and Mike Cuellar, Robinson helped lead Baltimore into the World Series in 1969, 1970 and 1971, averaging 28 homers and 92 RBIs per year. Upset by the "Amazin' Mets" in 1969, the Orioles claimed their second Series title in 1970, getting another two homers from Robinson

After returning to Baltimore as a coach, Robinson took over as manager early in the 1988 season. He managed the Orioles until 1991.

Robinson's Milestone Home Runs

	Date	Place	Pitcher	Club
1	April 28, 1956	Cincinnati	Paul Minner	Chicago
100	April 18, 1959	Cincinnati	Seth Morehead	Philadelphia
200	Aug. 26, 1961	Cincinnati	Johnny Podres	Los Angeles
300	June 10, 1965	St. Louis	Ray Sadecki	St. Louis
400	Sept. 9, 1967	Baltimore	Jim Kaat	Minnesota
500	Sept. 13, 1971	Baltimore	Fred Scherman	Detroit
Last	July 6, 1976	California	Sid Monge	California

in a five-game decision over Cincinnati. Less than two months after losing to Pittsburgh in 1971, however, they traded the veteran slugger to the Dodgers.

Robinson spent only one season in Los Angeles before being dealt to the California Angels, with whom he hit 30 home runs in 1972, the 11th and final time he reached the 30-homer mark. Near the end of the 1974 season, he was released on waivers to the Cleveland Indians. Now 39 years old, Robinson's playing days were numbered, but just ahead lay a historic appointment.

On October 3, 1974, Robinson was selected to succeed Ken Aspromonte as the Indians' manager, thus becoming major league baseball's first black manager. U.S. President Gerald Ford, in a congratulatory telegram to Robby, described the selection as "welcome news for baseball fans across the nation" and a "tribute to you personally, to your athletic skills and to your unsurpassed leadership."

Robinson had made it known in the 1960s that a managing opportunity for a black man was long overdue, but he wanted his appointment kept in perspective.

"I am black, and I don't ignore that fact," he said. "But I'm not going out there as a black manager, I'm going out there to manage. Judge me by how I do my job. If I don't do it, fire me."

Robinson made his managing debut on April 8, 1975, when the Indians played their season opener against the New York Yankees. In the lineup as a designated hitter, he homered in the first inning and the Tribe went on to a 5-3 victory. "By the time I got to third base," he said, "I thought to myself, 'Wow, will miracles never cease?'"

Robinson guided the Indians to back-to-back fourth-place finishes (closing out his playing career with a handful of appearances in 1976), but on June 19, 1977, baseball's first black manager became the first black manager fired. Nevertheless, he became the first black pilot in N.L. history on April 9, 1981, when he made his debut for the San Francisco Giants. In three full seasons, the Giants played close to .500 baseball, finishing only two games out of first in 1982, but a poor start in 1984 cost Robinson his job. Early in 1988, he returned for a third managerial stint when he took over the struggling Orioles in the midst of a 21-game losing streak, a major

league record from the start of one season. Robinson managed the Orioles until 1991.

A star in the American and National leagues, Robinson is the only player in major league history to hit more than 200 home runs in each league. With 343 N.L. blasts and 243 in the American League, he ranks fourth on the all-time list with 586 home runs, trailing only Aaron, Ruth and Mays.

"I don't want people to say Mickey Mantle, Willie Mays and Hank Aaron in one breath and then in the next, Frank Robinson," he had said after his first season in Baltimore. "I want them to say, Mantle, Mays, Aaron and Robinson in the same breath."

ROBINSON'S CAREER RECORD
Born August 31, 1935, at Beaumont, Tex.
Batted and threw righthanded.　　Elected to Hall of Fame, 1982.

Year	Club	League	G.	AB.	R.	H.	HR.	RBI.	B.A.
1953—Ogden		Pion.	72	270	70	94	17	83	.348
1954—Tulsa		Tex.	8	30	4	8	0	1	.267
1954—Columbia		Sally	132	491	*112	165	25	110	.336
1955—Columbia		Sally	80	243	50	64	12	52	.263
1956—Cincinnati		Nat.	152	572	*122	166	38	83	.290
1957—Cincinnati		Nat.	150	611	97	197	29	75	.322
1958—Cincinnati		Nat.	148	554	90	149	31	83	.269
1959—Cincinnati		Nat.	146	540	106	168	36	125	.311
1960—Cincinnati		Nat.	139	464	86	138	31	83	.297
1961—Cincinnati		Nat.	153	545	117	176	37	124	.323
1962—Cincinnati		Nat.	162	609	*134	208	39	136	.342
1963—Cincinnati		Nat.	140	482	79	125	21	91	.259
1964—Cincinnati		Nat.	156	568	103	174	29	96	.306
1965—Cincinnati		Nat.	156	582	109	172	33	113	.296
1966—Baltimore		Amer.	155	576	*122	182	*49	*122	*.316
1967—Baltimore		Amer.	129	479	83	149	30	94	.311
1968—Baltimore		Amer.	130	421	69	113	15	52	.268
1969—Baltimore		Amer.	148	539	111	166	32	100	.308
1970—Baltimore		Amer.	132	471	88	144	25	78	.306
1971—Baltimore		Amer.	133	455	82	128	28	99	.281
1972—Los Angeles		Nat.	103	342	41	86	19	59	.251
1973—California		Amer.	147	534	85	142	30	97	.266
1974—Calif.-Cleve.		Amer.	144	477	81	117	22	68	.245
1975—Cleveland		Amer.	49	118	19	28	9	24	.237
1976—Cleveland		Amer.	36	67	5	15	3	10	.224
National League Totals			1605	5869	1084	1759	343	1068	.300
American League Totals			1203	4137	745	1184	243	744	.286
Major League Totals			2808	10006	1829	2943	586	1812	.294

CHAMPIONSHIP SERIES RECORD

Year	Club	League	G.	AB.	R.	H.	HR.	RBI.	B.A.
1969—Baltimore		Amer.	3	12	1	4	1	2	.333
1970—Baltimore		Amer.	3	10	3	2	1	2	.200
1971—Baltimore		Amer.	3	12	2	1	0	1	.083
LCS Totals			9	34	6	7	2	5	.206

WORLD SERIES RECORD

Year	Club	League	G.	AB.	R.	H.	HR.	RBI.	B.A.
1961—Cincinnati		Nat.	5	15	3	3	1	4	.200
1966—Baltimore		Amer.	4	14	4	4	2	3	.286
1969—Baltimore		Amer.	5	16	2	3	1	1	.188
1970—Baltimore		Amer.	5	22	5	6	2	4	.273
1971—Baltimore		Amer.	7	25	5	7	2	2	.280
World Series Totals			26	92	19	23	8	14	.250

Another Ted Williams

The veteran baseball man, a two-time National League batting champion, had suggested that the lanky kid playing at Phoenix just might be in the same class with Ted Williams.

It was, clearly, the kind of statement certain to startle anyone within earshot. After all, the Phoenix Giants' first baseman—while no doubt possessing immense potential—had yet to play an inning of major league baseball. Furthermore, the man playing his position with the parent San Francisco Giants had been named Rookie of the Year in the National League the season before.

Lefty O'Doul, the sage baseball man, knew more than a little about hitting, though. In 970 major league games, he had fashioned a .349 batting average. O'Doul, a longtime Pacific Coast League player and manager, also knew more than a little about Williams. When the Splendid Splinter was breaking into professional ball with the San Diego Padres of the PCL in 1936 and 1937, O'Doul was managing the rival San Francisco Seals.

And, as it turned out, O'Doul knew more than a little about Willie Lee McCovey, the 21-year-old slugger who had caught his eye when Lefty served as a special hitting coach for the Giants' organization in the summer of 1959. By the end of July that year, McCovey had been summoned to the majors.

"Before McCovey came up," Giants coach Bill Posedel said, "Lefty O'Doul told me about a kid in Phoenix who reminded him of Williams. Lefty said this McCovey had the same swing and the same knowledge of the strike zone that he saw in Williams when Ted was with San Diego. He predicted this kid could be just as great—and from what I've seen, Lefty could be right."

Posedel's remarks came three weeks after McCovey's recall, when the man they called "Stretch" boasted a .395 average in 21 games with San Francisco. McCovey's power statistics were equally impressive: seven home runs, 22 runs batted in.

Veteran Hank Sauer, a basher of considerable note who was nearing the end of a long and productive big-league career, also saw some of Ted Williams in his young Giants teammate.

"He doesn't back up—he gets his hips and shoulders into the swing," Sauer said of McCovey. "His timing is excellent, like Ted's, and he gets that bat in front of him, where the power is."

Being compared to Williams was a staggering tribute for a neophyte major leaguer, one who years later would reflect on his career ambitions in considerably simpler terms: "All I ever wanted in my whole life, ever since I knew what a baseball was, was to be a baseball player."

For McCovey, that quest began on the sun-baked playgrounds of Mobile, Ala., where Hank Aaron,

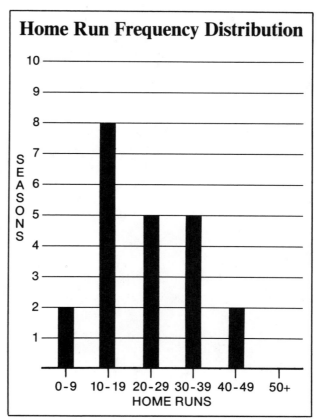

Powerful Willie McCovey.

McCovey was a young first baseman for the Texas League's Dallas Eagles in 1957.

four years older than Willie, had first given hint of his skills. McCovey, born in Mobile on January 10, 1938, was multi-gifted in athletics, playing football and basketball for Mobile's Central High School, as well as baseball.

For an Alabama boy, in the deepest regions of Dixie, the major leagues must have seemed an enchanting but faraway dream, particularly for a black youngster, who could not even begin the dream until 1947, when Jackie Robinson came to the big leagues with the Brooklyn Dodgers. Jackie was no doubt part of McCovey's reveries, for despite idolizing Williams and Stan Musial, Willie grew up a Brooklyn fan, with fantasies of game-winning home runs at Ebbets Field, a park that would be abandoned by the time he reached the top.

"That was my inspiration," said McCovey, remembering his boyhood reaction to Robinson's entry into the big leagues. "I knew right then that a door had been opened wide and I wanted to pass through it."

At the age of 14, McCovey was playing semipro ball. The youngest player on the team, he was the cleanup hitter—and highly noticeable. Willie attracted attention because of his height—he was well on his way to the 6-foot-4 stature of his pro playing days—and ferocious swing, an unmistakable home-plate signature that will always rivet the practiced baseball eye.

A playground director eventually recommended McCovey to the New York Giants, and the club that had struck gold on the playing fields of Alabama with Birmingham-bred Willie Mays was about to uncover another nugget. Scout Alex Pompez gave McCovey a bus ticket and an invitation to the Giants' minor league training camp at Melbourne, Fla., in March 1955.

The Giants were immediately impressed with Willie's power. There was a stand of trees beyond right field, some 400 feet away, and the new recruit began depositing baseballs among the timber.

"We weren't used to seeing an unknown kid putting them that far away," one of the club's scouts said. "It got to the point that during batting practice, whenever he stepped into the cage, guys on the sidelines would stop what they were doing and watch. That's a sure sign."

For the 17-year-old McCovey, it was like curtains parting and a bright new world appearing around him. He was away from home for the first time, standing amid the people and the props that had been the figments of his yearning just a few months before. In the beginning, he could hardly believe where he was and at times behaved more like spectator than participant. Salty Parker, then a manager in the Giants' farm system, remembered Willie's ingenuous fascination.

"When he first came into camp, he didn't seem to care about the game he was in," Parker recalled. "There were four diamonds at Melbourne, and he's playing on one and watching the games on the

other ones. So there's a meeting one night, and all we talk about is Stretch. What are we going to do to get him interested? So finally one fellow said, 'Let's not worry about Stretch. All this is new to him. He'll come around eventually.' So we let him alone, and he did."

Willie broke into pro ball with the Sandersville club of the Class-D Georgia State League. Salary: $175 per month. He was worth every penny. And, again, he drew attention to himself.

In fact, before he had played a full month in the pro ranks, McCovey was the focal point of a newspaper column—in the Atlanta Constitution, no less. Sports Editor Furman Bisher, in a trek to Sandersville, wrote a column bearing the headline "Another Giant Named Willie." In the piece, Sandersville Manager Peter Pavlick, while acknowledging that McCovey was the No. 1 prospect in the league, wasn't about to go overboard. "I don't guess you can call him another Willie Mays," Pavlick said, "but at least he's another Willie."

Bisher himself reserved judgment on the raw Alabamian. Winding up his column with the whys and wherefores of Pavlick's placement in Sandersville and the manager's chance association with a potential star, the Atlanta journalist commented: "And so he (Pavlick) came into a thin slip of a 17-year-old Negro boy named Willie McCovey, who may never be great to anybody else, but at least he's great in Sandersville."

McCovey, of course, was taking the first step on the journey to a level of greatness that would be recognized by virtually everyone else. He drove in a league-leading 113 runs (in 107 games) for Sandersville and batted .305 with 19 home runs. The banner season earned Willie a promotion to Class-B ball the next year.

Playing for Danville of the Carolina League in 1956, McCovey continued to hone his skills. He finished with a .310 average, 29 homers and 89 RBIs. The fact that a teammate walloped 22 more homers and knocked in 77 more runs than Willie didn't detract from McCovey's accomplishments. Fittingly, Leon Wagner, the man with the extraordinary numbers (51 homers and 166 RBIs), would be a teammate of McCovey's in the big leagues.

Willie advanced to Class AA in 1957, only to be plagued by knee injuries, which would prove bothersome throughout his career, and ankle problems. Performing for Dallas of the Texas League, he batted .281 and hit just 11 home runs. The following season saw him in major league baseball's anteroom, Class AAA, playing with the Phoenix club. Finding himself far from home (about 1,600 miles) for the first time, the still-maturing McCovey adjusted nicely and batted .319 with 14 home runs and 89 RBIs.

With most organizations, McCovey's year at Phoenix would have merited serious consideration for a job with the big club in spring training; the Giants, however, happened to be in the midst of remarkable first-base wealth in the spring of 1959.

The man called "Stretch" could really live up to that nickname.

San Francisco's potent power men: (left to right) McCovey, Willie Mays and Orlando Cepeda.

San Francisco already had a young, power-hitting first baseman in 21-year-old Orlando Cepeda, good enough to have been the National League's Rookie of the Year in 1958 and a player with a seemingly limitless future. In addition, the team also had Bill White, who had begun his big-league career with a 22-homer season for the Giants in 1956 (the franchise's next-to-last season in New York), then entered the service and recently had rejoined the club.

The Giants, in need of pitching help, resolved their enviable logjam at the end of March by trading White to the St. Louis Cardinals—the deal netted curveballing Sam Jones—and returning McCovey to the minors. The moves were understandable. Cepeda was a star and, furthermore, held forth as the team's most popular player in San Francisco, Willie Mays notwithstanding.

So McCovey went back to Phoenix and became like smoke in the basement—impossible to ignore.

"He has a perfect swing," O'Doul emphasized. "Never reaches out for a ball. Stays on top of it and never uppercuts it."

Through July 29, that swing was lethal. In 95 games, the big ripper from Mobile had hit 29 home runs, driven in 92 runs and batted .372. Finally, a telephone rang in Phoenix and Willie McCovey gathered his belongings and headed for San Francisco.

Manager Bill Rigney told Willie he was going right into the lineup. As an immediate answer to their pleasant "problem," the Giants switched Cepeda to third base and benched Jim Davenport, a superb fielder. This move was short-lived; after a few games, Cepeda was stationed in left field and Davenport was returned to third. Orlando didn't like his positioning in the outfield—nor did his fans—but there were few options, considering that McCovey apparently lacked the skills to play anywhere but first base. And the Giants quickly realized that Willie had to be in the lineup.

On July 30, McCovey made one of the most impressive debuts in big-league history. Facing the Philadelphia Phillies' formidable Robin Roberts at Seals Stadium in San Francisco, Willie slammed two singles and two triples. From this auspicious beginning, Willie kept hammering away. After his first seven games in a Giants uniform, McCovey boasted a .467 average and had two doubles, two triples, three homers and nine RBIs.

McCovey went on to bat .354 in 52 games, hitting 13 home runs and knocking in 38 runs. Despite playing just one third of the season, he was voted the National League's Rookie of the Year, giving the Giants unanimous winners two years in a row. Willie also achieved another highly remarkable distinction. With his 29 home runs holding up as the season high in the Pacific Coast League, he was the home run leader in one league and Rookie of the Year in another in the same season.

Still, the San Francisco club had a problem that would not resolve itself. In order to field their best lineup, the Giants had to play Cepeda in left field, a position the All-Star first baseman had trouble adjusting to. Complicating the matter was McCovey's inability to get going in 1960, the year in which the Giants moved into Candlestick Park. The big man hit just .238, although he managed creditable power figures with 13 home runs and 51 RBIs in 260 at-bats. Nevertheless, his year included a brief visit to the Pacific Coast League, a disappointing dip for the N.L.'s leading rookie of '59.

Rigney had been canned before the midway point of the 1960 season, and Tom Sheehan, the Giants' interim manager, was moved to this summation of his struggling young slugger: "He can't run, he can't field and he can't hit."

San Francisco fans' affection for Cepeda—coupled with Orlando's mounting unhappiness over his outfield duty—surely put added pressure on McCovey as he attempted to beat the "sophomore jinx."

When the Giants transferred to the West Coast in 1958, San Franciscans seemed to resent being force-fed Willie Mays as their reigning hero and focused instead on Cepeda. Some even went out of their way to be unimpressed with the Say Hey Kid, the sentiment being, "We have seen great center fielders—Joe DiMaggio played here." It was nothing against Mays, who certainly was admired, but simply that the Californians didn't want their preferences being decided in the East. So when Cepeda broke into the majors with a sensational season in '58, he was quickly adopted as a genuine homegrown hero, untainted by the accolades of the East.

McCovey's troubles continued in 1961 when it became the conclusion of new Manager Alvin Dark that Willie couldn't hit lefthanders. Consequently, Willie played in just 106 games and wound up with a .271 average, 18 home runs and 50 RBIs. Cepeda, dividing his time almost evenly between first base and the outfield, turned in a spectacular year by leading the league with 46 home runs and 142 RBIs. With Mays swatting 40 homers and driving home 123 runs, McCovey's decline seemed even more precipitous.

With Cepeda back at first base full time in 1962, McCovey platooned in left field with Harvey Kuenn. Dark was by this time so disenchanted with Willie that he was hoping someone would take the big guy off the club's hands in a trade. When the Cardinals reportedly made an offer for McCovey, it was Giants Owner Horace Stoneham who turned it down. The boss was still fascinated by the power in Willie's bat, latent though it might be.

Playing in just 91 games and getting only 229 at-bats in 1962, McCovey turned in highly impressive figures: .293 average, 20 home runs and 54 runs batted in. The production helped the Giants win the pennant, giving Willie the opportunity to play in what proved to be the only World Series of his 22-year major league career.

The Giants engaged the Yankees in a seven-game Series. Willie played in four of the games and started at three positions—right field, left field and first

Los Angeles Dodger Manager Walter Alston: "He looked menacing up there."

A familiar sight in San Francisco—Willie greeting Willie at the plate.

Although his slugging prowess has become almost legendary, McCovey's best-remembered moment came in 1962 when he lined out to Yankee second baseman Bobby Richardson to end a dramatic World Series.

base. He had only three hits in 15 at-bats, but included a triple and home run among them. Given the vagaries of baseball, however, those power hits long have been forgotten and the most vivid memory and talked-about moment of the 1962 World Series is the final out of Game 7. The man who made it was Willie McCovey.

The situation was this: It was the bottom of the ninth inning, the Yankees were leading 1-0, the Giants had men on second and third with two out, McCovey was the batter, Cepeda was on deck and righthander Ralph Terry was on the mound. Strategy dictated McCovey be purposely passed, allowing Terry to work on the righthanded-hitting Cepeda. After a conference on the mound, however, the consensus between Yankees Manager Ralph Houk and Terry was to pitch to McCovey. It was a case of that wonderful old baseball wisdom: "Don't walk him, but don't give him anything good to hit." In other words: "Do your best and I'll be praying in the dugout."

Terry pitched and McCovey hit a blur of a line drive that, for an instant, seemed headed to right field. Second baseman Bobby Richardson moved slightly to his left, threw up his glove and caught the vicious smash. The difference between a game-winning hit—a World Series-winning hit—and an out was breathtakingly slight. Of his more than 9,500 major league plate appearances, this was to be McCovey's most memorable.

It was almost as if that famous line drive had effected some sort of personal breakthrough, for a year later, in 1963, McCovey finally began hitting with the booming power that eventually would carry him to the Hall of Fame. Playing a full season for the first time (most of it still in the outfield), he tied Hank Aaron for the league home run lead. In a numerologist's delight, McCovey and Aaron, each wearing uniform number 44, socked 44 homers apiece.

McCovey demonstrated more than power in '63. His batting eye picking up virtually everything in sight, he reeled off a 24-game hitting streak at mid-season.

A combination of injuries and the death of his father helped diminish Willie's 1964 season—18 home runs, .220 batting average. There was no question, however, that this was a temporary lull in a burgeoning career.

A year later, an early-season injury sidelined Cepeda for most of the campaign and McCovey was able to return to his most suitable position. He never left it. Willie hit 39 home runs and drove in 92 runs in 1965, and this solid season brought the Giants to a decision. After seven years, they finally resolved their longstanding "problem." Early in May 1966, Cepeda was traded to the Cardinals for lefthander Ray Sadecki.

For McCovey, 1966 was another big season—as 36 home runs and 96 RBIs would attest. The big man was in a groove now, hitting all types of pitching, and his greatest seasons loomed just ahead. In 1967, Willie's notable figures included 31 and 91, his homer and RBI totals, and 500-plus, the number of feet he drove a Jim Bunning pitch in a game at Philadelphia.

Willie's tape-measure shot at Connie Mack Stadium merely added to his growing reputation as the league's most powerful hitter. Batting against Bunning in a May 22 contest, Willie rocketed the ball over the scoreboard in right-center. The blast was to the left of the clock that jutted high above the top of the massive scoreboard. It was an area that, according to old-timers, the likes of Babe Ruth, Jimmie Foxx and Al Simmons never reached.

"Stretch is the strongest man in baseball," Mays said. "Guys like Frank Howard and Harmon Killebrew can hit them far, but they're pull hitters. Stretch can hit them deep to any part of the ball park."

Once asked how he liked getting an occasional wind-swept homer in his home stadium, gale-ravaged Candlestick Park, McCovey cracked: "I don't have to have help from the wind."

In 1968, Willie took his second home-run crown with 36 long-distance shots and also topped the National League with 105 RBIs and a .545 slugging mark. Not bad in major league baseball's "Year of the Pitcher." The following season was his greatest. He made it back-to-back titles in home runs (45), RBIs (126) and slugging (.656) and batted a robust .320, the highest full-season mark of his career. Additionally, he received 45 intentional bases on balls, a major league record. It all added up to a Most Valuable Player award for McCovey in 1969.

"You hear a lot of talk about natural ability," said McCovey, a Wunderkind a decade earlier and now a seasoned veteran. "But I've found there's no substitute for experience. Hitting is about 90 percent knowledge. It's knowing the pitchers, knowing what they throw in a certain situation...."

McCovey continued his mayhem in 1970, hitting 39 home runs, driving in 126 runs and leading in slugging for a third straight year with .612. Another highly noticeable McCovey statistic was his 137 bases on balls (11 under the league record).

"In a close game," Los Angeles Manager Walter Alston said, "there was no point in fooling around with him."

Alston said McCovey was the object of more than mere deference.

"Sure, we respected him," said Alston, who managed the Dodgers for 23 seasons, "but more than that, he scared you half to death. (Don) Drysdale, for instance—he was one of the great pitchers in the league, but McCovey ate him alive."

Longtime Dodgers pitcher Don Sutton agreed about Willie's impact on Drysdale.

"Willie was the one guy Don was reluctant to face," Sutton said. "In the years I played with Don, I think McCovey is the only player he was afraid of physically."

There may have been better hitters among McCovey's peers—Willie Mays, Hank Aaron, Frank Rob-

McCovey being greeted after one of his National League-record 18 career grand slams.

In 1976, McCovey wore the uniforms of both the San Diego Padres and Oakland Athletics. But he still possessed one of baseball's "most aesthetically pure power swings ever."

inson—but none whose appearance at home plate was more intimidating.

At 6-4 and 225 pounds, McCovey was big enough, but in a tough situation, pitchers said, he looked enormous standing up there, close to the plate, bat cocked, ready to lash out with one of the most aesthetically pure power swings in baseball history.

"He looked menacing up there, no doubt about it," Alston said. "You know, that pitcher-batter confrontation is often more subtle than fans realize. Among the things a smart pitcher is doing out there is trying to get inside the batter's head, cause a few doubts, a few distractions. About McCovey, I used to say to my pitchers, 'Try to get his attention,' and they'd answer, 'How can I get his attention when he's got all of mine?'"

Pitchers got a bit of a reprieve in 1971 and 1972 as injuries cut into McCovey's playing time and reduced his effectiveness. After hitting a total of only 32 homers in those seasons, Willie came back to hit 29 homers in 1973. By now, though, Stoneham was beginning to feel financial pressures and had decided to unload his high-salaried stars. Mays was the first to go, departing early in the 1972 season, and then after the '73 season both McCovey and one-time ace pitcher Juan Marichal left the Giants.

Almost 36 years old, McCovey was traded to the San Diego Padres, for whom he put in two so-so years, hitting 22 and 23 home runs, before slumping badly in 1976. In late August of that year, he was sold to the Oakland Athletics. After appearing in 11 games with the A's, Willie seemed at the end of the

McCovey in 1978, after his triumphant return to San Francisco.

McCovey's Milestone Home Runs

	Date	Place	Pitcher	Club
1	Aug. 2, 1959	San Francisco	Ron Kline	Pittsburgh
100	Sept. 5, 1963	San Francisco	Don Nottebart	Houston
200	Sept. 26, 1966	Atlanta	Ron Reed	Atlanta
300	July 29, 1969	Chicago	Jim Colborn	Chicago
400	July 15, 1973	San Francisco	Bob Moose	Pittsburgh
500	June 30, 1978	Atlanta	Jamie Easterly	Atlanta
Last	May 3, 1980	Montreal	Scott Sanderson	Montreal

line.

McCovey felt he still had some good baseball left in him and appealed to the Giants for a chance. The club, now under the ownership of Bob Lurie, agreed and signed its former star as a free agent. Some thought it was simply a sentimental gesture on the team's part, that Willie would go through spring training with the Giants, draw his release and then be offered a job with the organization.

McCovey, however, surprised everyone—except himself. Reporting to camp in great shape, he won back his old job and began ripping the ball with his old-time authority. Suddenly, pitchers around the league were being haunted by an old ghost they thought had been laid to rest. In a season of triumph and personal satisfaction, the 39-year-old McCovey surged to 28 home runs, 86 RBIs, a .280 batting average and designation as The Sporting News' Comeback Player of the Year.

"Being in good shape at that age was no big deal," McCovey said. "I was able to do it by not burning the candle at both ends during my career. I worked hard to stay in shape, and it paid off . . . I sacrificed for what I did in 1977."

It was a marvelous summer for Willie, with the thunder of days past echoing once again. He played 2½ more seasons before retiring midway through 1980, his 22nd year in the big leagues.

"The Giants had guys like Mays, Cepeda and (Jim) Hart, but it always came down to McCovey," said Sutton, a member of the majors' 300-victory club. "He was awesome. There's a tendency to say a player is underrated, but I think it's fair to say McCovey has never been as highly acclaimed as he deserved. He easily was the most feared hitter in the league."

Before leaving the majors as a rare four-decade player, McCovey had earned many badges of distinction, otherwise known as records. Like geographical areas, these records are rightfully claimed and proudly possessed.

McCovey, for instance, can boast of being among the select group of players hitting two home runs in one inning, and he's one of only two men to have accomplished that feat twice (Andre Dawson is the other). His 18 bases-loaded homers constitute a National League record, and his three pinch-hit grand slams rank as a record-tying achievement in the

majors. Also in the record books under "McCovey" is the entry of 45 intentional walks in one season.

There's more, of course. A lot more. Above all else, though, is Willie's total of 521 home runs, the most ever by a lefthanded hitter in the National League. Among lefthanded batsmen in big-league history, only Babe Ruth and Reggie Jackson slugged more homers than McCovey.

The big man from Mobile made it big, all right, proving Lefty O'Doul's long-ago contention that, in many ways, he had the makings of another Ted Williams.

Indeed, one last check of the record book reveals that Willie Lee McCovey stands in a 10th-place tie on the majors' all-time homer list. His companion in that slot? None other than Williams himself.

McCOVEY'S CAREER RECORD

Born January 10, 1938, at Mobile, Ala.

Batted and threw lefthanded.   Elected to Hall of Fame, 1986.

Year Club	League	G.	AB.	R.	H.	HR.	RBI.	B.A.
1955—Sandersville	Ga. St.	107	410	82	125	19	*113	.305
1956—Danville	Carol.	152	519	119	161	29	89	.310
1957—Dallas	Texas	115	395	63	111	11	65	.281
1958—Phoenix	P. C.	146	527	91	168	14	89	.319
1959—Phoenix	P. C.	95	349	84	130	*29	●92	.372
1959—San Francisco	Nat.	52	192	32	68	13	38	.354
1960—San Francisco	Nat.	101	260	37	62	13	51	.238
1960—Tacoma	P. C.	17	63	14	18	3	16	.286
1961—San Francisco	Nat.	106	328	59	89	18	50	.271
1962—San Francisco	Nat.	91	229	41	67	20	54	.293
1963—San Francisco	Nat.	152	564	103	158	●44	102	.280
1964—San Francisco	Nat.	130	364	55	80	18	54	.220
1965—San Francisco	Nat.	160	540	93	149	39	92	.276
1966—San Francisco	Nat.	150	502	85	148	36	96	.295
1967—San Francisco	Nat.	135	456	73	126	31	91	.276
1968—San Francisco	Nat.	148	523	81	153	*36	*105	.293
1969—San Francisco	Nat.	149	491	101	157	*45	*126	.320
1970—San Francisco	Nat.	152	495	98	143	39	126	.289
1971—San Francisco	Nat.	105	329	45	91	18	70	.277
1972—San Francisco	Nat.	81	263	30	56	14	35	.213
1973—San Francisco	Nat.	130	383	52	102	29	75	.266
1974—San Diego	Nat.	128	344	53	87	22	63	.253
1975—San Diego	Nat.	122	413	43	104	23	68	.252
1976—San Diego	Nat.	71	202	20	41	7	36	.203
1976—Oakland	Amer.	11	24	0	5	0	0	.208
1977—San Francisco	Nat.	141	478	54	134	28	86	.280
1978—San Francisco	Nat.	108	351	32	80	12	64	.228
1979—San Francisco	Nat.	117	353	34	88	15	57	.249
1980—San Francisco	Nat.	48	113	8	23	1	16	.204
National League Totals		2577	8173	1229	2206	521	1555	.270
American League Totals		11	24	0	5	0	0	.208
Major League Totals		2588	8197	1229	2211	521	1555	.270

CHAMPIONSHIP SERIES RECORD

Year Club	League	G.	AB.	R.	H.	HR.	RBI.	B.A.
1971—San Francisco	Nat.	4	14	2	6	2	6	.429

WORLD SERIES RECORD

Year Club	League	G.	AB.	R.	H.	HR.	RBI.	B.A.
1962—San Francisco	Nat.	4	15	2	3	1	1	.200

A 'Family' Man

"Listen. Pittsburgh isn't fancy, but it's real. It's a working town, and money doesn't come easy. They don't warm up to quick turnovers. They want a guy to be around.

"I feel as much a part of this city as the cobblestone streets and the steel mills. I've lived a plain, simple life, and I've treated people how they like to be treated. People in this town expect an honest day's work, and I've given it to them for a long, long time.

At that juncture of his career, the man doing the talking, one Wilver Dornel Stargell, was nearing the end of his 17th full season with the Pirates. And what he was talking about in 1979, in a single word, was commitment, the act of pledging to do a job. For Willie Stargell, the word meant more than vowing to take on a task—it meant performing that task to the very best of his ability.

Stargell's commitment to a cause, while evident from the start of his career, probably reached its zenith in '79, a year in which Willie, at age 38, wound up with 32 homers and helped Pittsburgh to the National League East championship. His regular-season contribution, though, seemed almost too good to be true. How much production could the tightly knit Pirates—the club that thought of itself as a family—expect from the veteran team leader, the man known as "Pops," in postseason play?

Whatever the Bucs and their fans hoped for, Willie clearly delivered more. A lot more. In a three-game Championship Series sweep of the Cincinnati Reds, Stargell merely bashed two home runs (the first a decisive three-run shot in the 11th inning of the opening game), knocked in six runs and batted .455. Then, in the World Series, he clubbed three homers, collected seven RBIs and hit .400.

Stargell, to no one's surprise, was named the Most Valuable Player of the 1979 World Series. It was an honor that would go nicely with other accolades he would win that year—including designations as Co-Most Valuable Player in the National

Promising young Pittsburgh slugger Willie Stargell in 1963.

League, Major League Player of the Year and Man of the Year, the latter two awards being bestowed by The Sporting News.

The honors and accompanying adulation were a far cry from what Willie Stargell had encountered when he started his climb up the professional baseball ladder 20 years earlier. And how.

In 1959, Willie made his professional debut with the Class-D San Angelo, Tex., club, a Sophomore League team that would shift to Roswell, N.M., in early June. Willie had experienced racial prejudice as a youngster in Oakland, but in the tough old frontier towns of the Southwest, he came up against something much more virulent and savage than he

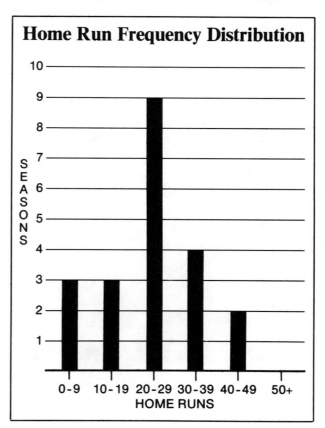

Home Run Frequency Distribution

A hard-hitting group of Pirates: (left to right) Roberto Clemente, Matty Alou,
Stargell and Manny Mota.

This Dodger Stadium diagram shows the landing points of two of Stargell's most
prolific clouts.

had ever experienced in his young life.

That life had begun 18 years earlier—March 6, 1941, to be exact—in Earlsboro, Okla., which was little more than a bump in the road in the middle of the Sooner State, a town of less than 300 people and hardly a citadel of opportunity, especially for blacks. The Stargell family left Earlsboro soon after the birth of robust little Wilver and moved to the Oakland area, where Willie grew up.

In high school, Willie played baseball and basketball and was a high jumper on the track team. But baseball was his game, and he played it so well at nearby Santa Rosa Junior College that the Pirates signed him late in the summer of 1958 for a $1,200 bonus and delivery into their farm system in 1959.

Stargell has never forgotten the insults and indignities of that first year.

During Sophomore League games, Willie would often hear shouts from the stands that he would be shot, lynched, tarred and feathered. It was scary, he said, and it was disheartening, and on more than one occasion the situation came close to sapping his resolve. Several times he considered leaving and returning home, but his parents counseled him to stay, reminding him that the path to success was never easy. Furthermore, they told Willie that if he wanted to succeed in baseball badly enough, he was going to have to tolerate the vituperation of scabbed minds.

"Black people would put us up in private homes," Stargell told writer Arnold Hano in 1971. "Except the blacks didn't have anything. When we played in Artesia, New Mexico, I stayed with a woman who raised her own fishing bait. She kept the bait in her house, and nailed down the windows. I guess she was afraid somebody would steal it. We had to stay in there with the heat, the odor. We didn't eat in any restaurant. One place downtown would serve us, but only out the back door. I refused. I bought food at local grocery stores, canned meat, lunch meat, sardines."

The hurt was obvious.

"I had my dreams of baseball," Willie said. "It was different from this." And between the clash of dream and reality, it was the dream that survived.

Despite the hardships and the catcalls of the fried-brain bunch, Willie did passably well in his first pro test, batting .274 and driving in 87 runs in 118 games, though hitting only seven home runs. Incredibly, he made 37 errors at first base, leading the Pirates to the conclusion that the big, strong youngster might be better off in the outfield, which was where he played in 1960 for Grand Forks, N.D., in the Class-C Northern League. The racial epithets disappeared with the change of venue and life was a little better, but the improved circumstances didn't help Stargell at the plate. He batted .260, with 11 home runs and 61 RBIs in 107 games.

Despite these indifferent outings, the Pirates promoted Willie to Asheville, N.C., in the Sally League. He responded with a .289 average, 22 home runs and 89 RBIs, entertaining Asheville fans along the

Big Pirate outfielder Dave Parker called Stargell "our stabilizer."

way with some prodigious wallops that crashed like meteorites onto a hill behind right field, earning him the nickname "On the Hill Will."

In 1962, On the Hill Will was On the Move Will, advancing two classifications and now playing for Columbus of the Class-AAA International League, where he hit 27 home runs and batted .276. The Pirates brought him up at the end of the season and he got into 10 games, batting .290. His 21-year major league career and trek to the Hall of Fame had begun.

Willie became a meaningful force in the National League in 1965, his third full season, when he smashed 27 home runs, the second of 13 consecutive years in which he would hit 20 or more homers, and drove in 107 runs. On June 24, he joined a select circle when he homered three times in one game, a feat he was to repeat on May 22, 1968, and twice in 1971 (April 10, 21).

The first of those three-homer cannonades thrust considerable attention upon Pittsburgh's young belter. The performance came against one of baseball's best teams and off the game's top pitching staff. Additionally, Stargell nearly hit a fourth home run in that '65 contest, played at Dodger Stadium.

All three of Willie's shots were long-distance drives, with the first one crashing four rows into the second deck down the right-field line. "This is the first time I ever saw one land there," marveled

Stargell checking some fan mail in the Pirates' clubhouse.

Pittsburgh's big bopper with teammate Richie Hebner in 1971.

Stargell gets a welcome-home hug from teammate Bill Robinson (left) after his homer in Game 7 of the 1979 World Series against Baltimore. By this time, he was known as "Pops."

Los Angeles outfielder Ron Fairly, whose service with the Dodgers predated the opening of the ball park in 1962.

Stargell socked his first two homers of the night off Dodgers star Don Drysdale, drilled No. 3 off rookie John Purdin and had his near-miss (an eighth-inning double that missed being a homer by a foot or so) against rookie Mike Kekich. He finished the evening with six RBIs.

Two nights earlier, Stargell had walloped two home runs in a game at San Francisco.

"I never have seen a batter who hits the ball any harder," Pirates Manager Harry Walker said. "For sheer crash of bat meeting the ball, Stargell simply is the best."

Stargell excelled again in 1966, rifling 33 homers, driving in 102 runs and batting .315 (which would stand up as his career high). In June 4-5 games against the Houston Astros in '66, Willie banged out nine consecutive hits at Pittsburgh's Forbes Field. After cooling off the next two seasons, Willie rebounded in 1969 and 1970 with homer/RBI figures of 29/92 and 31/85. In August of '69, he gave Los Angeles fans another night to remember when he became the first player to hit a ball out of Dodger Stadium. (In 1973, Stargell sent another ball winging out of the Los Angeles park. Through the 1992 season, only Stargell had hammered a ball beyond Dodger Stadium's confines—and he, of course, had done it twice.)

It was during the 1970 season that the Pirates moved out of Forbes Field, their home for more than 60 years, and into spanking-new Three Rivers Stadium. While some fans and players waxed nostalgic over the switch, Stargell had reason to be enthusiastic. At Forbes Field, it was 457 feet to the center-field wall and a homer to any locale except right down the right-field line required a poke of at least 365-375 feet. The power alleys took on airport dimensions. Three Rivers was considerably cozier, with the center-field barrier only 410 feet away—later, it would be moved 10 feet closer—and the power-alley fences within comfortable range.

"Forbes Field actually helped me to be a better hitter," said Stargell, "although my wife used to chart all the 450-foot outs I hit and there were about 20 a year. That's 160 (homers) I didn't get. But I learned to stroke the ball. . . ."

The figures would tell the story on the impact of the change in parks. With Forbes Field as the Bucs' home, Willie had highs of 33 home runs overall in one year and 14 at home in a single season. At Three Rivers, Stargell shot into the 40s overall in two of his first three full seasons in the new facility and drilled 15 or more homers at home five times after leaving Forbes.

In 1971, Stargell became a home run factory. He set a major league record by hitting 11 home runs in April, wound up with a league-leading 48 and helped the Pirates to the National League pennant and World Series crown. In 1972, Willie had 33 crowd-pleasers, then came back a year later to top the league once more with 44 homers (he also led N.L. batsmen in 1973 with 43 doubles, 119 RBIs and a slugging percentage of .646). In '71, he cracked 21 homers at Three Rivers and in '73 he walloped 24 there.

Stargell was the big bopper on heavy-hitting Pittsburgh teams that won six division titles, two pennants and two World Series in the 1970s. There was nothing subtle about these clubs; generally light on pitching, they were known as "The Lumber Company," and in addition to Stargell, these Pirate aggregations boasted Roberto Clemente, Al Oliver, Richie Zisk, Dave Parker and others.

On this team of hitters, Stargell was known for his cannon shots. Willie accounted for four of the first five upper-deck homers hit at Three Rivers Stadium. He also detonated some tremendous blasts at Forbes Field; in fact, of the 18 balls hit over the right-field roof there, Willie touched off seven of them. Additionally, he was the first to reach the upper-right-field tier at Busch Stadium in St. Louis and, of course, he struck those mammoth blows at Dodger Stadium. One of his home runs in Los Angeles traveled so far that Dodgers announcer Vin Scully, aware that many fans brought transistor radios to the games, asked the fan who had caught the ball to stand up and wave it, so everyone could have a second, more believing appreciation of what Willie had done.

Stargell's career slipped in the mid-1970s—from 1974 through 1977 he averaged only 20 homers—but he rebounded in 1978 with a 28-homer, 97-RBI season that netted him The Sporting News' honor as Comeback Player of the Year in the National League.

After following up with a banner season in 1979, Willie spent three more years in the majors and finished with 475 home runs in his big-league career. But despite the monstrous homer total, the postseason heroics and the many awards, Stargell, at the end of his playing days, was most known and admired for his character and his capacity to inspire teammates.

He was a natural leader in the clubhouse, a man who gradually won the respect of whites, blacks and Spanish-speaking players, and probably no team had a larger mix of the three than the Pirates. People in the Pittsburgh organization said the positive elements of Stargell's presence in the clubhouse could not be overstated.

"Those teams went through one pennant race after another in the 1970s," one writer said, "and you know what kind of pressure that can build. But Willie never let it get out of hand. He was able to defuse or lighten any situation with a few quiet, soothing words. 'If you win like men, you got to lose like men.' He'd say things like that, and people paid attention."

Dave Parker called Willie "our stabilizer." The ebullient Parker also viewed Stargell as "the silent leader of the club. I'm the noisy leader."

According to Stargell, "People don't realize that

The Stargell spirit was contagious and especially evident in the Pirates' 1979 title campaign.

Stargell receiving an award for his work in the fight against sickle-cell anemia.

there are a lot of emotions in baseball or how much pride and deep feelings are worth." The statement touches upon some of the intangibles Stargell brought to work with him. Pride is indeed a power motivator, a constant and positive exploration of one's self. In Stargell, it flowered in abundance and was a source of his leadership.

Willie looked at things with a gentle, compassionate realism. He was a leader in the fight against sickle-cell anemia, a disease that attacks the blood cells, with blacks the primary victims. In the early 1970s, he was part of a contingent that flew in and out of Vietnam war zones to visit GIs. He visited schools and youth groups and inner-city problem spots and warned the kids about drugs and alcohol and crime and all the snares and pitfalls so temptingly close to them. He was an impressive figure, though not so terribly impressed with himself. When asked about his big days at home plate, he was apt to say something like, "Am I swinging where they are throwing, or are they throwing where I am swinging?"

Stargell's leadership qualities were different from those of a Frank Robinson. Whereas Robinson helped motivate his teammates by aggressive, combative play, Willie simply let it happen.

"People just naturally gravitated to him," Pirates broadcaster Bob Prince said. "Just like in every family there's some strong focal point, be it the father, mother, older brother, somebody; on the Pirates, it became Willie, who simply was being himself."

Longtime teammates Oliver and Richie Hebner focused on Stargell's special attributes.

"If Willie told us to jump off the Fort Pitt Bridge, we'd ask him what kind of dive he wanted," Oliver said. "That's how much respect we have for the man."

Hebner, commenting on baseball's ebbs and flows and Stargell's reaction to same, said: "He takes it all in stride. It's four shots, a shower and back the next day, even if some of those shots look like they come from Cape Kennedy."

In 1979, Stargell's standing as a player and leader seemed to become officially sanctioned, at least as far as the public at large was concerned. It was the World Series—that vast and glittering national stage—that brought home to fans nationwide the stature of Willie Stargell.

"Pops" was more than just a spiritual leader.

Willie bids a fond farewell to a packed Three Rivers Stadium crowd as John W. Galbreath, the Pirates' chairman of the board, presides over the retirement ceremony.

Stargell's Milestone Home Runs

	Date	Place	Pitcher	Club
1	May 8, 1963	Chicago	Lindy McDaniel	Chicago
100	June 7, 1967	Pittsburgh	Jack Fisher	New York
200	April 10, 1971	Atlanta	George Stone	Atlanta
300	June 28, 1973	Pittsburgh	Rick Wise	St. Louis
400	June 29, 1977	St. Louis	Eric Rasmussen	St. Louis
Last	July 21, 1982	Cincinnati	Tom Hume	Cincinnati

Character and dignity are noble and admirable, but in the brutally competitive world of professional sports, the leader has to lead by example. In decisive Game 7 of the 1979 World Series, Stargell gave a graphic demonstration of just such leadership.

The Pirates had scrambled back from a three-games-to-one deficit to tie the Series, but they found themselves trailing Baltimore by a 1-0 score in the sixth inning of the final contest. Stargell was at the plate with a man on first base. Cranking up his bat in his familiar windmill style, Willie unloaded on a delivery from Orioles lefthander Scott McGregor and sent the ball on a one-way trip over the wall in right-center. The Pirates went on from there to a 4-1 triumph, wrapping up the Series championship.

When Willie learned that he had been voted the Series MVP, he said, "I know only one person can receive the award, but if I could, I would divide it among the entire organization."

When he heard what Stargell had said, one teammate commented, "A lot of guys say things like that. But this guy means it."

Perspective, then, was yet another Stargell trait. Willie's reaction to the Series honor brought back memories of his early-1970s reflection on the "pressure" he felt—or didn't feel—on the diamond.

"Pressure is being raised in a government project, the way I was," Stargell had said. "Pressure is thinking about whether something will turn up for dinner that night. Pressure is having to worry about paying your bills."

Baseball meant good times—and basically worry-free times—for "Pops."

"We do want to have fun," Stargell said of the baseball-playing fraternity. "We only have a few years in the game. There's so much to learn, to enjoy. You can't be tied up in knots and play baseball."

"When that umpire hollers 'Play ball,' he says 'Play' . . . That means fun, relaxation. He doesn't say 'Work ball.'"

"It's talent that gets a player here and mentality that keeps him here. You come into the game without ulcers. It's important to leave the game without ulcers."

"And each game should be cherished as a highlight of one's life."

Make no mistake, Willie wanted to succeed—indeed, he wanted to excel—on the ball field. However, a strikeout, even one in a key situation, didn't ruin his life. There would be another day, another chance.

Stargell struck out a lot, too, but the power hitters often do. In his explanation for this, Stargell unwittingly voiced his credo of life:

"I strike out because I commit myself early. Big swingers have that tendency. I don't sit back and wait on a pitch. I see it leave the pitcher's hand and I commit before I can be sure of what the pitch is. It's an aggressive action. The power comes out of the commitment."

Without question, commitment was an approach to life that Wilver Stargell knew something about.

STARGELL'S CAREER RECORD

Born March 6, 1941, at Earlsboro, Okla.
Batted and threw lefthanded.   Elected to Hall of Fame, 1988.

Year—Club	League	G.	AB.	R.	H.	HR.	RBI.	B.A.
1959—S. A'gelo-R'well ...Soph.		118	431	66	118	7	87	.274
1960—Grand Forks........North.		107	396	63	103	11	61	.260
1961—Asheville.............. Sally		130	453	78	131	22	89	.289
1962—Columbus.............. Int.		138	497	97	137	27	82	.276
1962—Pittsburgh............. Nat.		10	31	1	9	0	4	.290
1963—Pittsburgh............. Nat.		108	304	34	74	11	47	.243
1964—Pittsburgh............. Nat.		117	421	53	115	21	78	.273
1965—Pittsburgh............. Nat.		144	533	68	145	27	107	.272
1966—Pittsburgh............. Nat.		140	485	84	153	33	102	.315
1967—Pittsburgh............. Nat.		134	462	54	125	20	73	.271
1968—Pittsburgh............. Nat.		128	435	57	103	24	67	.237
1969—Pittsburgh............. Nat.		145	522	89	160	29	92	.307
1970—Pittsburgh............. Nat.		136	474	70	125	31	85	.264
1971—Pittsburgh............. Nat.		141	511	104	151	*48	125	.295
1972—Pittsburgh............. Nat.		138	495	75	145	33	112	.293
1973—Pittsburgh............. Nat.		148	522	106	156	*44	*119	.299
1974—Pittsburgh............. Nat.		140	508	90	153	25	96	.301
1975—Pittsburgh............. Nat.		124	461	71	136	22	90	.295
1976—Pittsburgh............. Nat.		117	428	54	110	20	65	.257
1977—Pittsburgh............. Nat.		63	186	29	51	13	35	.274
1978—Pittsburgh............. Nat.		122	390	60	115	28	97	.295
1979—Pittsburgh............. Nat.		126	424	60	119	32	82	.281
1980—Pittsburgh............. Nat.		67	202	28	53	11	38	.262
1981—Pittsburgh............. Nat.		38	60	2	17	0	9	.283
1982—Pittsburgh............. Nat.		74	73	6	17	3	17	.233
Major League Totals............		2360	7927	1195	2232	475	1540	.282

CHAMPIONSHIP SERIES RECORD

Year Club	League	G.	AB.	R.	H.	HR.	RBI.	B.A.
1970—Pittsburgh............. Nat.		3	12	0	6	0	1	.500
1971—Pittsburgh............. Nat.		4	14	1	0	0	0	.000
1972—Pittsburgh............. Nat.		5	16	1	1	0	1	.063
1974—Pittsburgh............. Nat.		4	15	3	6	2	4	.400
1975—Pittsburgh............. Nat.		3	11	1	2	0	0	.182
1979—Pittsburgh............. Nat.		3	11	2	5	2	6	.455
LCS Totals....................		22	79	8	20	4	12	.253

WORLD SERIES RECORD

Year Club	League	G.	AB.	R.	H.	HR.	RBI.	B.A.
1971—Pittsburgh............. Nat.		7	24	3	5	0	1	.208
1979—Pittsburgh............. Nat.		7	30	7	12	3	7	.400
World Series Totals.............		14	54	10	17	3	8	.315

Mr. October

Reggie Jackson (left) as a rookie with the Oakland A's in 1968. He was a product of Arizona State (above), where he starred as a talented but undisciplined power hitter for the Sun Devils.

In baseball, if you're going to be named after a month, then October is the one to hope for, because this is the game's pinnacle time, when only the best are left to compete, the spoils are grandest and the nation's attention is most rapt. Because of the pressure, the caliber of the competition and the fact that relatively few games are involved, it's a difficult time to excel, and not even the greatest players can be assured of succeeding on demand.

Reggie Jackson played in five World Series and never had a bad one. Indeed, he had one that crashed the record books. Reggie hit a lot of home runs in October and he did it with a flair, meaning that a Jackson home run was an occasion more fes-

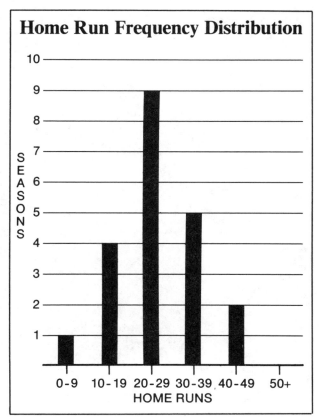

217

Young Reggie exploded for 47 homers in 1969, finishing third in the American League behind Minnesota's Harmon Killebrew and Washington's Frank Howard (right).

Jackson is greeted at the plate by Oakland teammate Sal Bando after one of his 563 career home runs.

tive than your usual four-bagger.

Reggie became a known quantity to the fans, a "first name" player, like Babe and Yogi. He was an extrovert; he also was intelligent and articulate, always available to the press. He had a lot of pride, also considerable ego. Since most ball players—most athletes—are faceless technicians, little known to the general fan beyond their statistics, the well-publicized and sharply defined Reggie became a towering figure on a ball field.

There was nothing subtle about Jackson, not in the way he operated at home plate (563 home runs and 2,597 strikeouts, the latter figure the highest in major league history), not in the way he preened before the public. It was said he could sense a note-pad or camera five miles away, and his statement about the All-Star Game is a succinct summation of the man: "I don't go there to compete, I go there to be seen."

Reggie was first seen in Wyncote, Pa., on May 18, 1946. He grew up in this Philadelphia suburb, raised primarily by his father after his parents had separated. Reggie's father, who was a tailor and with whom Reggie was always extremely close, encouraged the youngster's athletic abilities. By the time he was in high school, Reggie was active on the baseball, football, basketball and track teams.

Word soon got around that there was an extremely gifted black athlete performing for Cheltenham Township High School. Baseball and football recruiters started coming around with offers and inducements and incentives. The football-playing Jackson (he was a hard runner) was good enough to receive inquiries from the University of Alabama and the University of Georgia, schools that had yet to integrate their football teams. He finally signed a letter of intent with Arizona State University, where he would play football for Frank Kush (whose approach to the game sometimes made Vince Lombardi look timid) and baseball for Bobby Winkles, who later managed the California Angels and Oakland Athletics.

The baseball program at Arizona State under Winkles was one of the most successful in the collegiate ranks, a veritable minor league franchise. From ASU came Sal Bando, Rick Monday, Floyd Bannister, Bob Horner and many others, including Reginald Martinez Jackson. According to Kush, Reggie could have had a career in professional football, but once at Arizona State, Jackson began leaning more and more toward baseball.

By the spring of 1966, the big-league scouts were crowding into ASU's ball park to watch the muscular young Jackson—just a sophomore then—send long, towering home runs into the dry, hot skies of the Southwest.

"He was totally undisciplined at home plate," one scout recalled. "A smart pitcher with a nickel curve could make him look bad. Reggie was raw as hell, but he had a powerhouse swing and terrific strength. It was all there. You could see it. It was just a matter of getting a harness on it."

What the scouts also saw was a positive lust to smash a baseball and a charismatic exultation when it had been done to satisfaction. Not only was he a star slugger in the making, but one who radiated self-confidence and personality.

"I go back to 1965 with Reggie," Monday said, "but I guess I don't go far enough back to remember when he was shy."

Reggie Jackson was available for major league baseball's amateur free-agent draft in the spring of 1966. Picking first were the New York Mets, second the Kansas City Athletics. The Mets opted for catcher Steve Chilcott. The A's picked Jackson. Chilcott soon developed a bad shoulder and never played for the Mets.

Reggie gave some thought to finishing college before signing a professional contract, but this notion melted under the persuasive powers of A's Owner Charles O. Finley, whose friendly persuasion included a bonus deal worth some $85,000.

Finley was an eminently successful insurance man who wandered into baseball and through a combination of shrewd trades, good luck and some remarkable baseball horse sense, put together a team that took five straight division titles and three straight World Series championships in the 1970s. These Oakland A's teams were not superstar conglomerates; rather, they were clubs that played with a cohesive unity (one of the things that unified them was a collective dislike of the sometimes sharp-tongued and abrasive Finley), overcame off-the-field disunity (strong personalities touched off many a fight among A's players, but all was forgotten once the game began), had very strong pitching and boasted several stars, the most prominent of whom was Reggie Jackson.

Reggie started out in pro ball with the Lewiston, Idaho, club in the Northwest League. The town had been named after Meriwether Lewis of the Lewis and Clark exploration team, which had used the area as a camp site in 1805. More than a century and a half later, another American hero arrived there, but did not remain very long—for just 12 games, during which he batted .292 and hit two home runs.

In July, the Athletics sent Reggie to Modesto in the California League, where he finished out the season. In 56 games, he batted .299 and hit an impressive 21 home runs. A teammate on the Modesto club was righthanded starter Rollie Fingers, later to become the relief ace of Oakland's championship teams.

Fingers' first impression of the new man? "Strength . . . muscles on muscles." And a desire not just to hit home runs, but "home runs the organization would recognize"—meaning baseballs that were hit extraordinarily hard and extraordinarily far. Even then, Fingers recalled, Reggie loved the attention and the challenge, he "lived for the chance to win the game as the big hero."

Jackson played most of the 1967 season with Birmingham, Ala., of the Southern League. In 114

From agony to joy: A disconsolate Jackson (left) after Oakland's loss to Baltimore
in the 1971 A.L. Championship Series and a triumphant Reggie (right) after the
A's 1973 World Series victory over the New York Mets.

Jackson's never-ending quest was to get the sweet part of the bat on the ball.

games, he batted .293, hit 17 home runs and led the league with 17 triples ("I could run like hell then," he was always proud to point out in later years). He finished the season in the big leagues, with Kansas City, but lit no bonfires. In 35 games with the A's, he batted only .178 and socked just one home run— at Anaheim Stadium on September 17, against left-hander Jim Weaver. It was the first of 563 big-league home runs he would hit.

In 1968, the Athletics moved to Oakland, where Finley began putting together the team that would dominate baseball in the early 1970s. Along with Reggie, the mainstays were outfielder Joe Rudi, third baseman Sal Bando, shortstop Bert Campaneris, catcher-first baseman Gene Tenace and pitchers Fingers, Catfish Hunter, Ken Holtzman and Vida Blue.

Reggie's first full season in the majors, 1968, was an approximate blueprint of the next two decades of his professional life: a solid total of home runs (29, a figure he would top seven times), a modest batting average (.250, 12 points under his lifetime mark) and a carload of strikeouts (171, which turned out to be a career high).

A year later, the 23-year-old Oakland muscle man exploded into the front ranks of big-league dynamiters. Jackson always knew who he was, and the entire universe of baseball had been alerted. It was a powerhouse year, perhaps his best ever. He had career highs in home runs (47) and runs batted in (118), batted .275 and led the league in slugging percentage (.608). Despite that glittering home run total, Reggie could do no better than place third in the league, behind Harmon Killebrew's 49 and Frank Howard's 48.

There were times during the 1969 season when it appeared the young belter would wind up No. 1— on the majors' all-time single-season homer chart, that is. With more than two months to play in the season, Jackson had 40 home runs. Roger Maris' 61-homer achievement of 1961 was within reach.

However, Jackson went into a tailspin at the plate. A severe rash didn't help matters, either. After July 29, he clubbed only seven home runs.

Reggie was disappointed at season's end, but undeterred. In fact, he displayed some of the braggadocio for which he would become famous.

"There was a lot of talk that I might break the record," Jackson said. "Well, I still think I'm capable of doing it. Hitting more than 60 home runs in one season is not out of the realm of my ability."

Behind Reggie's missile launching in '69, the A's finished second in the American League West. Oakland placed second again in 1970, with its prime slugger slumping off to 23 home runs, 66 RBIs and a .237 average.

In 1971, the A's roared to the first of their five straight division titles, tearing apart the league for 101 victories and a 16-game lead over divisional runner-up Kansas City. It was halfway through the '71 season, during the All-Star Game at Detroit's Tiger Stadium, that a national audience had a defin-

itive look at Reggie Jackson the hitter and Reggie Jackson the showman. Playing in the second of his 12 All-Star Games, the Oakland slugger came to bat as a pinch-hitter in the bottom of the third inning. The pitcher was Pittsburgh righthander Dock Ellis. There was a runner on first base.

Ellis delivered and then Jackson delivered, connecting with terrific impact. It is doubtful if he ever hit a ball harder or farther. The ball attained great height in a dazzling instant, kept traveling, kept climbing, finally hitting a light tower on the roof in right-center. This gargantuan blast was estimated to have gone some 520 feet. And at home plate, the author of this awesome clout, knowing full well what he had done, paused, bat in hand, to watch and admire. This was to become a typical Jackson response to a job performed extremely well—an admiring, appreciative gaze after making a ball disappear. It bespoke the pride and pleasure and deep satisfaction he felt in doing what he always was trying to do.

"Taters," Reggie said. "That's where the money is."

There also was money to be made by winning the World Series. After the fractious-but-formidable A's had won their third consecutive Series in 1974, Reggie reflected on the success he had enjoyed.

"I don't like to talk about specifics because individual statistics aren't that important," Reggie said. "The important thing is that I have become a winner.

"There's nothing tangible about it. Being a winner is a state of mind. It's knowing how to go about winning. It's mental.

"It's knowing what to do at the right time and not panicking, to play your own style of game, not to force anything. That's the fellow who's a winner...."

Definitely a winner, Jackson also became known for his ego, his flamboyance, his self-proclaimed 160 I.Q., but it all meant little without something that was more basic, something that was primal—his ability to bash a baseball distant places. He was admired and reviled, but never ignored, and of this he made certain when he finally went to New York in 1977. "Finally" seems to apply because the Jackson/New York matchup appeared inevitable, a kind of fulfilling of a sports destiny in the mold of Babe Ruth and the Big Town. Though never a king of sluggers like Ruth, Jackson was surely a crown prince and indisputably the game's premier attention-getter.

After eight years with the Oakland A's, seasons that included those three consecutive World Series crowns, Jackson was traded to Baltimore as increasing payroll demands prompted Finley to break up his winning team. Reggie marked time as an Orioles outfielder for one year. Free agency had by now come to baseball, and an eligible man could go where he chose. That, too, was a factor in the dismantling of the A's; facing the risk of losing star players to free agency and getting nothing in re-

Jackson during his one year of service with the
Baltimore Orioles.

Jackson and Yankee catcher Thurman Munson.
Reggie was the straw that stirred the drink.

Reggie with Yankee Manager Billy Martin (right):
the calm before the storm.

Jackson launching his third home run in Game 6 of the 1977 World Series against the Los Angeles Dodgers.

turn, Finley sought to obtain something of value via the trade mart.

Reggie was one of those men who was granted his "freedom" after the 1976 season. Courted by many teams, his destination nonetheless seemed a foregone conclusion. George Steinbrenner's obsession to possess the best, backed up by the Yankee owner's wide-open checkbook and the seductive promises of New York, brought Reggie to the city of Ruth and DiMaggio and Mantle where, he promised, a candy bar would be named after him. (And that's just what happened, although one writer said the candy bar tasted like a hot dog, "hotdog" being baseball parlance for showboat, which led to another well-known crack about Reggie: "There isn't enough mustard in the world to cover him.")

It was a case of a lion walking into a lion's den. There was Steinbrenner himself, a man who could pay a player millions of dollars and then belittle him (see the Dave Winfield file), and there was the manager, Billy Martin, a testy, short-tempered man who believed religiously in "Yankee tradition" and "Yankee pride," abstractions he saw embodied most prominently in the quiet leadership of DiMaggio and Mantle.

For Martin, the Yankee uniform was a vestment designed to imbue its wearer with pride and humility. A Yankee wasn't supposed to say, "I didn't come to New York to become a star, I brought my star with me," which Reggie had boldly announced.

Martin was, in fact, against the signing of Jackson; the Yankees had won the pennant without him in 1976, Billy reminded George. But Steinbrenner was determined: The Big Apple would have The Big Knocker.

So the lion entered the lion's den not with a walk, but a swagger. Plus, he headed straight for the choice seat. In Oakland, Reggie always had been the leader, but the Yankees already had one in catcher Thurman Munson, a tough, grumpy, sensitive man who had the admiration of his teammates. So when Reggie told a magazine writer in spring training that he, Jackson, was "the straw that stirs the drink" and that Munson "really doesn't enter into it," it sent Munson into a sullen and hostile shell, offended many new teammates, enraged Martin and delighted the New York press, which settled in for what would be five years of fireworks.

Catfish Hunter, Reggie's teammate in Oakland and now with the Yankees, pointed out the difference between the Athletics and Yankees and, in a larger sense, between Oakland and New York. By implication, he also touched upon the pitfalls of the situation.

"The difference with the Yankees," Hunter said, "is guys paid attention to what he said. At Oakland, nobody listened to him. We just watched him hit."

Those who traveled with the Yankees through the spring of 1977 could see the tension building within the ball club; it was Reggie versus almost

A couple of New York heroes: the Mets' Tom Seaver (left) and Jackson.

everybody, and Jackson against Martin in particular. When the first explosion came, it took place—appropriately enough—on national television.

The Yankees were playing the Red Sox in Fenway Park, under any circumstances a highly charged occasion. In the sixth inning of a June 18 game, Boston's Jim Rice looped a fly ball into short right field—Reggie's sector. In the opinion of Martin, Jackson did not put enough hustle into his retrieval of the ball. Reggie later admitted that he "could have played the ball better," but nevertheless maintained he gave 100 percent effort.

An infuriated Martin immediately pulled Reggie out of the game, sending Paul Blair out to play right field. When a bewildered Jackson came into the dugout, Martin began screaming at him. The pent-up animosity between the two men suddenly erupted, and only the intervention of coaches Yogi Berra and Elston Howard and a few players prevented fisticuffs right then and there, with the big, unblinking eye of NBC television relaying the pictures throughout an enthralled America.

No accord of understanding was ever reached between Jackson and Martin, nor was any possible. By temperament, intellect and background, by their very chemistry, it was impossible.

Nevertheless, a pennant race transcends all, and in 1977 the Yankees found themselves in a good one. The Yanks wrapped up the American League East title on the season's final weekend and then bested the Kansas City Royals in a thrilling playoff series, during which Reggie was a minor contributor. (Jackson's "Mr. October" status was earned in World Series and not playoff action; in 11 Championship Series, he averaged just .227, batting under .200 six times.)

For Reggie, his first year in New York, rapidly drawing to a conclusion, had been one of tension, bitterness and confusion. With a few exceptions, he had never been accepted by his teammates. But whatever the season had brought—and statistically it had been a success, as his 32 home runs and 110 RBIs indicate—it ended on a drama-filled note of triumph.

It was the night of October 18, 1977, at Yankee Stadium, Game 6 of a World Series that saw the Yankees leading the Los Angeles Dodgers three games to two. In the second inning, Jackson walked and scored on Chris Chambliss' home run, tying the score at 2-2. In the fourth, with the Dodgers ahead 3-2, Jackson hit the first pitch from righthander Burt Hooton into the right-field stands for a two-run homer. In the bottom of the fifth, with the Yankees ahead 5-3, Jackson hit the first pitch from righthander Elias Sosa into the right-field stands for another two-run homer, his fourth of the Series, tying a record. In the eighth, Jackson hit the first pitch from righthander Charlie Hough into the center-field bleachers, giving the Yankees their final run in a Series-deciding 8-4 victory.

Three pitchers, three swings, three home runs. World Series records were broken like china hitting a marble floor. Having homered in his final at-bat in Game 5 in Los Angeles, Jackson had belted four "taters" in a row and five for the Series, both records. Additionally, he established various marks for slugging and total bases.

Reggie's years in New York remained a blend of heroics and frustrations, of feuding with Martin (who eventually left, only to reappear), of gradual acceptance by his teammates, of a deteriorating relationship with Steinbrenner.

In 1978, the Yankees came from 14 games behind in July to overtake the Red Sox in September. Eventually, the teams met in a one-game Fenway shoot-out to decide the division championship. The Yankees getting a game-swinging three-run homer from Bucky Dent, won an unforgettable battle, 5-4, with what proved to be the deciding run coming on Reggie's solo home run. Not surprisingly, the calendar now read "October."

Even when Jackson struck out, it could be memorable. His "High Noon" duel with young Dodger fastballer Bob Welch in the ninth inning of Game 2 of the '78 World Series was as dramatic as any Jackson home run. Batting with two men on base and the Yankees trailing by one run, Jackson fouled off three two-strike pitches before fanning on a 3-2 count to end the game.

Reggie, at his theatrical best, got revenge in Game 6. He rifled a crushing two-run homer of Welch in the seventh inning of that contest, a blow that all but sealed the Yankees' championship victory.

Jackson had now been with the Yanks for two seasons—and the New Yorkers had won two World Series titles. Before Reginald Martinez Jackson's arrival in Gotham, the Yankees had not ruled as Series champions since 1962.

Clearly, Mr. October was doing his thing. In 12 Series games in a Yankee uniform, Reggie had seven home runs, 16 RBIs and a .419 batting average. This, of course, came on top of some pretty impressive fall-classic hitting that Jackson had done while with Oakland. After missing the 1972 Series because of a hamstring injury, Reggie batted .302 overall in the 1973 and 1974 Series and contributed two homers and seven RBIs.

After batting .297 in 1979 but dropping off to 89 RBIs (his lowest total since 1972), Jackson muscled up again in 1980. He drove in 111 runs and led the league in home runs for the third time with 41. In addition, he batted .300 (on the nose) for the only time in his career.

Accustomed to turbulent conditions and considerable criticism in his first three seasons with the Yankees, Reggie found acceptance during the 1980 season. The presence of Dick Howser, the third manager for whom he had played while with New York (Martin and Bob Lemon were the others), proved a boon to Jackson.

"I am more at peace with myself than at any time I can remember in my career," Reggie said. "The manager here . . . he's been really helpful to me. Dick Howser makes me feel like I'm better than I

Jackson welcomes new Yankee slugger Dave Winfield (left) to the fold.

Reggie playing to the crowd as a member of the California Angels in 1986.

Mr. October still was smiling when he returned to Oakland to write his closing chapter.

Jackson's Milestone Home Runs

	Date	Place	Pitcher	Club
1	Sept. 17, 1967	California	Jim Weaver	California
100	Sept. 27, 1970	California	Greg Garrett	California
200	May 6, 1974	Oakland	Mike Cuellar	Baltimore
300	Aug. 5, 1977	Seattle	Dick Pole	Seattle
400	Aug. 11, 1980	New York	Britt Burns	Chicago
500	Sept. 17, 1984	California	Bud Black	Kansas City
Last	Aug. 17, 1987	California	Mike Witt	California

really am. That was Earl Weaver's way in Baltimore when I was there. . . . More than that, though, I can finally feel that the fans and the players here are for me—really for me."

Yankee batting instructor Charley Lau spoke almost reverently about Jackson that summer.

"Each at-bat is a pleasure to behold," Lau said. "He's getting better and better with age. The preparation, the discipline, the concentration. At-bat after at-bat after at-bat. When everything is in place, in the proper sequence, he's awesome. In a season of 450 at-bats, maybe 1,200 swings, you can only count on maybe 20 perfect swings a year. When he does it, I get goose pimples."

Unfortunately for Reggie, the 1981 season was as bad as the 1980 campaign had been good. And Jackson's five-year, $3 million contract with the Yanks was expiring after a season in which the Wyncote product played in his fifth and last World Series (his first with a losing team).

Steinbrenner chose not to offer Reggie a new pact, a decision the Yankee owner later called "my biggest mistake." So, the 35-year-old slugger accepted a long-term contract from the California Angels.

Jackson helped the Angels to a West Division title in 1982 with a league-leading 39 home runs—actually, he shared the lead, as he did three of the four times he was atop the A.L. homer standings—but there would be no more World Series appearances for Mr. October. The Angels lost in the A.L. playoffs in '82 and again in 1986. (Reggie's major league career Series statistics, then, wound up this way for 27 games: 10 homers, 24 RBIs, a .357 average and a record .755 slugging percentage.)

Jackson took his legend and his excitement back to Oakland for his 21st and final big-league season in 1987. In spring training that year, he pondered his stature and his legacy.

"Yeah, I think I'm a little special," he said. "I think I have some credibility, some credentials. I think there's something about my ability to compete that can rub off on some of the kids. . . ."

Struggling at the plate, though, the 41-year-old Reggie hit just 15 home runs and batted .220 in his farewell trip through the American League schedule. Retirement came quietly and without fanfare after the season.

Jackson took with him into retirement one of baseball's noisiest and most entertaining careers, including that glamorous autumnal nickname, the World Series triumphs, his 563 home runs and the riveted attention of fans who never ignored him, no matter how they felt about him. And, of course, there was that candy bar, which inspired this observation: "When you unwrapped it," one writer cracked, "it told you how good it was."

JACKSON'S CAREER RECORD
Born May 18, 1946, at Wyncote, Pa.
Batted and threw lefthanded.   Elected to Hall of Fame, 1993.

Year	Club	League	G.	AB.	R.	H.	HR.	RBI.	B.A.
1966—Lewiston	N'west	12	48	14	14	2	11	.292
1966—Modesto	Calif.	56	221	50	66	21	60	.299
1967—Birmingham	South.	114	413	*84	121	17	58	.293
1967—Kansas City	Amer.	35	118	13	21	1	6	.178
1968—Oakland	Amer.	154	553	82	138	29	74	.250
1969—Oakland	Amer.	152	549	*123	151	47	118	.275
1970—Oakland	Amer.	149	426	57	101	23	66	.237
1971—Oakland	Amer.	150	567	87	157	32	80	.277
1972—Oakland	Amer.	135	499	72	132	25	75	.265
1973—Oakland	Amer.	151	539	*99	158	*32	*117	.293
1974—Oakland	Amer.	148	506	90	146	29	93	.289
1975—Oakland	Amer.	157	593	91	150	●36	104	.253
1976—Baltimore	Amer.	134	498	84	138	27	91	.277
1977—New York	Amer.	146	525	93	150	32	110	.286
1978—New York	Amer.	139	511	82	140	27	97	.274
1979—New York	Amer.	131	465	78	138	29	89	.297
1980—New York	Amer.	143	514	94	154	●41	111	.300
1981—New York	Amer.	94	334	33	79	15	54	.237
1982—California	Amer.	153	530	92	146	●39	101	.275
1983—California	Amer.	116	397	43	77	14	49	.194
1984—California	Amer.	143	525	67	117	25	81	.223
1985—California	Amer.	143	460	64	116	27	85	.252
1986—California	Amer.	132	419	65	101	18	58	.241
1987—Oakland	Amer.	115	336	42	74	15	43	.220
Major League Totals			2820	9864	1551	2584	563	1702	.262

DIVISION SERIES RECORD

Year	Club	League	G.	AB.	R.	H.	HR.	RBI.	B.A.
1981—New York	Amer.	5	20	4	6	2	4	.300

CHAMPIONSHIP SERIES RECORD

Year	Club	League	G.	AB.	R.	H.	HR.	RBI.	B.A.
1971—Oakland	Amer.	3	12	2	4	2	2	.333
1972—Oakland	Amer.	5	18	1	5	0	2	.278
1973—Oakland	Amer.	5	21	0	3	0	0	.143
1974—Oakland	Amer.	4	12	0	2	0	1	.167
1975—Oakland	Amer.	3	12	1	5	1	3	.417
1977—New York	Amer.	5	16	1	2	0	1	.125
1978—New York	Amer.	4	13	5	6	2	6	.462
1980—New York	Amer.	3	11	1	3	0	0	.273
1981—New York	Amer.	2	4	1	0	0	1	.000
1982—California	Amer.	5	18	2	2	1	2	.111
1986—California	Amer.	6	26	2	5	0	2	.192
LCS Totals		45	163	16	37	6	20	.227

WORLD SERIES RECORD

Year	Club	League	G.	AB.	R.	H.	HR.	RBI.	B.A.
1973—Oakland	Amer.	7	29	3	9	1	6	.310
1974—Oakland	Amer.	5	14	3	4	1	1	.286
1977—New York	Amer.	6	20	10	9	5	8	.450
1978—New York	Amer.	6	23	2	9	2	8	.391
1981—New York	Amer.	3	12	3	4	1	1	.333
World Series Totals		27	98	21	35	10	24	.357

The Late Bloomer

A favorite parlor pastime for baseball fans has always been the selection of an all-time all-star team. Several candidates emerge at each position, each nominee supported by partisans armed with statistics and lists of achievements.

For decades, the automatic selection at third base was the longtime Pittsburgh star for the 1920s and early 1930s, Hall of Famer Pie Traynor. As the 1950s gave way to the 1960s, however, that appointment ceased being uncontested. When the home run guns of summer cracked the air throughout the 1950s, many fans championed the cause of Eddie Mathews. By the end of the 1960s, Brooks Robinson had taken the baseball public to a higher level of consciousness with his fielding magic.

Beginning in the 1980s, even those choices seemed debatable, if not completely outdated. The logical selection in the opinion of many was the big third baseman with the golden glove *and* the booming home run bat—the Philadelphia Phillies' Mike Schmidt.

Among his contemporaries, there is little doubt where Schmidt fits in.

"There's nobody in baseball who can do all the things Mike Schmidt can do," said fellow third baseman Bill Madlock, a four-time National League batting titlist. "There are four things you can do in this game—run, hit, field and hit with power, and nobody can do it all except Mike Schmidt."

It hadn't always been that way, according to Schmidt, who considered himself "your basic late bloomer." His first minor and major league seasons would have discouraged lesser men (batting averages near .200 usually do) but Schmidt had overcome obstacles before.

"I was about the fourth or fifth best baseball player in school—a .250 hitter, and if you don't hit .400 in high school, nobody knows you're alive," he said. "I was always the kid with potential. The only time I was really a star was in Little League. After that, I just seemed to be missing something."

Schmidt had nurtured a dream of becoming a

professional athlete, "but I went off to Ohio University with a T square and a portfolio," he said. "I was dead serious about becoming an architect. All I did my freshman year was stay up nights constructing little models of buildings and doing projects for my art courses."

Like a couple of other former students of architecture—Lou Gehrig at Columbia and Sandy Koufax at the University of Cincinnati—Schmidt was destined to erect not buildings but a career in baseball. After undergoing a successful program to rehabilitate the knees that had been battered in high school football, he joined Ohio's baseball team—as a shortstop.

Philadelphia's Mike Schmidt.

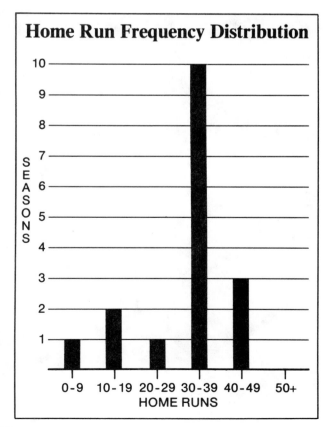

Schmidt (center) with Ohio University teammate Mike Hannah (left) and Coach Bob Wren in 1971.

The swing that put Schmidt among the elite all-time power hitters.

Schmidt with slugging teammate Dick Allen in 1976.

With Schmidt as their catalyst, the Bobcats were champions of the Mid-American Conference in 1969, 1970 and 1971, and finished fourth in the 1970 College World Series. Schmidt set a standing school record with 27 career homers, was a first-team All-America selection his junior year and, as a senior, was named the shortstop on The Sporting News' 1971 All-America squad, a team chosen by the scouting directors of the 24 major league clubs.

Longtime major league scout Tony Lucadello was mesmerized by Schmidt and convinced Philadelphia farm director Paul Owens (later the club's manager and general manager) to make a trip to the Ohio campus.

"I hit a home run, made a good defensive play in the hole and took an extra base on a single," said Schmidt, recalling the visit. "I did three real pivotal things they're looking for in a prospect." The Phillies made him their second-round pick in the June 1971 draft.

A business degree in hand, Schmidt decided to give his attention to professional baseball "to see how good I was." Assigned to Reading in the Class-AA Eastern League, he batted .211 and hit only eight home runs—hardly numbers to launch a career. His inauspicious debut hardly fazed the Phillies, however.

"We didn't look at the statistics from his first year," one club official said. "We looked at the player, and when we did, all we saw was talent."

Schmidt responded with numbers more indicative of that talent after a promotion to the Class-AAA Pacific Coast League in 1972: 26 home runs, 91 runs batted in and a .291 batting average as a second and third baseman for the club's Eugene, Ore., outpost. That winter, the Phils created a vacancy for Schmidt at third by trading Don Money to the Milwaukee Brewers.

Schmidt sliding safely as Dodger third baseman Ron Cey awaits the throw.

Schmidt watches intently as his fourth straight home run leaves the park in an April 17, 1976, game against Chicago at Wrigley Field.

The Phillies' third baseman gets a grand reception from teammates Greg Luzinski, Larry Bowa and Jerry Martin after hitting a home run.

Schmidt makes a valiant but vain attempt to get Baltimore pinch-hitter Benny Ayala's single in Game 3 of the 1983 World Series.

No great career was ever begun in more dismal fashion. Near the end of spring training, he dislocated his left shoulder and missed the opening of the 1973 season. Once healthy, he played himself into Manager Danny Ozark's doghouse by striking out too often, then taking his batting woes out on the field. Schmidt batted just .196 and struck out 136 times in 367 at-bats, though he did show occasional power with 18 home runs.

"I can't get relaxed," he had complained. "Hell, I want to do good so much, I'm trying too damn hard. I go up to the plate telling myself to take it easy, but when the first pitch comes in there, I swing like my life depends on it."

His rookie season would have buried many players, but the Phillies remained fascinated by Schmidt's potential. Ozark, once he'd recovered from the previous game's strikeouts, bragged openly about the natural ability of his strong, young third baseman.

"Danny and I would occasionally have dinner together when the Dodgers were in Philadelphia," Los Angeles Manager Walter Alston said. "One night he was going on and on about Mike, who I don't think was hitting his weight at the time. Finally, I said to him, 'Who are you trying to convince, Danny? Yourself or me? Because if you're trying to convince me, you don't have to. Everybody in the league knows this kid is going to be a star.' "

That winter, playing for Bobby Wine's championship Caguas team in Puerto Rico, Schmidt committed himself to an adjustment that would

**It's celebration time as Schmidt rounds third base and gets a pat from
Philadelphia coach Jim Davenport after hitting career home run No. 500 in 1987.**

bring the talent from the shadows of potential into the sunlight of stardom: he learned to relax at the plate. That spring, he wisely resisted all of the accumulated wisdom of the Phillies' coaching staff, which, conceivably, could have undone his composure.

"I stopped acting as though every trip to the plate was a life-or-death proposition," Schmidt explained. "Instead of thinking I had to hit every pitch with every ounce of strength, I tried to pick out a good pitch and swing naturally."

Schmidt's leap to stardom was sudden and genuine. In 1974, his second year in the big leagues, he won his first of three straight home run titles with 36 homers. It marked the return of an era of home run dominance in the National League, a period in which Schmidt would rule the circuit with consistency not seen since the days of Ralph Kiner. In the 14 seasons from 1974 through 1987, Schmidt hit more than 30 homers 13 times and established a league record by leading in home runs eight times. And he did it because he was "putting the ability and confidence together."

"Everything started falling into place," he said. "I was able to relax more when I batted, had a clear head and allowed my natural instincts to take over. What it amounted to was that I stopped thinking so much and I started hitting." (Perhaps further vindication for Yogi Berra's axiom about not being able to think and hit at the same time.)

Schmidt, actually one of the game's most introspective players, followed his turnabout of 1974 with three successive 38-homer seasons, including those long-ball titles in 1975 and 1976. On April 17, 1976, he inscribed his name on the walls of one of baseball's most exclusive chambers by becoming only the 10th major leaguer to hoist four home runs in one game. Schmidt, who didn't hit his first homer until the fifth inning, shot four home runs out of Wrigley Field in a 10-inning victory over the Chicago Cubs, joining a cast of four N.L. hitters who had previously accomplished the feat in the modern era: Chuck Klein, Gil Hodges, Joe Adcock and Willie Mays.

Always on an even keel, Schmidt (known as "Captain Cool" to teammates) never paused to dwell on personal achievements. "When a batter strikes out four times in a game, they tell him to forget it," he said after rocking Wrigley. "Well, I'd like to forget about the homers. I want to concentrate on the games ahead."

And while the strikeout also was a Schmidt trademark—he led N.L. hitters in strikeouts four times and fanned more than 100 times in a dozen seasons —the home run feats are the hallmark of his legend. Such was the case in 1980, when he whaled a career-high 48 to establish a single-season major league record for third basemen, leading the Phillies to the pennant and, ultimately, their first-ever World Series championship.

Schmidt's clutch hitting down the stretch (13 home runs and 28 RBIs from September 1 through

Schmidt receives the 1981 National League Most Valuable Player award as Phillies President Bill Giles watches.

the end of the season) helped Philadelphia edge the Montreal Expos in a sizzling N.L. East division race that was decided in a head-to-head title bout on the season's final weekend. Tied for first with Montreal entering the three-game series, the Phillies won the opener, 2-1, on Schmidt's sacrifice fly and home run. The following day, he belted a two-run homer in the top of the 11th inning that clinched the division crown (and shattered Mathews' home run mark for third basemen).

The Phillies toppled the Houston Astros in a gripping five-game playoff, easing the disappointment of losses in the N.L. Championship Series of 1976, 1977 and 1978, and advanced into only their third World Series in club history.

Schmidt came through in a big way in baseball's biggest event. He doubled home the go-ahead run in Philadelphia's second-game victory over the Kansas City Royals and homered and scored the tying run in a fifth-game win. In the decisive sixth contest, he delivered a two-run single that gave the early lead to the Phillies, who hung on for a 4-1 victory and laid claim to that elusive championship of baseball.

Schmidt, voted the World Series Most Valuable Player on the merit of two homers, seven RBIs and a .381 batting average, also received his first of three N.L. MVP awards. Coupled with his fourth home

"I've tried to play the game the way it was meant to be played my entire career."

Schmidt's Milestone Home Runs

	Date	Place	Pitcher	Club
1	Sept. 16, 1972	Philadelphia	Balor Moore	Montreal
100	April 20, 1976	Pittsburgh	John Candelaria	Pittsburgh
200	May 13, 1979	San Francisco	Vida Blue	San Francisco
300	Aug. 14, 1981	New York	Mike Scott	New York
400	May 15, 1984	Los Angeles	Bob Welch	Los Angeles
500	April 18, 1987	Pittsburgh	Don Robinson	Pittsburgh
Last	May 2, 1989	Philadelphia	Jim Deshaies	Houston

run title, Schmidt drove home a league-high (and career-best) 121 runs to put together the first of four career "doubles"—seasons in which he would lead (or co-lead) the circuit in both homers and RBIs. "That's what counts, the RBIs," he said. "Hitting a ball 500 feet with nobody on seems a waste."

Often overlooked in the wake of Schmidt's heavy hitting was his defensive work, which was good enough to earn 10 Gold Gloves, second only to Brooks Robinson's 16 among third basemen. Discussing his fielding, Schmidt sounded like a creature of instinct.

"You know how it is when you're a kid," he said. "You always like to be tossing a ball around. You like to do things with it—catch it between your legs, behind your back. It's fun. Well, I'm good at fielding because I take it lightly. I just go out there and field. I don't even do things fundamentally right, and I hate infield practice—it's nothing more than pregame entertainment. . . . On defense, I guess you could say I'm something of a flake."

In the strike-shortened 1981 season, Schmidt became only the third back-to-back MVP winner in N.L. history (joining Ernie Banks, 1958-59, and Joe Morgan, 1975-76) as he paced the league in both home runs (31 in only 102 games) and RBIs (91). In 1983, he slugged the Phillies into another World Series, topping the circuit with 40 homers along the way, but couldn't duplicate the magic he had created in the 1980 classic. He collected only one hit in 20 at-bats against the Baltimore Orioles, who dispatched the Phils in five games.

Schmidt added two more home run and RBI "doubles" to his career list: in 1984, when he co-led the circuit with 36 homers and 106 RBIs, and in 1986, when his 37 homers and 119 RBIs earned him MVP honors for the third time. In N.L. history, only St. Louis' Stan Musial and Brooklyn's Roy Campanella had won the award as many times.

At this stage, Schmidt's career was decorated with illustrious honors. In 1986, he had eclipsed Kiner's league record by claiming his eighth home run crown. In 1987, he surpassed Mathews' career home run record for third basemen and, with 35 homers overall, posted his 13th season of 30 or more homers, tied for second with Ruth behind Aaron's 15 seasons.

At the close of his career, the Phillies slugger had

rung up 548 career home runs, placing him seventh on baseball's most glamorous scroll of honor. And Schmidt had made it there without compromising his principles.

"My whole career I've been concerned for my team and for myself, playing the game the way it's supposed to be played," he once said. "There have been many, many times I've taken 2-0 pitches down the middle of the plate because I'm leading off the ninth inning and we're down two or three runs. The situation calls for me to get on base, so I look for a walk. I understand that's the way the game is supposed to be played.

"All in all, I've tried to play the game the way it was meant to be played my entire career. The things I've accomplished statistically are a direct result of that."

SCHMIDT'S CAREER RECORD
Born September 27, 1949, at Dayton, O.
Batted and threw righthanded.

Year	Club	League	G.	AB.	R.	H.	HR.	RBI.	B.A.
1971—Reading	East.	74	237	27	50	8	31	.211
1972—Eugene	P.C.	131	436	80	127	26	91	.291
1972—Philadelphia	Nat.	13	34	2	7	1	3	.206
1973—Philadelphia	Nat.	132	367	43	72	18	52	.196
1974—Philadelphia	Nat.	162	568	108	160	*36	116	.282
1975—Philadelphia	Nat.	158	562	93	140	*38	95	.249
1976—Philadelphia	Nat.	160	584	112	153	*38	107	.262
1977—Philadelphia	Nat.	154	544	114	149	38	101	.274
1978—Philadelphia	Nat.	145	513	93	129	21	78	.251
1979—Philadelphia	Nat.	160	541	109	137	45	114	.253
1980—Philadelphia	Nat.	150	548	104	157	*48	*121	.286
1981—Philadelphia	Nat.	102	354	*78	112	*31	*91	.316
1982—Philadelphia	Nat.	148	514	108	144	35	87	.280
1983—Philadelphia	Nat.	154	534	104	136	*40	109	.255
1984—Philadelphia	Nat.	151	528	93	146	•36	•106	.277
1985—Philadelphia	Nat.	158	549	89	152	33	93	.277
1986—Philadelphia	Nat.	160	552	97	160	*37	*119	.290
1987—Philadelphia	Nat.	147	522	88	153	35	113	.293
1988—Philadelphia	Nat.	108	390	52	97	12	62	.249
1989—Philadelphia	Nat.	42	148	19	30	6	28	.203
Major League Totals		2404	8352	1506	2234	548	1595	.267

DIVISION SERIES RECORD

Year	Club	League	G.	AB.	R.	H.	HR.	RBI.	B.A.
1981—Philadelphia	Nat.	5	16	3	4	1	2	.250

CHAMPIONSHIP SERIES RECORD

Year	Club	League	G.	AB.	R.	H.	HR.	RBI.	B.A.
1976—Philadelphia	Nat.	3	13	1	4	0	2	.308
1977—Philadelphia	Nat.	4	16	2	1	0	1	.063
1978—Philadelphia	Nat.	4	15	1	3	0	1	.200
1980—Philadelphia	Nat.	5	24	1	5	0	1	.208
1983—Philadelphia	Nat.	4	15	5	7	1	2	.467
LCS Totals		20	83	10	20	1	7	.241

WORLD SERIES RECORD

Year	Club	League	G.	AB.	R.	H.	HR.	RBI.	B.A.
1980—Philadelphia	Nat.	6	21	6	8	2	7	.381
1983—Philadelphia	Nat.	5	20	0	1	0	0	.050
World Series Totals		11	41	6	9	2	7	.220

Yearly Home Run Leaders Since 1920

(Beginning of Babe Ruth's domination and the lively ball era)

1920

American League		National League	
Ruth, New York	54	Williams, Philadelphia	15
Sisler, St. Louis	19	Meusel, Philadelphia	14
Walker, Philadelphia	17	Kelly, New York	11
Felsch, Chicago	14	McHenry, St. Louis	10
2 tied with	12	Robertson, Chicago	10

1921

American League		National League	
Ruth, New York	59	Kelly, New York	23
Meusel, New York	24	Hornsby, St. Louis	21
Williams, St. Louis	24	Williams, Philadelphia	18
Walker, Philadelphia	23	McHenry, St. Louis	17
Heilmann, Detroit	19	Fournier, St. Louis	16

1922

American League		National League	
Williams, St. Louis	39	Hornsby, St. Louis	42
Walker, Philadelphia	37	Williams, Philadelphia	26
Ruth, New York	35	Kelly, New York	17
Heilmann, Detroit	21	Lee, Philadelphia	17
Miller, Philadelphia	21	2 tied with	16

1923

American League		National League	
Ruth, New York	41	Williams, Philadelphia	41
Williams, St. Louis	29	Fournier, Brooklyn	22
Heilmann, Detroit	18	Miller, Chicago	20
Speaker, Cleveland	17	Meusel, New York	19
2 tied with	16	Hornsby, St. Louis	17

1924

American League		National League	
Ruth, New York	46	Fournier, Brooklyn	27
Hauser, Philadelphia	27	Hornsby, St. Louis	25
Jacobson, St. Louis	19	Williams, Philadelphia	24
Williams, St. Louis	18	Kelly, New York	21
Boone, Boston	13	2 tied with	16

1925

American League		National League	
Meusel, New York	33	Hornsby, St. Louis	39
Ruth, New York	25	Hartnett, Chicago	24
Williams, St. Louis	25	Fournier, Brooklyn	22
Simmons, Philadelphia	24	Bottomley, St. Louis	21
Gehrig, New York	20	Meusel, New York	21

1926

American League		National League	
Ruth, New York	47	Wilson, Chicago	21
Simmons, Philadelphia	19	Bottomley, St. Louis	19
Lazzeri, New York	18	Williams, Philadelphia	18
Goslin, Washington	17	Bell, St. Louis	17
Williams, St. Louis	17	Southworth, New York-St. Louis	16

1927

American League		National League	
Ruth, New York	60	Williams, Philadelphia	30
Gehrig, New York	47	Wilson, Chicago	30
Lazzeri, New York	18	Hornsby, New York	26
Williams, St. Louis	17	Terry, New York	20
Simmons, Philadelphia	15	Bottomley, St. Louis	19

1928

American League		National League	
Ruth, New York	54	Bottomley, St. Louis	31
Gehrig, New York	27	Wilson, Chicago	31
Goslin, Washington	17	Hafey, St. Louis	27
Hauser, Philadelphia	16	Bissonette, Brooklyn	25
Simmons, Philadelphia	15	Hornsby, Boston	21

1929

American League		National League	
Ruth, New York	46	Klein, Philadelphia	43
Gehrig, New York	35	**Ott, New York**	42
Simmons, Philadelphia	34	Hornsby, Chicago	39
Foxx, Philadelphia	33	Wilson, Chicago	39
Alexander, Detroit	25	O'Doul, Philadelphia	32

1930

American League		National League	
Ruth, New York	49	Wilson, Chicago	56
Gehrig, New York	41	Klein, Philadelphia	40
Foxx, Philadelphia	37	Berger, Boston	38
Goslin, Washington-St. Louis	37	Hartnett, Chicago	37
Simmons, Philadelphia	36	Herman, Brooklyn	35

1931

American League		National League	
Gehrig, New York	46	Klein, Philadelphia	31
Ruth, New York	46	**Ott, New York**	29
Averill, Cleveland	32	Berger, Boston	19
Foxx, Philadelphia	30	Arlett, Philadelphia	18
Goslin, St. Louis	24	Herman, Brooklyn	18

1932

American League		National League	
Foxx, Philadelphia	58	Klein, Philadelphia	38
Ruth, New York	41	**Ott, New York**	38
Simmons, Philadelphia	35	Terry, New York	28
Gehrig, New York	34	Hurst, Philadelphia	24
Averill, Cleveland	32	Wilson, Brooklyn	23

1933

American League		National League	
Foxx, Philadelphia	48	Klein, Philadelphia	28
Ruth, New York	34	Berger, Boston	27
Gehrig, New York	32	**Ott, New York**	23
Johnson, Philadelphia	21	Medwick, St. Louis	18
Lazzeri, New York	18	3 tied with	16

1934

American League		National League	
Gehrig, New York	49	Collins, St. Louis	35
Foxx, Philadelphia	44	**Ott, New York**	35
Trosky, Cleveland	35	Berger, Boston	34
Johnson, Philadelphia	34	Hartnett, Chicago	22
Averill, Cleveland	31	Klein, Chicago	20

1935

American League		National League	
Foxx, Philadelphia	36	Berger, Boston	34
Greenberg, Detroit	36	**Ott, New York**	31
Gehrig, New York	30	Camilli, Philadelphia	25
Johnson, Philadelphia	28	Collins, St. Louis	23
Trosky, Cleveland	26	Medwick, St. Louis	23

1936

American League		National League	
Gehrig, New York	49	**Ott, New York**	33
Trosky, Cleveland	42	Camilli, Philadelphia	28
Foxx, Boston	41	Berger, Boston	25
DiMaggio, New York	29	Klein, Chicago-Philadelphia	25
Averill, Cleveland	28	Mize, St. Louis	19

1937

American League		National League	
DiMaggio, New York	46	Medwick, St. Louis	31
Greenberg, Detroit	40	**Ott, New York**	31
Gehrig, New York	37	Camilli, Philadelphia	27
Foxx, Boston	36	Mize, St. Louis	25
York, Detroit	35	Galan, Chicago	18

1938

American League		National League	
Greenberg, Detroit	58	**Ott, New York**	36
Foxx, Boston	50	Goodman, Cincinnati	30
Clift, St. Louis	34	Mize, St. Louis	27
York, Detroit	33	Camilli, Brooklyn	24
DiMaggio, New York	32	Rizzo, Pittsburgh	23

1939

American League		National League	
Foxx, Boston	35	Mize, St. Louis	28
Greenberg, Detroit	33	**Ott, New York**	27
Williams, Boston	31	Camilli, Brooklyn	26
DiMaggio, New York	30	Leiber, Chicago	24
Gordon, New York	28	Lombardi, Cincinnati	20

1940

American League		National League	
Greenberg, Detroit	41	Mize, St. Louis	43
Foxx, Boston	36	Nicholson, Chicago	25
York, Detroit	33	Rizzo, Pit.-Cin.-Phil.	24
DiMaggio, New York	31	Camilli, Brooklyn	23
Johnson, Philadelphia	31	3 tied with	19

1941

American League		National League	
Williams, Boston	37	Camilli, Brooklyn	34
Keller, New York	33	**Ott, New York**	27
Henrich, New York	31	Nicholson, Chicago	26
DiMaggio, New York	30	Young, New York	25
York, Detroit	27	Dahlgren, Boston-Chicago	23

1942

American League		National League	
Williams, Boston	36	Ott, New York	30
Laabs, St. Louis	27	Camilli, Brooklyn	26
Keller, New York	26	Mize, New York	26
DiMaggio, New York	21	Nicholson, Chicago	21
York, Detroit	21	West, Boston	16

1943

American League		National League	
York, Detroit	34	Nicholson, Chicago	29
Keller, New York	31	Ott, New York	18
Stephens, St. Louis	22	Northey, Philadelphia	16
Heath, Cleveland	18	DiMaggio, Pittsburgh	15
2 tied with	17	Triplett, St. Louis-Philadelphia	15

1944

American League		National League	
Etten, New York	22	Nicholson, Chicago	33
Stephens, St. Louis	20	Ott, New York	26
Lindell, New York	18	Northey, Philadelphia	22
Spence, Washington	18	Kurowski, St. Louis	20
York, Detroit	18	McCormick, Cincinnati	20

1945

American League		National League	
Stephens, St. Louis	24	Holmes, Boston	28
Cullenbine, Cleveland-Detroit	18	Workman, Boston	25
Etten, New York	18	Adams, Philadelphia-St. Louis	22
York, Detroit	18	Kurowski, St. Louis	21
Heath, Cleveland	15	Ott, New York	21

1946

American League		National League	
Greenberg, Detroit	44	Kiner, Pittsburgh	23
Williams, Boston	38	Mize, New York	22
Keller, New York	30	Slaughter, St. Louis	18
Seerey, Cleveland	26	Ennis, Philadelphia	17
DiMaggio, New York	25	2 tied with	16

1947

American League		National League	
Williams, Boston	32	**Kiner, Pittsburgh**	51
Gordon, Cleveland	29	Mize, New York	51
Heath, St. Louis	27	Marshall, New York	36
Cullenbine, Detroit	24	Cooper, New York	35
York, Boston-Chicago	21	Thomson, New York	29

1948

American League		National League	
DiMaggio, New York	39	**Kiner, Pittsburgh**	40
Gordon, Cleveland	32	Mize, New York	40
Keltner, Cleveland	31	Musial, St. Louis	39
Stephens, Boston	29	Sauer, Cincinnati	35
Doerr, Boston	27	2 tied with	30

1949

American League		National League	
Williams, Boston	43	**Kiner, Pittsburgh**	54
Stephens, Boston	39	Musial, St. Louis	36
4 tied with	24	Sauer, Cincinnati-Chicago	31
		Thomson, New York	27
		Gordon, New York	26

1950

American League		National League	
Rosen, Cleveland	37	**Kiner, Pittsburgh**	47
Dropo, Boston	34	Pafko, Chicago	36
DiMaggio, New York	32	Hodges, Brooklyn	32
Stephens, Boston	30	Sauer, Chicago	32
Zernial, Chicago	29	3 tied with	31

1951

American League		National League	
Zernial, Chicago-Philadelphia	33	**Kiner, Pittsburgh**	42
Williams, Boston	30	Hodges, Brooklyn	40
Robinson, Chicago	29	Campanella, Brooklyn	33
3 tied with	27	Musial, St. Louis	32
		Thomson, New York	32

1952

American League		National League	
Doby, Cleveland	32	**Kiner, Pittsburgh**	37
Easter, Cleveland	31	Sauer, Chicago	37
Berra, New York	30	Hodges, Brooklyn	32
Zernial, Philadelphia	29	Gordon, Boston	25
Dropo, Boston-Detroit	29	**Mathews, Boston**	25

1953

American League		National League	
Rosen, Cleveland	43	Mathews, Milwaukee	47
Zernial, Philadelphia	42	Snider, Brooklyn	42
Doby, Cleveland	29	Campanella, Brooklyn	41
Berra, New York	27	Kluszewski, Cincinnati	40
Boone, Cleveland-Detroit	26	**Kiner, Pittsburgh-Chicago**	35

1954

American League		National League	
Doby, Cleveland	32	Kluszewski, Cincinnati	49
Williams, Boston	29	Hodges, Brooklyn	42
Mantle, New York	27	**Mays, New York**	41
Jensen, Boston	25	Sauer, Chicago	41
2 tied with	24	2 tied with	40

1955

American League		National League	
Mantle, New York	37	**Mays, New York**	51
Zernial, Kansas City	30	Kluszewski, Cincinnati	47
Williams, Boston	28	**Banks, Chicago**	44
3 tied with	27	Snider, Brooklyn	42
		Mathews, Milwaukee	41

1956

American League		National League	
Mantle, New York	52	Snider, Brooklyn	43
Wertz, Cleveland	32	Adcock, Milwaukee	38
Berra, New York	30	**Robinson, Cincinnati**	38
Sievers, Washington	29	**Mathews, Milwaukee**	37
Maxwell, Detroit	28	2 tied with	36

1957

American League		National League	
Sievers, Washington	42	**Aaron, Milwaukee**	44
Williams, Boston	38	**Banks, Chicago**	43
Mantle, New York	34	Snider, Brooklyn	40
Wertz, Cleveland	28	Mays, New York	35
Zernial, Kansas City	27	**Mathews, Milwaukee**	32

1958

American League		National League	
Mantle, New York	42	**Banks, Chicago**	47
Colavito, Cleveland	41	Thomas, Pittsburgh	35
Sievers, Washington	39	**Mathews, Milwaukee**	31
Cerv, Kansas City	38	**Robinson, Cincinnati**	31
Jensen, Boston	35	**Aaron, Milwaukee**	30

1959

American League		National League	
Colavito, Cleveland	42	**Mathews, Milwaukee**	46
Killebrew, Washington	42	**Banks, Chicago**	45
Lemon, Washington	33	Aaron, Milwaukee	39
Mantle, New York	31	**Robinson, Cincinnati**	36
Maxwell, Detroit	31	**Mays, San Francisco**	34

1960

American League		National League	
Mantle, New York	40	**Banks, Chicago**	41
Maris, New York	39	**Aaron, Milwaukee**	40
Lemon, Washington	38	**Mathews, Milwaukee**	39
Colavito, Detroit	35	Boyer, St. Louis	32
Killebrew, Washington	31	**Robinson, Cincinnati**	31

1961

American League		National League	
Maris, New York	61	Cepeda, San Francisco	46
Mantle, New York	54	**Mays, San Francisco**	40
Gentile, Baltimore	46	**Robinson, Cincinnati**	37
Killebrew, Minnesota	46	Adcock, Milwaukee	35
Colavito, Detroit	45	Stuart, Pittsburgh	35

1962

American League		National League	
Killebrew, Minnesota	48	**Mays, San Francisco**	49
Cash, Detroit	39	**Aaron, Milwaukee**	45
Colavito, Detroit	37	**Robinson, Cincinnati**	39
Wagner, Los Angeles	37	**Banks, Chicago**	37
2 tied with	33	Cepeda, San Francisco	35

1963

American League		National League	
Killebrew, Minnesota	45	**Aaron, Milwaukee**	44
Stuart, Boston	42	**McCovey, San Francisco**	44
Allison, Minnesota	35	**Mays, San Francisco**	38
Hall, Minnesota	33	Cepeda, San Francisco	34
Howard, New York	28	Howard, Los Angeles	28

1964

American League		National League	
Killebrew, Minnesota	49	**Mays, San Francisco**	47
Powell, Baltimore	39	Williams, Chicago	33
Mantle, New York	35	Callison, Philadelphia	31
Colavito, Kansas City	34	Cepeda, San Francisco	31
Stuart, Boston	33	Hart, San Francisco	31

1965

American League		National League	
Conigliaro, Boston	32	**Mays, San Francisco**	52
Cash, Detroit	30	**McCovey, San Francisco**	39
Horton, Detroit	29	Williams, Chicago	34
Wagner, Cleveland	28	**Robinson, Cincinnati**	33
3 tied with	26	Santo, Chicago	33

1966

American League		National League	
F. Robinson, Baltimore	49	**Aaron, Atlanta**	44
Killebrew, Minnesota	39	Allen, Philadelphia	40
Powell, Baltimore	34	**Mays, San Francisco**	37
Cash, Detroit	32	**McCovey, San Francisco**	36
Pepitone, New York	31	Torre, Atlanta	36

1967

American League		National League	
Killebrew, Minnesota	44	**Aaron, Atlanta**	39
Yastrzemski, Boston	44	Wynn, Houston	37
Howard, Washington	36	**McCovey, San Francisco**	31
F. Robinson, Baltimore	30	Santo, Chicago	31
2 tied with	25	Hart, San Francisco	29

1968

American League		National League	
Howard, Washington	44	**McCovey, San Francisco**	36
Horton, Detroit	36	Allen, Philadelphia	33
Harrelson, Boston	35	**Banks, Chicago**	32
Jackson, Oakland	29	Williams, Chicago	30
2 tied with	25	**Aaron, Atlanta**	29

1969

American League		National League	
Killebrew, Minnesota	49	**McCovey, San Francisco**	45
Howard, Washington	48	**Aaron, Atlanta**	44
Jackson, Oakland	47	May, Cincinnati	38
Petrocelli, Boston	40	Perez, Cincinnati	37
Yastrzemski, Boston	40	Wynn, Houston	33

1970

American League		National League	
Howard, Washington	44	Bench, Cincinnati	45
Killebrew, Minnesota	41	Williams, Chicago	42
Yastrzemski, Boston	40	Perez, Cincinnati	40
T. Conigliaro, Boston	36	**McCovey, San Francisco**	39
Powell, Baltimore	35	2 tied with	38

1971

American League		National League	
Melton, Chicago	33	**Stargell, Pittsburgh**	48
Cash, Detroit	32	**Aaron, Atlanta**	47
Jackson, Oakland	32	May, Cincinnati	39
Smith, Boston	30	Johnson, Philadelphia	34
4 tied with	28	2 tied with	33

1972

American League		National League	
Allen, Chicago	37	Bench, Cincinnati	40
Murcer, New York	33	Colbert, San Diego	38
Epstein, Oakland	26	Williams, Chicago	37
Killebrew, Minnesota	26	**Aaron, Atlanta**	34
2 tied with	25	**Stargell, Pittsburgh**	33

1973

American League		National League	
Jackson, Oakland	32	**Stargell, Pittsburgh**	44
Burroughs, Texas	30	Johnson, Atlanta	43
Robinson, California	30	Evans, Atlanta	41
Bando, Oakland	29	**Aaron, Atlanta**	40
3 tied with	26	Bonds, San Francisco	39

1974

American League		National League	
Allen, Chicago	32	**Schmidt, Philadelphia**	36
Jackson, Oakland	29	Bench, Cincinnati	33
Tenace, Oakland	26	Wynn, Los Angeles	32
Burroughs, Texas	25	Perez, Cincinnati	28
Darwin, Minnesota	25	Cedeno, Houston	26

1975

American League		National League	
Jackson, Oakland	36	**Schmidt, Philadelphia**	38
Scott, Milwaukee	36	Kingman, New York	36
Mayberry, Kansas City	34	Luzinski, Philadelphia	34
Bonds, New York	32	Bench, Cincinnati	28
2 tied with	29	2 tied with	25

1976

American League		National League	
Nettles, New York	32	**Schmidt, Philadelphia**	38
Bando, Oakland	27	Kingman, New York	37
Jackson, Baltimore	27	Monday, Chicago	32
3 tied with	25	Foster, Cincinnati	29
		Morgan, Cincinnati	27

1977

American League		National League	
Rice, Boston	39	Foster, Cincinnati	52
Bonds, California	37	Burroughs, Atlanta	41
Nettles, New York	37	Luzinski, Philadelphia	39
Scott, Boston	33	**Schmidt, Philadelphia**	38
Jackson, New York	32	Garvey, Los Angeles	33

1978

American League		National League	
Rice, Boston	46	Foster, Cincinnati	40
Baylor, California	34	Luzinski, Philadelphia	35
Hisle, Milwaukee	34	Parker, Pittsburgh	30
Thornton, Cleveland	33	Smith, Los Angeles	29
Thomas, Milwaukee	32	2 tied with	28

1979

American League		National League	
Thomas, Milwaukee	45	Kingman, Chicago	48
Lynn, Boston	39	**Schmidt, Philadelphia**	45
Rice, Boston	39	Winfield, San Diego	34
Baylor, California	36	Horner, Atlanta	33
Singleton, Baltimore	35	**Stargell, Pittsburgh**	32

1980

American League		National League	
Jackson, New York	41	**Schmidt, Philadelphia**	48
Oglivie, Milwaukee	41	Horner, Atlanta	35
Thomas, Milwaukee	38	Murphy, Atlanta	33
Armas, Oakland	35	Baker, Los Angeles	29
Murray, Baltimore	32	Carter, Montreal	29

1981

American League		National League	
Armas, Oakland	22	**Schmidt, Philadelphia**	31
Evans, Boston	22	Dawson, Montreal	24
Grich, California	22	Foster, Cincinnati	22
Murray, Baltimore	22	Kingman, New York	22
2 tied with	21	Hendrick, St. Louis	18

1982

American League		National League	
Jackson, California	39	Kingman, New York	37
Thomas, Milwaukee	39	Murphy, Atlanta	36
Winfield, New York	37	**Schmidt, Philadelphia**	35
Oglivie, Milwaukee	34	Guerrero, Los Angeles	32
5 tied with	32	Horner, Atlanta	32

1983

American League		National League	
Rice, Boston	39	**Schmidt, Philadelphia**	40
Armas, Boston	36	Murphy, Atlanta	36
Kittle, Chicago	35	Dawson, Montreal	32
Murray, Baltimore	33	Guerrero, Los Angeles	32
2 tied with	32	Evans, San Francisco	30

1984

American League		National League	
Armas, Boston	43	Murphy, Atlanta	36
Kingman, Oakland	35	**Schmidt, Philadelphia**	36
Murphy, Oakland	33	Carter, Montreal	27
Parrish, Detroit	33	Strawberry, New York	26
Thornton, Cleveland	33	Cey, Chicago	25

1985

American League		National League	
Evans, Detroit	40	Murphy, Atlanta	37
Fisk, Chicago	37	Parker, Cincinnati	34
Balboni, Kansas City	36	Guerrero, Los Angeles	33
Mattingly, New York	35	**Schmidt, Philadelphia**	33
Thomas, Seattle	32	Carter, New York	32

1986

American League		National League	
Barfield, Toronto	40	**Schmidt, Philadelphia**	37
Kingman, Oakland	35	Davis, Houston	31
Gaetti, Minnesota	34	Parker, Cincinnati	31
Canseco, Oakland	33	Murphy, Atlanta	29
Deer, Milwaukee	33	3 tied with	27

1987

American League		National League	
McGwire, Oakland	49	Dawson, Chicago	49
Bell, Toronto	47	Murphy, Atlanta	44
5 tied with	34	Strawberry, New York	39
		Davis, Cincinnati	37
		Johnson, New York	36

1988

American League		National League	
Canseco, Oakland	42	Strawberry, New York	39
McGriff, Toronto	34	Davis, Houston	30
McGwire, Oakland	32	Clark, San Francisco	29
Gaetti, Minnesota	28	Galarraga, Montreal	29
Murray, Baltimore	28	McReynolds, New York	27

1989

American League		National League	
McGriff, Toronto	36	Mitchell, San Francisco	47
Carter, Cleveland	35	Johnson, New York	36
McGwire, Oakland	33	Davis, Cincinnati	34
Jackson, Kansas City	32	Davis, Houston	34
Esasky, Boston	30	Sandberg, Chicago	30